North Sámi

North Sámi: An Essential Grammar is a unique English-medium resource on the North Sámi language.

The book provides:

- A clear and comprehensive overview of modern North Sámi grammar including examples drawn from authentic texts of various genres.
- A systematic order of topics beginning with the alphabet and phonology, continuing with nominal and verbal morphology and syntax, and concluding with more advanced topics such as discourse particles, complex sentences, and word formation.
- Full explanations of the grammatical terminology for the benefit of readers without a background in linguistics.

Suitable for linguists, as well as independent and classroom-based students, *North Sámi: An Essential Grammar* is an accessible but thorough introduction to the essential morphology and syntax of modern North Sámi, the largest of the Sámi languages.

Riitta-Liisa Valijärvi is Senior Teaching Fellow in Finnish at University College London and Senior Lecturer in Finnish/Finno-Ugric Languages at Uppsala University, Sweden.

Lily Kahn is Reader in Hebrew and Jewish Languages, University College London.

Routledge Essential Grammars

Essential Grammars are available for the following languages:

Arabic
Chinese
Czech
Danish
Dutch
English
Finnish
German
Greek
Hindi
Hungarian
Korean
Latvian
Modern Hebrew
North Sámi
Norwegian
Polish
Portuguese
Romanian
Serbian
Spanish
Swedish
Thai
Turkish
Urdu

North Sámi

An Essential Grammar

Riitta-Liisa Valijärvi and Lily Kahn

LONDON AND NEW YORK

First published 2017
by Routledge
2 Park Square, Milton Park, Abingdon, Oxon OX14 4RN

and by Routledge
711 Third Avenue, New York, NY 10017

Routledge is an imprint of the Taylor & Francis Group, an informa business

© 2017 Riitta-Liisa Valijärvi and Lily Kahn

The right of Riitta-Liisa Valijärvi and Lily Kahn to be identified as authors of this work has been asserted by them in accordance with sections 77 and 78 of the Copyright, Designs and Patents Act 1988.

All rights reserved. No part of this book may be reprinted or reproduced or utilised in any form or by any electronic, mechanical, or other means, now known or hereafter invented, including photocopying and recording, or in any information storage or retrieval system, without permission in writing from the publishers.

Trademark notice: Product or corporate names may be trademarks or registered trademarks, and are used only for identification and explanation without intent to infringe.

British Library Cataloguing-in-Publication Data
A catalogue record for this book is available from the British Library

Library of Congress Cataloging-in-Publication Data
A catalog record for this book has been requested

ISBN: 978-1-138-83936-6 (hbk)
ISBN: 978-1-138-83937-3 (pbk)
ISBN: 978-1-315-73348-7 (ebk)

Typeset in Sabon and Gill Sans
by Apex CoVantage, LLC

Contents

Preface	**xi**
Acknowledgements	**xiii**
Abbreviations	**xiv**

Chapter 1	**Introduction**		**1**
1.1	Sámi within the Uralic language family		1
1.2	Sámi language variants		2
1.3	Historical and sociolinguistic introduction to North Sámi		5
	1.3.1	Early history of North Sámi	5
	1.3.2	Written North Sámi	6
	1.3.3	Dialects of modern North Sámi	8
	1.3.4	Sociolinguistic situation of North Sámi	9
	1.3.5	North Sámi culture, literature, and music	10
Chapter 2	**Phonology and orthography**		**13**
2.1	The alphabet		13
2.2	Vowels		13
2.3	Diphthongs		14
2.4	Consonants		14
2.5	Stress, syllables, and intonation		18
2.6	Consonant gradation		20
Chapter 3	**Nouns**		**27**
3.1	Noun types		27
	3.1.1	Even-syllable	28
	3.1.2	Odd-syllable	37
	3.1.3	Contracted	47

3.2	Cases		51
	3.2.1	Nominative	51
	3.2.2	Accusative	51
	3.2.3	Genitive	52
	3.2.4	Illative	53
	3.2.5	Locative	55
	3.2.6	Comitative	57
	3.2.7	Essive	58

Chapter 4 Adjectives 60

4.1	Predicative adjective types	60
4.2	Attributive adjective types	61
4.3	Comparative	64
4.4	Superlative	66
4.5	Demonstrative	68

Chapter 5 Pronouns 69

5.1	Personal		69
5.2	Possessive		71
	5.2.1	Pronouns	71
	5.2.2	Suffixes	71
5.3	Demonstrative		95
5.4	Interrogative		96
5.5	Relative		98
5.6	Indefinite		99
5.7	Distributive		103
5.8	Reflexive		104
5.9	Reciprocal		105

Chapter 6 Numerals 110

6.1	Cardinal	110
6.2	Ordinal	114
6.3	Derived	115

Chapter 7 Verbs 117

7.1	Tense		117
	7.1.1	Present	117

		7.1.1.1	Form	117
		7.1.1.2	Usage	120
	7.1.2	Past		120
		7.1.2.1	Form	120
		7.1.2.2	Usage	123
	7.1.3	Perfect		124
		7.1.3.1	Form	124
		7.1.3.2	Usage	125
	7.1.4	Pluperfect		125
		7.1.4.1	Form	125
		7.1.4.2	Usage	126
	7.1.5	Progressive		126
		7.1.5.1	Form	126
		7.1.5.2	Usage	127
	7.1.6	Alternative ways of expressing tense		128
	7.1.7	Tense in reported speech		128
7.2	Mood			129
	7.2.1	Indicative		129
	7.2.2	Potential		129
		7.2.2.1	Form	129
		7.2.2.2	Usage	132
	7.2.3	Conditional		133
		7.2.3.1	Form	133
		7.2.3.2	Usage	136
	7.2.4	Imperative		137
		7.2.4.1	Form	138
		7.2.4.2	Usage	141
	7.2.5	Alternative ways of expressing modality		142
7.3	Negation			143
	7.3.1	Indicative present		143
	7.3.2	Indicative past, perfect, and pluperfect		144
	7.3.3	Potential		145
	7.3.4	Conditional		146
	7.3.5	Progressive		147
	7.3.6	Imperative		147
7.4	Non-finite verb forms			148
	7.4.1	Infinitive		148
		7.4.1.1	Form	148
		7.4.1.2	Usage	149
	7.4.2	Verbal nouns		154

		7.4.2.1	Form	155
		7.4.2.2	Usage	155
	7.4.3	Actio essive		156
		7.4.3.1	Form	156
		7.4.3.2	Usage	156
	7.4.4	Actio locative		158
		7.4.4.1	Form	158
		7.4.4.2	Usage	158
	7.4.5	Actio comitative		160
		7.4.5.1	Form	160
		7.4.5.2	Usage	161
	7.4.6	Gerund		161
		7.4.6.1	Form	161
		7.4.6.2	Usage	162
	7.4.7	Verbal genitive		163
		7.4.7.1	Form	163
		7.4.7.2	Usage	164
	7.4.8	Verbal abessive		165
		7.4.8.1	Form	165
		7.4.8.2	Usage	165
	7.4.9	Purposive (supine)		168
		7.4.9.1	Positive	168
		7.4.9.2	Negative	168
	7.4.10	Participles		169
		7.4.10.1	Present participle	169
			7.4.10.1.1 Form	169
			7.4.10.1.2 Usage	170
		7.4.10.2	Past participle	171
			7.4.10.2.1 Form	171
			7.4.10.2.2 Usage	172

Chapter 8   Adverbs   174

8.1	Manner	175
8.2	Time	180
8.3	Place	188
8.4	Degree, measure, and quantity	202
8.5	Interrogative	205
8.6	Other	210

Chapter 9   Adpositions   213

    9.1   Adpositions of place   213
    9.2   Adpositions of time   217
    9.3   Adpositions with other meanings   219
    9.4   Adpositions with possessive suffixes   221

Chapter 10   Conjunctions   224

    10.1 Coordinate   224
    10.2 Subordinate   225
          10.2.1 Complementisers   225
          10.2.2 Adverbial   226

Chapter 11   Particles   230

    11.1 Discourse particles   230
          11.1.1 Enclitic particles   230
          11.1.2 Independent particles   234
    11.2 Interjections   236

Chapter 12   Clauses   237

    12.1 Word order   237
    12.2 Intransitive   238
    12.3 Transitive   239
    12.4 Other two-place verbal clauses   239
    12.5 Habitive   239
    12.6 Existential   240
    12.7 Predicative   240
    12.8 Subjectless   241
    12.9 Interrogative   241

Chapter 13   Word formation   244

    13.1 Derivative suffixes   244
          13.1.1 Verb suffixes   244
                  13.1.1.1 Verbs derived from verbs   244
                            13.1.1.1.1 Valency-changing
                                        suffixes   244
                                  13.1.1.1.1.1 Passive   245

			13.1.1.1.1.2	Adversative passive	250
			13.1.1.1.1.3	Reflexive	251
			13.1.1.1.1.4	Reciprocal	252
			13.1.1.1.1.5	Causative	252
			13.1.1.1.1.6	Applicative	255
			13.1.1.1.1.7	Anti-applicative	256
			13.1.1.1.1.8	Desiderative	257
		13.1.1.1.2	Aspectual suffixes		257
			13.1.1.1.2.1	Subitive and diminutive	257
			13.1.1.1.2.2	Momentaneous	259
			13.1.1.1.2.3	Frequentative	259
			13.1.1.1.2.4	Inchoative	261
	13.1.1.2	Verbs derived from nominals			262
13.1.2	Noun suffixes				264
	13.1.2.1	Nouns derived from verbs			264
	13.1.2.2	Nouns derived from nouns			268
	13.1.2.3	Nouns derived from adjectives			270
13.1.3	Adjective suffixes				271
	13.1.3.1	Adjectives derived from verbs			271
	13.1.3.2	Adjectives derived from nouns			273
	13.1.3.3	Adjectives derived from adjectives			275
	13.1.3.4	Adjectives derived from adverbs			276
13.2 Compounding					277
13.2.1 Compound nouns					277
13.2.2 Compound adjectives					280
13.2.3 Compound verbs					281

Suggested resources — **283**
Index — **285**

Preface

The purpose of this grammar is to provide students and scholars of Sámi and Uralic languages with the first accessible, up-to-date, and reasonably comprehensive presentation of North Sámi grammar in English. The project was born out of our love of Sámi language and culture: Riitta studied Sámi at Uppsala University (Sweden) and Lily learned North Sámi while living in Kautokeino (Norway) as a teenager.

In writing this grammar our approach has been descriptive rather than prescriptive, so we have tended to present the language as it is used rather than giving preference to normative considerations. However, where relevant we have drawn the reader's attention to regional and colloquial variations. Most of the examples in this book have been drawn from authentic online North Sámi-language sources from Norway, Sweden, and Finland including media such as NRK Sápmi, YLE Sápmi, the *Ávvir* newspaper, and institutional websites, as well as material from blogs and forums. Because the examples illustrate North Sámi as spoken and written by bilingual speakers in three different countries, they naturally exhibit some lexical and grammatical variations. For example, you will find both the Western dialect form of the actio essive **-me** and its Eastern equivalent **-min**; similarly, administrative terminology from all regions can be seen. The enclitic particles are typically written as separate words, following the Norwegian North Sámi convention, but in examples taken from Finnish sources they are attached to the preceding word. The decision to include examples from the different dialect regions and all three countries is rooted in a desire to familiarise the reader with the natural variations exhibited in North Sámi. The book's content has been checked by two North Sámi native speaker language professionals.

Preface

The English name for the language varieties and people can be spelt in a number of different ways, i.e. Sámi, Same, Saami, Samic, Saamic, and Saame. We use the spelling Sámi in keeping with North Sámi orthographic conventions. Note that Sámi was historically referred to in English as Lappish, and the Sámi people were known as Lapps. These terms are now considered inappropriate and are no longer used.

Acknowledgements

We are extremely grateful to Andrea Hartill at Routledge for her continual support of this project from its inception through to its publication. Likewise, our deepest gratitude goes to Outi Länsman and Ellen Pautamo for expertly proofreading and helping us to improve the volume, and to the British Academy for funding their work. We would also like to thank the anonymous reviewer for numerous helpful suggestions. We are grateful to James Holz for drawing the maps of the Sámi-speaking regions as well as for his patience, encouragement, and cheer throughout the writing process. Finally, a gigantic thank you to Tails and Panda for reminding us of the importance of exercise and food, which are easily neglected while working on a grammar book.

Abbreviations

Acc	accusative case
Acc/Gen	accusative-genitive case
Com	comitative case
Ess	essive case
Gen	genitive case
Ill	illative case
Loc	locative case
Nom	nominative case

Chapter 1

Introduction

1.1 Sámi within the Uralic language family

Sámi is a member of the Uralic language family. The Uralic family consists of two main branches. One is Samoyedic, which includes a number of languages spoken in Siberia, and the other is Finno-Ugric, which includes languages spoken to the west of the Ural Mountains. The Uralic languages are spoken by approximately 25 million people in total in a broad geographical area stretching from Siberia to the Atlantic coast of Norway. The Uralic languages with the largest numbers of speakers are Hungarian (approximately 14 million speakers), Finnish (5.4 million speakers), and Estonian (1.2 million speakers). These three languages are the only members of the Uralic family with official national status in an independent country; in addition, they are official languages of the European Union. Certain other Uralic languages with relatively large numbers of speakers, such as Mordvin (Erzya and Moksha), Mari, Udmurt, Komi, and Karelian, have official status in various regions of Russia. There are also a number of highly endangered Uralic languages, such as Selkup and Nenets in Siberia and Veps and Votic by the Baltic Sea.

As a typical Uralic language, Sámi has a rich morphological and derivational system, including seven nominal cases, four verbal moods, a negative verb, a variety of postpositions, possessive suffixes, and an extensive array of derivative suffixes for both nouns and verbs. In addition to these core grammatical features, the basic Sámi lexicon is of Uralic stock. For example, the verb 'to go' is **mannat** in North Sámi, **mennä** in Finnish, and **menni** in Hungarian; the noun 'fish' is **guolli** in North Sámi, **kala** in Finnish, and **hal** in Hungarian; and the noun 'blood' is **varra** in North Sámi, **veri** in Finnish, and **vér** in Hungarian. As it is spoken in the periphery of the Uralic geographical area, Sámi has retained some original Uralic features

1 Introduction

that have been lost in many other Uralic languages, such as the dual form of pronouns and verbs.

Sámi belongs to the Finno-Ugric branch of the Uralic family. It is generally assumed to be most closely related to the Fennic subgroup of languages, which includes Finnish, Estonian, and Karelian. It is debatable whether the similarities between Sámi and Fennic are due to historical relatedness or are contact-induced. Sámi differs from its supposed closest relatives in that its vowel system has undergone radical changes, it possesses a rich inventory of consonants not found in Fennic languages, and it has a considerably smaller number of cases.

1.2 Sámi language variants

Sámi is not a single unified language but rather comprises nine distinct living linguistic varieties as well as two extinct ones. All of these varieties can be traced back to a reconstructed proto-Sámi language which is assumed to have originated in what is now southern Finland approximately 2,500 years ago, from where they spread into northern Fenno-Scandia over the course of subsequent centuries. The distinct Sámi language varieties are believed to have emerged in approximately 800 CE. However, there is a hypothesis that one of the varieties, South Sámi, may have diverged earlier, based on its archaic case suffixes and more complicated vowel system than the other Sámi varieties. The Sámi language varieties all reflect early contact with speakers of Baltic and Germanic (particularly Nordic) languages, as well as proto-Fennic in the form of loanwords.

These varieties are spoken in the region known as Sápmi, which stretches from central Scandinavia in the southwest to the Kola Peninsula in the northeast, in territory belonging to present-day Norway, Sweden, Finland, and Russia. The majority of Sámi speakers live in Norway. The Sámi language varieties form a continuum in which those forms spoken next to each other are usually mutually intelligible, whereas speakers of more geographically distant varieties cannot communicate with each other. Overall, the degree of difference between the Sámi language varieties can be compared to that of the Romance or Scandinavian languages. The Sámi linguistic varieties can be divided into two main groups, Western and Eastern. The Western Sámi varieties can be further divided into two subgroups, South (South and Ume Sámi) and Central (Pite, Lule, and North Sámi). The Eastern Sámi varieties can similarly be divided into two subgroups, Mainland

Introduction

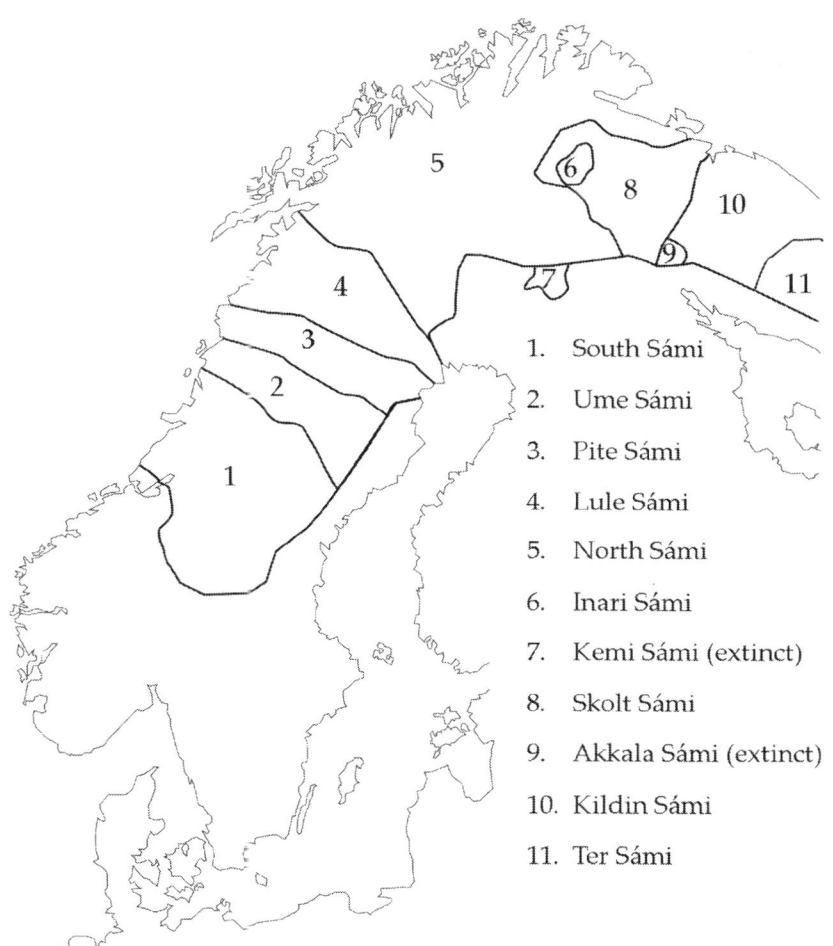

SAMI MAP 1.1 Sámi-speaking regions

(Inari, Kemi, Skolt, and Akkala Sámi) and Peninsular (Kildin and Ter Sámi) (see map 1.1).

There is significant variation in speaker numbers among the nine Sámi language varieties: North Sámi has by far the largest number of speakers, whereas other varieties, such as Pite and Ter Sámi, are extremely endangered. Kemi Sámi became extinct in the nineteenth century, while the last known speaker of Akkala Sámi died in 2003. The Sámi language varieties and their approximate numbers of speakers are shown here.

1 Introduction

Sámi language variety	Approximate number of speakers
South Sámi	600
Ume Sámi	20
Pite Sámi	20
Lule Sámi	1,000–2,000
North Sámi	20,000
Inari Sámi	300
Kemi Sámi	extinct
Skolt Sámi	420
Akkala Sámi	extinct
Kildin Sámi	500
Ter Sámi	2–10

The largest six Sámi varieties, namely South Sámi, Lule Sámi, North Sámi, Inari Sámi, Skolt Sámi, and Kildin Sámi, all have an established literary standard with a distinct orthography. In addition, an official orthography was launched for Ume Sámi in 2016, and an orthography for Pite Sámi has recently been established as well. Some of these language varieties have a relatively long literary tradition. For example, an ABC and Mass book in South/Ume Sámi was published in 1619. This was the first book published in any Sámi language variety. Written North Sámi dates to the seventeenth century as well (see section 1.3.2 for details). The current South Sámi, Lule Sámi, North Sámi, Inari Sámi, and Skolt Sámi orthographies are all based on the Roman alphabet, with the addition of a number of special characters. By contrast, Kildin Sámi uses an extended version of the Cyrillic alphabet.

The Sámi language varieties spoken in Norway, Sweden, and Finland all have a degree of official recognition in those countries. In Norway, the Constitution guarantees the right of the Sámi people to preserve and develop their language, and moreover the Sámi Language Act of 1990 made Sámi an official language of six northern counties. In Sweden, Sámi became an officially recognised minority language in 2000. Moreover, a law concerning national minorities from 2009 guarantees Sámi speakers the right to receive care for children and the elderly in Sámi and states that the language can be used when dealing with the authorities in a number of municipalities. In Norway and Sweden, these laws do not specify any particular varieties of Sámi, and most resources are spent on North Sámi, which has the greatest number of speakers. In Finland, the Sámi Language Act of 1992 and the revised version of 2002 guarantee children the right to study Sámi in school and guarantee Sámi speakers the right to use Sámi in all government services in certain municipalities. This act refers specifically to three particular language varieties, North Sámi, Inari Sámi, and Skolt Sámi. In Russia, Sámi has no official status, and the Sámi language varieties spoken there receive little or no government support.

The following table provides a sample of the eight Sámi language varieties with an independent orthography while giving an indication of the resemblances and differences between them.

	'bird'	'I come'
South Sámi	**ledtie**	**boatam**
Lule Sámi	**ládde**	**boadáv**
North Sámi	**loddi**	**boađán**
Inari Sámi	**lodde**	**poađám**
Skolt Sámi	**lä'dd**	**puäđám**
Kildin Sámi	**ло'нд**	**поадам**
Ume Sámi	**láddie**	**bádáv**
Pite Sámi	**ládde**	**bádav**

1.3 Historical and sociolinguistic introduction to North Sámi

1.3.1 Early history of North Sámi

North Sámi has long been spoken above the Arctic Circle in Norway, Sweden, and Finland. However, very little is known about the history of the language before the earliest written attestations.

1.3.2 Written North Sámi

Written records of North Sámi are relatively late, beginning with missionary activity in the seventeenth century. The first book in North Sámi is a collection of prayers and confessions published in 1638 (first edition) and 1640 (second edition) entitled *Swenske och lappeske ABC-book* 'Swedish and Lappish ABC Book'. This was followed by *Manuale Lapponicum* (published in 1648), written by the priest Johan Tornaeus (early 1600s–1691). This seminal volume contained a number of religious texts written in a language based primarily on Swedish varieties of North Sámi.

The North Sámi language itself began to attract scholarly attention in the same period. The first grammar of North Sámi was written by the Norwegian priest and linguist Knut Leem (1696/1697–1774) and published in 1748, and the first dictionaries were published in 1756 and 1768. A contemporary of Knut Leem was Anders Porsanger (1735–80). He was the first Sámi to receive higher education, assisted Leem in his research, and translated portions of the Bible into North Sámi. Unfortunately, most of his work has now been lost. In the same period, the Swedish priest Per Fjellström (1697–1764) attempted to create a common orthography for all the Sámi language varieties spoken in Sweden. This variety was based primarily on South Sámi but incorporated elements of North Sámi and was used in Sweden throughout the eighteenth and nineteenth centuries.

In the 1820s the Danish linguist Rasmus Rask (1787–1842) devised an orthographic system for North Sámi which included for the first time the use of special consonants to denote sounds particular to the language. His work, which was published in 1832, was based on Leem's grammar. Rask collaborated with the Norwegian priest Nils Vibe Stockfleth (1787–1866), and the latter put the system into use in a range of North Sámi publications, including Luther's Small Catechism (published in 1837), the New Testament (published in 1840), a grammar (published in 1840), a Norwegian–North Sámi dictionary (published in 1851), and Luther's Postil (published in 1857). Stockfleth also translated parts of the Old Testament.

However, the first complete North Sámi Bible translation was not published until 1895. A significant role in this translation was played by Jens Andreas Friis (1821–96), a Norwegian linguist who was a professor of Sámi and Finnish at the University of Kristiania (now the University of Oslo). He was one of the pioneers of academic study of the Sámi language. Friis also published a grammar of Sámi (1856), a dictionary (1887), an anthology of

Sámi mythology (1871), and a prominent novel about Sámi life called *Lajla* (1881). In addition, he published travel descriptions and ethnographic maps. Another important figure from this period of Sámi literary history was Lars Jacobsen Hætta (1834–96), a Sámi reindeer herder who served as Friis' language consultant and worked on the 1895 Bible translation. In addition, he and Friis published two books of psalms together.

Over the course of the twentieth century several different orthographies have been used to write North Sámi in Norway, Sweden, and Finland. The first modern orthography in widespread use in Norway was the one launched by Friis. This orthography was used, for example, in the first North Sámi newspaper, *Sagai Muittalægje* (1904–11), and in *Nuorttanaste*, a religious publication first published in 1898 (and still in print today). Subsequently, the Norwegian linguist Just Qvigstad (1853–1957) developed a modified orthography including the use of an apostrophe to mark the strong and extra strong grade of consonants (see section 2.6 for discussion of this phenomenon in North Sámi), e.g. **oap'pat** 'to learn' vs. modern orthography **oahppat**. In the 1920s another Norwegian linguist, Konrad Nielsen (1875–1953), developed a new orthography incorporating Qvigstad's system of apostrophes which was intended to provide a closer correspondence between North Sámi sounds and graphemes. Nielsen published a three-volume textbook of North Sámi, *Lærebok i lappisk* 'Lapp Textbook' (1926–9) and a five-volume dictionary, *Lappisk ordbook* 'Lapp Dictionary' (1932–62) using this orthography.

In Sweden, orthographic work in the first half of the twentieth century focused on South, Ume, and Lule Sámi rather than on North Sámi. In 1948 there was an orthography reform initiated by the Norwegian linguist Knut Bergsland (1914–98) and the Swedish Pite Sámi linguist Israel Ruong (1903–86). The so-called Bergsland-Ruong orthography was based on the Kautokeino dialect and remained in use in the Swedish and Norwegian Sámi school systems until 1979.

Meanwhile, in Finland an orthography was developed in the 1930s by the Finnish linguist Paavo Ravila (1902–74). The orthography, which was based on eastern dialects of North Sámi, was modified in the 1950s by another Finnish linguist, Erkki Itkonen (1913–92). These Finnish orthographies differed from their Norwegian and Swedish counterparts in that they lacked the consonants **b, g,** and **d,** using instead **p, k, t** (under influence from Finnish orthography) and did not use the apostrophe or Norwegian/Swedish-derived letter å (in contrast to the Bergsland-Ruong orthography used at the same time in Norway and Sweden).

1 Introduction

A major landmark in the history of North Sámi orthography occurred in 1979, when a new unified writing system for the language was developed for use in Norway, Sweden, and Finland. The new orthography was approved by the Nordic Sámi Council and quickly came to replace all existing North Sámi orthographies. The orthography underwent minor revisions in 1985 and continues to serve as the standard orthography for North Sámi in all of the Nordic countries.

1.3.3 Dialects of modern North Sámi

Modern North Sámi is spoken in northern Norway, Sweden, and Finland, with its heartland in the Norwegian county of Finnmark (see map 1.2). The number of speakers is estimated to be approximately 20,000, with 2,000 in Finland, 5,000–6,000 in Sweden, and 12,000–13,000 in Norway. North Sámi is usually divided into two main dialect areas, Western (centred around the town of Kautokeino in Finnmark and covering the municipalities of Alta, Enontekiö, and parts of Sodankylä and Inari) and Eastern (centred around the town of Karasjok in Finnmark and covering the municipalities of Porsanger, Tana, Utsjoki, and parts of Inari). Additionally, smaller dialectal areas can be distinguished; e.g. within the Western group there is Torne (centred around Kiruna, Karesuando, and Jukkasjärvi in Sweden), and all along the coast there is Sea Sámi. The standard written language is based primarily on the Western dialect, with incorporation of some features of the Eastern dialect. The Torne and Sea dialects are now relatively restricted in use. Noteworthy features of the Torne dialect include the absence of the sound š /ʃ/, the replacement of the sounds č /tʃ/ and ž /dʒ/ with c /ts/ and z /dz/ respectively, the use of the suffix -n instead of -s for the locative singular case of nouns (see section 3.2.5), and the ending -o instead of -u in the third person singular form of the present tense (see section 7.1.1). Noteworthy features of the Sea dialect include the replacement of the consonant clusters -pm-, -tn-, -kŋ-, and -dg- with the nasals and glides -mm-, -nn-, -ŋŋ-, and -jj- (for example, the standard written form sápmelaš 'Sámi person' is pronounced sámmelaš) and the use of the suffix -st instead of -s for the locative singular case of nouns. The Western dialect closely resembles the written standard but has a few distinguishing features. For example, ŋ /ŋ/ is consistently replaced by nj /ɲ/, and t /θ/ is often pronounced as s /s/. One of the most characteristic features of the Eastern dialect is that the diphthongs ea / eæ/, oa /oɑ/, and uo /uo/ are pronounced as ie /ie/, uo /uo/ or /ua/, and ue /ue/. In addition, the letter á is often pronounced as /æ/, while between vowels the consonant g /g/ disappears and the consonant b /b/ is pronounced as /v/.

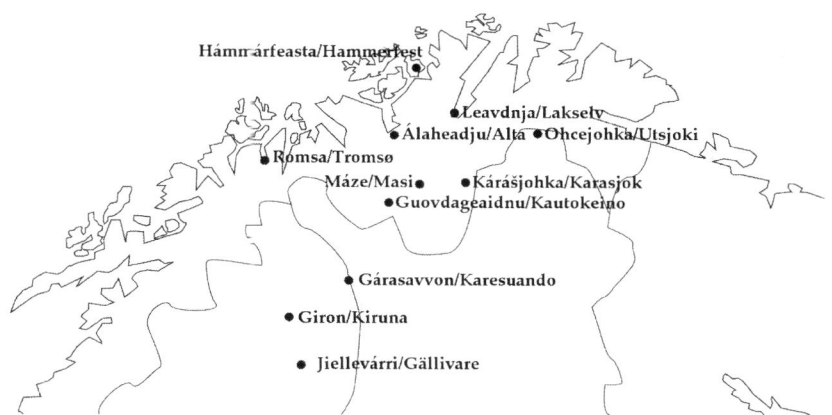

SAMI MAP 1.2 North Sámi region

There are also some grammatical differences between the Western and Eastern dialects, which will be pointed out in the relevant sections of this volume. In addition, there are some lexical differences between the two variants, e.g. Western **mánnodat** 'Monday' and **disdat** 'Tuesday' vs. Eastern **vuossárga** and **maŋŋebárga**, respectively.

1.3.4 Sociolinguistic situation of North Sámi

The North Sámi language suffered from oppression for many centuries in Norway, Sweden, and Finland. Lutheran missionary activity in Sápmi was widespread throughout the early modern period and typically involved attempts to eradicate traditional Sámi culture, religion, and language. In the nineteenth and twentieth centuries, the national governments actively discouraged the use of Sámi through a variety of measures including banning the language from education and other public arenas. Sámi children were routinely taken away from their families and sent to boarding schools, where they were punished for speaking Sámi. In addition, the Sámi suffered other types of oppression and discrimination such as denial of land and water rights, intensive logging and mining in their traditional lands, and racial segregation. They were also subjected to state-sponsored biological research. The 1970s saw the emergence of a strong grassroots Sámi cultural and political activist movement with the goal of obtaining land and water rights as well as greater cultural and linguistic autonomy. This movement led to the establishment of Sámi organisations including the Sámi parliaments (**Sámediggi**) in Norway, Sweden, and Finland. Over the course of the 1980s and 1990s the position of the Sámi language was improved significantly: North Sámi became the main language of instruction in schools in its heartland, and there was increased government support for Sámi-language radio programming.

In the twenty-first century North Sámi enjoys a relatively secure position in Norway, Sweden, and Finland. As mentioned earlier, it benefits from a certain amount of legal protection in the three countries: Sámi children are entitled to mother-tongue education; Sámi is taught at several universities such as at the Giellagas Institute in Oulu (Finland), Umeå and Uppsala (Sweden), and Tromsø (Norway); and there is a Sámi institute of higher education, the **Sámi allaskuvla** (Sámi University College) in Kautokeino. The Norwegian, Swedish, and Finnish national television stations all offer some Sámi programming (mostly news and children's TV) in addition to radio and online news. A list of links to these online media outlets can be found in the section on suggested resources at the back of this book. The language has a good rate of intergenerational transmission and, despite its small speaker base, its future seems secure.

1.3.5 North Sámi culture, literature, and music

Although, as mentioned in 1.3.2, literature in Sámi dates back to the early seventeenth century, the first non-religious book written by a Sámi author was published in 1910. The book, entitled *Muitalus sámiid birra* 'An Account of the Sámi', was written by Johan Turi (1854–1936), a reindeer herder from Kautokeino, and paints a picture of Sámi life in Northern Sweden in the early 1900s. Over the course of the twentieth century, North Sámi developed a thriving literary culture. The 1970s and 1980s saw the emergence of a number of prominent North Sámi-language authors, such as Kirsti Paltto, Nils-Aslak Valkeapää (discussed further later), and Elle-Márjá Vars, some of whom have remained active until the present day. Contemporary North Sámi literature includes novels, short stories, poetry, and plays. There are several online shops selling North Sámi-language literature; links to these can be found in the suggested resources section at the end of this book.

The traditional pre-Christian Sámi religion is animistic and shamanistic. It involves reverence for sacred sites, including natural features such as rock formations and springs, as well as for animals such as the bear. The key Sámi spiritual figure is the **noaidi**, a shaman who plays a ritual drum in order to connect with the spiritual world. Following the arrival of Christian missionaries in Sápmi in the early modern period, there were intensive ongoing attempts to eradicate the Sámi religion. Nowadays most Sámi are Lutheran, and some are active churchgoers. Christmas and Easter are important Sámi holidays. A prominent figure in traditional Sámi mythology and folklore is the **stállu**, a giant troll-like creature who eats humans. The **juovlastállu** (lit: Christmas **stállu**) is the Sámi version of Santa Claus but is a menacing figure who should be avoided.

The Sámi have a long and vibrant musical tradition based around the genre of joik, a form of singing without instrumental accompaniment that may or may not have words. Joiks are often based on or dedicated to individual people or animals. As joiking was associated with the traditional Sámi religion, it was banned for much of Sámi history. The renaissance of Sámi culture in the second half of the twentieth century led to a renewed appreciation of joik and the appearance of commercially successful joik singers, as well as the growth of Sámi music of other genres. Perhaps the most well-known contemporary Sámi musician is Mari Boine, who has gained widespread international recognition. There are a number of other singers and bands who sing in Sámi in a variety of genres, including rock, metal, folk, and modern interpretations of joik. There is a Sámi music competition, the Sámi Grand Prix, which has taken place in Kautokeino annually since 1990.

There is a Sámi-language theatre, **Beaivváš Sámi Našunálateáhter**, which is based in Kautokeino and puts on dramatic performances in various genres. There have also been two North Sámi-language feature films, both written and directed by the Norwegian Sámi Nils Gaup. The first, *Ofelaš* (Pathfinder, 1987), tells the story of a thousand-year-old legend about a Sámi community under threat from **čuđit**, the Chudes, a marauding enemy people based in Russia and possibly of Finnic origin. The second, *Guovdageainnu Stuimmit* (The Kautokeino Rebellion, 2008), relates the true story of a Sámi uprising that took place in Kautokeino in 1852 in the face of Norwegian oppression.

Nils-Aslak Valkeapää or Áillohaš (1943–2001) is one of the most prominent North Sámi cultural figures of the second half of the twentieth century. Áillohaš, who was born in Finnish Sápmi, played a hugely influential role in the renaissance of Sámi culture from the 1970s onwards. He was active in many areas of Sámi culture, including music, drama, poetry, and art. As a musician, he modernised the traditional joik genre and wrote the music for the film *Ofelaš*. His literary activity includes winning the Nordic Council of Literature Prize in 1991 for his collection *Beaivi áhčážan* 'The Sun, My Father'. He also performed in the Sámi theatre and played a major role in *Ofelaš*.

Introduction

Another important aspect of Sámi culture is **duodji**, the traditional style of handicrafts, which includes woven baskets and belts as well as carved cups (called **guksi**, plural **guvssit**), bowls, and knives made from wood burl, reindeer bone, and antlers. Traditional Sámi clothes include the **gákti**, a tunic with colourful decorations that vary from location to location, as well as reindeer-skin trousers and boots. Nowadays the **gákti** is typically worn only at Easter, weddings, confirmations, and on other special occasions. **Duodji** items are often sold to tourists as well as at annual markets, which commonly take place around Easter and include snowmobile and reindeer racing.

Traditionally the Sámi were often nomadic reindeer herders who lived in the inland regions in the winter and migrated with the flocks to the coast for the summer. Other traditional Sámi livelihoods include fishing and farming. The nomadic Sámi traditionally lived in a **goahti**, a tipi-like hut built out of wooden poles with a covering of turf, moss, or timber, and at times of migration built a smaller and more temporary tipi-like construction called a **lávvu**, made of wooden poles with a leather or fabric covering. Nomadic Sámi society was organised around the **siida**, a group of families that worked cooperatively and migrated together. Nowadays many Sámi live in cities, and only relatively small numbers herd reindeer for a living.

Chapter 2
Phonology and orthography

While North Sámi has a standard orthography, the underlying phonology varies according to dialect area. The following presentation is based on the Western dialect. A more thorough treatment of the North Sámi phonology is beyond the scope of this book. For a more detailed analysis see Pekka Sammallahti's (1998) *The Saami Languages: An Introduction*, listed in the Suggested Resources section at the end of the volume.

2.1 The alphabet

The North Sámi alphabet is as follows:

a á b c č d đ e f g h i j k l m n ŋ o p r s š t ŧ u v z ž

2.2 Vowels

Vowel	IPA	Description
a	/ɑ/	open back unrounded
á	/ɛ:/, /a/ or /æ/	open front unrounded
e	/e/ or /e:/	close-mid front unrounded
i	/ɪ/ or /i:/	close front unrounded
o	/o/ or /o:/	close-mid back rounded
u	/u/ or /u:/	back close rounded

2 Phonology and orthography

Points to note:

- The vowel **á** is pronounced as a long /aː/ in western parts of the North Sámi-speaking region (e.g. Kautokeino) and as /æ/ in the Eastern dialect region in the final syllable and in the first syllable except when followed by /a/, /o/, or /u/.
- When following a vowel, the symbol **i** represents the consonant /j/, e.g. **láibi** /lajpi/ 'bread'.
- An epenthetic schwa usually appears between a consonant cluster beginning with **đ, l,** or **r**, e.g. **geađgi** /keæđəki/ 'stone', **golbma** /koləpmɑ/ 'three', **bárdni** /parətni/ 'boy'.

2.3 Diphthongs

Diphthong	IPA	Example
ea	/eæ/	**beana** 'dog'
ie	/ie/	**giella** 'language'
oa	/oa/	**boazu** 'reindeer'
uo	/uo/	**muohta** 'snow'

Points to note:

- Diphthongs are regularly reduced to a lengthened form of the first vowel of the diphthong in the following two circumstances: a) when followed by **ii** or **ui**, e.g. **giehta** 'hand' : **gihtii** 'to a hand' or b) when followed by **e** that has shifted from **i**, e.g. **vuolgit** 'to leave' : **vulge** 'they left' or **o** that has shifted from **u**, e.g. **goarrut** 'to sew' : **gorro** 'they sewed'.
- In Eastern North Sámi **ea** /eæ/, **oa** /oɑ/, and **uo** /uo/ are pronounced as **ie** /ie/, **uo** /uo/ or /ua/, and **ue** /ue/.

2.4 Consonants

Consonant	IPA	Description	English equivalent
b	/p/	voiceless bilabial stop	s**p**ort
c	/ts/	voiceless alveolar sibilant affricate	ca**ts**

2 Phonology and orthography

č	/tʃ/	voiceless palato-alveolar sibilant affricate	**ch**urch
d	/t/	voiceless alveolar stop	**s**tar
đ	/ð/	voiced dental fricative	**th**is
f	/f/	voiceless labio-dental fricative	**f**un
g	/k/	voiceless velar stop	s**k**in
h	/h/	voiceless glottal fricative	**h**ello
j	/j/	voiced palatal glide	**y**arn
k	/k/	voiceless velar stop	s**k**in
l	/l/	voiced alveolar lateral	**l**uck
m	/m/	voiced bilabial nasal	**m**other
n	/n/	voiced alveolar nasal	**n**ose
ŋ	/ŋ/	voiced velar nasal	si**ng**er
p	/p/	voiceless bilabial stop	s**p**ort
r	/r/	voiced alveolar trill	as in Spanish or Italian
s	/s/	voiceless alveolar sibilant	**s**un
š	/ʃ/	voiceless palato-alveolar sibilant	**sh**op
t	/t/	voiceless alveolar stop	**s**tar
ŧ	/θ/	voiceless dental fricative	**th**in
v	/v/	voiced labio-dental fricative	**v**ery
z	/ts/	voiced alveolar sibilant affricate	ca**ts**
ž	/tʃ/	voiceless palato-alveolar sibilant affricate	**ch**urch

2 Phonology and orthography

Points to note:

Consonant length

- All consonants can be doubled. Double consonants are written with two symbols, e.g. **geassi** /keæssi/ 'summer'.
- Some consonants can also be tripled. However, this is not represented in the orthography; instead, triple consonants look identical to double consonants, e.g. **guossi** /kuosssi/ 'guest'.

Stops and affricates

- The stops **b**, **g**, and **d**, and the affricates **z** and **ž** are typically voiceless.
- The consonant **h** often appears before **k**, **p**, **t**, **c**, and **č**. This indicates a phenomenon called preaspiration, i.e. a /h/ sound preceding the stop or affricate. When appearing before a double consonant, the /h/ is actually pronounced twice and the other consonant is pronounced once, e.g. **áhkku** /a^{hh}ku/ 'grandmother', **bohccot** /po^{hh}tso^{h}t/ 'reindeer (plural)'.
- The only difference in pronunciation between **b**, **g**, **d**, **z**, and **ž** on the one hand and **k**, **p**, **t**, **c**, and **č** on the other is that the latter are typically accompanied by unwritten preaspiration in consonant clusters and after the vowel **i** as well as before word-final **t**. For example, compare **álgit** /aləkit/ 'to begin' with **mielki** /mielə^{h}ki/ 'milk'.
- The letters **k**, **p**, and **t** do not appear at the beginning of words except in some recent borrowings, e.g. **telefovdna** 'telephone'.
- The stops are unaspirated, i.e. without an accompanying puff of air. This resembles English stops after **s**, as indicated in the table.
- When the stops **b**, **g**, and **d** and the affricates **z** and **ž** are doubled, the first one is voiced, e.g. **oabbá** /oɑbpa/ 'sister', **vázzit** /vadztsi^{h}t/ 'to walk'.
- If the stops **k**, **p**, and **t** are preceded by a sibilant or another stop, there is no preaspiration, e.g. **astat** /asta^{h}t/ 'to have time', **luokta** /luoktɑ/ 'bay'.
- In the Eastern dialect area, the stops **b** and **g** are pronounced as /v/ and /j/ or /Ø/ between vowels, e.g. **stobus** 'in the house' is pronounced as /stovus/ and **logan** 'I read' is pronounced as /lo.an/.

Other

- The consonant **v** sounds like /w/ before the vowel **u**, e.g. **vuordit** /wuorə-ti^{h}t/ 'to wait' and before voiced consonants, e.g. **guovža** /kuowtʃa/ 'bear'.
- There is another phenomenon called postaspiration, whereby a consonant is followed by an unwritten /h/ sound. Examples include **okta** /ok^{h}ta/ 'one', **čakča** /tʃak^{h}tʃa/ 'autumn'.

- The consonant combinations **dj**, **lj**, and **nj** are pronounced palatalised (with an inherent /ʲ/ element), i.e. /tʲ/, /lʲ/, /nʲ/.
- Word-final **t** is typically pronounced just as /h/ within a sentence, e.g. **mannat ruoktot** /mannaʰ ruokʰtoʰt/ 'to go home'.
- The consonant **ŋ** is pronounced like the 'ng' in the Standard English word 'singer'. However, in the Western dialect it is typically pronounced as /nʲ/, e.g. **maŋis** 'behind' is pronounced as /manʲis/.

Note that only the following consonants can occur at the end of North Sámi:

l, n, r, s, š, t (and also **-id** in the accusative-genitive plural of nouns; see section 3.2).

Words ending in these consonants may display a different consonant in their inflected forms (discussed in subsequent chapters). This is actually the original consonant that is not allowed in word-final position. Typical alternations are listed in the following table.

Word-final	Non-final	Example	Translation
-n	-m-	**eallin : eallima**	life
-š	-ž-	**nieiddaš : nieiddaža**	little girl
-t	-b-	**unnit : unnibu**	smaller
-t	-d-	**vielgat : vielgada**	white
-t	-g-	**servodat : servodaga**	society
-t	-h-	**alit : aliha**	blue

Similarly, North Sámi words cannot end in a double consonant. Only the first consonant appears in word-final position, and the consonant cluster reappears in other inflected forms.

Word-final	Non-final	Example	Translation
-l	-ld-	**in oaivvil : oaivvildit**	I don't have an opinion : to have an opinion

2 Phonology and orthography

-r	-rd-	in ipmir : ipmirdit	I don't understand : understand
-s	-ss-	buoremus : buoremussan	best : as the best
-s	-st-	in ráhkis : ráhkistit	I don't love : to love
-š	-šš-	borramuš : borramuššan	food : as food
-š	-št-	in beroš : beroštit	I don't care : to care

Finally, word-final -š can also become -čč- in non-word-final position:

Word-final	Non-final	Example	Translation
-š	-čč-	sápmelaš : sápmelačča	Sámi person

2.5 Stress, syllables, and intonation

The stress in North Sámi is always on the first syllable. A stressed syllable is followed by one or two unstressed syllables.

    ***guok*-te**   two

    ***or*-rut**   to live

    ***beat*-na-gat**   dog

    ***sá*-gas-tit**   to chat

If a word has four or more syllables, every other syllable is stressed.

    ***jea*-ral-*da*-gat**   questions

    ***dárb*-ba-*šeh*-pet**   you (plural) need

2 Phonology and orthography

North Sámi has the following syllable types:

CV	go	interrogative particle
VC	ik-te	yesterday
VCC	olg-gos	towards out
VVC	ean	not (first person dual)
VVCC	oahp-pi	pupil
VVV	eai	not (third person plural)
CVV	lea	is
CVVV	moai	we (dual)
CVC	mán-ná	child
CVVC	giel-la	language
CVCC	guht-ta	six
CCVC	spáb-ba	ball
CVVCC	meahc-ci	wilderness
CCVCC	smáhk-ka	taste, flavour
CCVVCC	spoahk-ka-lit	to knock once

In compound words the main stress is on the first syllable of the first word and the secondary stress is on the first syllables of the following word(s).

boa-zo-doal-lu   reindeer herding

má-náid-gár-di   nursery, kindergarten, preschool

The same applies to derivative suffixes, which have their own secondary stress.

oah-pa-head-dji   teacher

ráh-kis-vuoh-ta   love

ve-jo-laš-vuoh-ta   possibility

Both statements and questions display a falling intonation.

2 Phonology and orthography

2.6 Consonant gradation

Consonant gradation is a phenomenon of sound alternations within words. Consonants have three possible grades: extra strong, strong, and weak. Consonants appear in one grade in the dictionary form of words and a different grade in inflected forms. Some words appear in the extra strong or strong grade in the dictionary form and shift to a weaker grade in the inflected forms, whereas others do the opposite. See sections 3.1 and 7 for paradigms illustrating consonant gradation in the infection of nouns and verbs respectively.

The following lists illustrate some of the most common types of consonant gradation.

1a Double consonant → single consonant

Strong	Weak	Example			
đđ	đ	oa*đđ*it	to sleep	oa*đ*án	I sleep
ff	f	gá*ff*e	coffee	gá*f*es	in the coffee
ll	l	guo*ll*i	fish	guo*l*is	in the fish
mm	m	na*mm*a	name	na*m*at	names
nn	n	má*nn*á	child	má*n*áin	with a child
rr	r	bo*rr*at	to eat	bo*r*an	I eat
ss	s	gu*ss*a	cow	gu*s*at	cows
tt	t	Ruo*tt*a	Sweden	Ruo*t*as	in Sweden
vv	v	go*vv*a	picture, photo	go*v*as	in the picture/photo

1b Triple consonant → double consonant

The consonants in category 1a also have an extra strong grade consisting of a triple consonant that alternates with the strong grade. The triple consonant in the extra strong grade is written with a double consonant so that it looks identical to the strong grade.

2 Phonology and orthography

Extra strong	Strong	Example			
ll /lll/	*ll*	**ja*ll*a** /ja*lll*a/	stupid	**ja*ll*at**	stupidly
nn /nnn/	*nn*	**u*nn*i** /u*nnn*i/	small	**u*nn*it**	smaller
ss /sss/	*ss*	**guo*ss*i** /guo*sss*i/	guest	**guo*ss*it**	guests

2a Double consonant with **h** → single voiced consonant

Strong	Weak	Example			
hc	*z*	**bá*hc*it**	to stay	**báze**	stay!
hk	*g*	**jo*hk*a**	river	**jogas**	in the river
hp	*b*	**sto*hp*u**	house	**stobut**	houses
ht	*đ*	**boa*ht*it**	to come	**boađán**	I come

2b Double consonant with **h** → single consonant with **h**

Extra strong	Strong	Example			
hcc	*hc*	**mea*hcc*i**	wilderness, forest	**mea*hc*is**	in the wilderness, in the forest
hčč	*hč*	**á*hčč*i**	father	**á*hč*it**	fathers
hkk	*hk*	**á*hkk*u**	grandmother	**á*hk*uin**	with grandmother
hpp	*hp*	**oa*hpp*at**	to learn	**oa*hp*an**	I learn
htt	*ht*	**sá*htt*it**	to be able	**sá*ht*ii**	he was able

2 Phonology and orthography

3 Double voiced consonant → its double voiceless equivalent

Extra strong	Strong	Example			
bb	pp	oa**bb**á	sister	oa**pp**át	sisters
dd	tt	gá**dd**i	shore	gá**tt**is	at the shore
gg	kk	bie**gg**a	wind	bie**kk**as	in the wind
zz	cc	vá**zz**it	to walk	vá**cc**ii	s/he walked
žž	čč	oa**žž**ut	to get, to receive	oa**čč**un	I get, I receive

4a Voiceless stop + nasal → nasal

Strong	Weak	Example			
pm	m	Sá**pm**i	Sámi land	Sá**m**is	in Sámi land
tn	n	a**tn**it	to use	a**n**ii	s/he used
tnj	nj	la**tn**ja	room	la**nj**at	rooms
kŋ	ŋ	jie**kŋ**a	ice	jie**ŋ**ain	with ice

4b Voiced stop + nasal → voiceless stop + nasal

Extra strong	Strong	Example			
bm	pm	bie**bm**u	food	bie**pm**uin	with food
dn	tn	ea**dn**i	mother	ea**tn**it	mothers

Point to note:

- There may be an additional consonant at the beginning of the cluster, which does not effect the alternations given earlier, e.g. **bárdni** 'boy', **bártnit** 'boys'

5 Consonant + consonant → consonant + double consonant

Extra strong	Strong	Example			
đg	đgg	gea*đ*gi	stone	gea*đgg*it	stones
ib	ibb	lá*i*bi	bread	lá*ibb*iin	with bread
id	idd	nie*i*da	girl	nie*idd*at	girls
ig	igg	á*i*gi	time	á*igg*it	times
ik	ikk	čuo*i*ka	mosquito	čuo*ikk*at	mosquitos
il	ill	bi*i*la	car	bi*ill*at	cars
it	itt	mu*i*tit	to remember	mu*itt*e	remember!
iv	ivv	bea*i*vi	day	bea*ivv*it	days
lb	lbb	há*l*bi	cheap	há*lbb*it	cheaper
lg	lgg	vuo*l*git	to leave	vuo*lgg*án	I leave
lk	lkk	mie*l*ki	milk	mie*lkk*is	in the milk
lp	lpp	vuo*l*pu	dress	vuo*lpp*ut	dresses
lv	lvv	gi*l*vu	competition	gi*lvv*ut	competitions
mp	mpp	lá*m*pá	lamp	lá*mpp*át	lamps
nd	ndd	gá*n*da	boy	gá*ndd*at	boys
ŋg	ŋgg	sea*ŋ*ga	bed	sea*ŋgg*as	in bed
rd	rdd	gi*r*dit	to fly	gi*rdd*ii	s/he flew
rf	rff	má*r*fi	sausage	má*rff*it	sausages
rg	rgg	ba*r*gat	to work	ba*rgg*an	I work

2 Phonology and orthography

2 Phonology and orthography

rj	rjj	*girji*	book	*girjjit*	books
sk	skk	o*sk*ut	to believe in	o*skk*un	I believe in
st	stt	oa*st*it	to buy	oa*stt*e	buy!
tk	tkk	má*tk*i	trip	má*tkk*it	trips
vd	vdd	bi*vd*it	to hunt	bi*vdd*ii	s/he hunted
vg	vgg	lea*vg*a	flag	lea*vgg*at	flags
vk	vkk	lá*vk*a	bag	lá*vkk*as	in the bag
vl	vll	sku*vl*a	school	sku*vll*at	schools
vp	vpp	gá*vp*i	shop	gá*vpp*is	in the shop
vr	vrr	já*vr*i	lake	já*vrr*it	lakes
vž	vžž	guo*vž*a	bear	guo*vžž*at	bears

Points to note:

- In the extra strong grade of all the consonant clusters listed, except those beginning with đ, l, or r, the first part of the cluster is pronounced double, whereas in the strong grade the second part is pronounced double, e.g. o**sk**ut /osskut/ 'to believe in', o**skk**un /oskkun/ 'I believe in'.
- In these combinations the consonant **j** is written as **i**.
- The preaspiration in the extra strong grade **it** becomes more prominent in the strong grade **itt**, e.g. muitit /mui^{h}ti^{h}t/ 'to remember', mui**tt**e /mui^{hh}te/ 'remember!'.
- There is an epenthetic vowel when the extra strong grade begins with đ, l, or r. The vowel disappears in the strong grade, e.g. geađgi /keæđ$^{\partial}$ki/ 'stone', geađggit /keađgki^{h}t/ 'stones'.
- There may be an additional consonant at the beginning of the cluster, which does not affect the alternations given here, e.g. **goansta** 'trick', **goansttat** 'tricks'.

6   Consonant + stop + nasal → consonant + double nasal

Extra strong	Strong	Example			
ibm	**imm**	**di*ib*mu**	clock	**di*im*mut**	clocks
idn	**inn**	**oa*id*nit**	to see	**oa*in*nán**	I see
lbm	**lmm**	**ča*lb*mi**	eye	**ča*lm*mit**	eyes
vdn	**vnn**	**i*vd*ni**	colour	**i*vn*nit**	colours

Point to note:

- As in category 5, in these combinations the consonant **j** is written as **i**.

7a   Single consonant + j → j

Strong	Weak	Example			
dj	**j**	**vuo*dj*it**	to drive	**vuo*j*án**	I drive

Point to note:

- The cluster **dj** represents a double palatalised **t**.

7b   Double consonant + j → single consonant + j

Extra strong	Strong	Example			
ddj	**dj**	**á*ddj*á**	grandfather	**á*dj*át**	grandfathers
llj	**lj**	**vie*llj*a**	brother	**vie*lj*ain**	with the brother

Points to note:

- The cluster **ddj** represents a double palatalised **d**.
- The cluster **llj** represents a triple palatalised **l**.
- The cluster **lj** represents a double palatalised **l**.

8   k + affricate, sibilant or t → v + double affricate, sibilant or t

Extra strong	Strong	Example			
kc	**vcc**	**lákca**	cream	**lávccas**	in the cream
kč	**včč**	**čakča**	autumn	**čavččas**	from autumn
ks	**vss**	**máksit**	to pay	**mávssán**	I pay
kt	**vtt**	**okta**	one	**ovttas**	together

Chapter 3
Nouns

3.1 Noun types

There are three types of nouns in North Sámi: even-syllable (also known as vowel-stem), odd-syllable (also known as consonant-stem), and contracted. Note that these patterns sometimes include adjectives. Each type of noun inflects (i.e. changes its form) differently. North Sámi nouns inflect in seven different cases, in the singular and in the plural. The basic case endings are as follows; see section 3.2 for examples of each case.

Even-syllable and contracted suffixes

	Singular	Plural
Nominative	—	**-t**
Accusative-genitive	—	**-id**
Illative	**-i**	**-ide**
Locative	**-s**	**-in**
Comitative	**-in**	**-iguin**
Essive	**-n**	

Odd-syllable suffixes

	Singular	Plural
Nominative	—	**-at**
Accusative-genitive	**-a**	**-iid**

Illative	-ii	-iidda
Locative	-is	-iin
Comitative	-iin	-iiguin
Essive		-in

Points to note:

- Addition of the case endings is often accompanied by consonant gradation (illustrated later).
- The accusative and genitive have the same form but different functions; see section 3.2.
- The essive is the same in the singular and the plural.
- The nominative is distinguished from the accusative-genitive by either consonant gradation, e.g. **guolli** : **guoli** 'fish', the addition of a syllable, e.g. **gahpir** : **gahpira** 'hat', or both, e.g. **beana** : **beatnaga** 'dog'.

3.1.1 Even-syllable

Even-syllable nouns have two or, more rarely, four syllables. They end in a vowel in the accusative-genitive case. The nominative and illative singular and the essive are in the strong grade. All other cases are in the weak grade.

mánná 'child'

	Singular	Plural
Nom	**mánná**	**máná-t**
Acc/Gen	**máná**	**máná-id**
Ill	**mánná-i**	**máná-ide**
Loc	**máná-s**	**máná-in**
Com	**máná-in**	**máná-iguin**
Ess		**mánná-n**

Here is a list of some other commonly used nouns that follow this pattern.

bussá	cat
muottá	aunt (mother's younger sister)
oabbá	sister
siessá	aunt (father's sister)

guovža 'bear'

	Singular	Plural
Nom	**guovža**	**guovžža-t**
Acc/Gen	**guovžža**	**guovžža-id**
Ill	**guvži-i**	**guovžža-ide**
Loc	**guovžža-s**	**guovžža-in**
Com	**guovžža-in**	**guovžža-iguin**
Ess		**guovža-n**

Points to note:

- The final vowel -a changes to -i in the illative, as in **guovža** : **guvžii**
- Diphthongs in the first syllable of nouns ending in -a are simplified before -ii-, in other words in the illative, as in **guovža** : **guvžii**

Here is a list of some other commonly used nouns that follow this pattern.

biila	car
čakča	autumn
dolla	fire
filbma	film
gánda	boy, son
giehta	hand

3 Nouns

giella	language, tongue
govva	photo, picture
idja	night
johka	river
latnja	room
lávka	bag
mearra	sea, ocean
nieida	girl, daughter
ruhta	money
skuovva	shoe
skuvla	school
vielja	brother

guolli 'fish'

	Singular	Plural
Nom	**guolli**	**guoli-t**
Acc/Gen	**guoli**	**guli-id**
Ill	**guollá-i**	**guli-ide**
Loc	**guoli-s**	**guli-in**
Com	**guli-in**	**guli-iguin**
Ess		**guolli-n**

Points to note:

- As in the case of nouns ending in -a, diphthongs in the first syllable of nouns ending in -i are simplified before -ii-, as in **guolli** : **guliin**.
- The final vowel -i becomes -á- in the illative.

3 Nouns

Here is a list of some other commonly used nouns that follow this pattern.

albmi	sky
áhčči	father
bárdni	boy, son
bátni	tooth
beaivi	day
čalbmi	eye
čáhci	water
čoavji	stomach
dálvi	winter
eadni	mother
gávpi	shop
geađgi	stone, rock
geassi	summer
girji	book
goahti	Sámi hut
irgi	boyfriend, fiancé
jahki	year
jávri	lake
juolgi	leg, foot
láibi	bread
niibi	knife
várri	mountain

3 Nouns

gáffe 'coffee'

	Singular	Plural
Nom	gáffe	gáfe-t
Acc/Gen	gáfe	gáfi-id
Ill	gáffi-i	gáfi-ide
Loc	gáfe-s	gáfi-in
Com	gáfi-in	gáfi-iguin
Ess	gáffe-n	

Point to note:

- The final vowel -e becomes -i in the illative.

Here is a list of some other commonly used nouns that follow this pattern.

baste	spoon
boraspire	predator
busse	bus
gumpe	wolf
reive	letter
skáhppe	wardrobe

ruvdno 'krone'

	Singular	Plural
Nom	ruvdno	ruvnno-t
Acc/Gen	ruvnno	ruvnnu-id
Ill	ruvdnu-i	ruvnnu-ide

Loc	**ruvnno-s**	**ruvnnu-in**
Com	**ruvnnu-in**	**ruvnnu-iguin**
Ess		**ruvdno-n**

Point to note:

- The final vowel -o becomes -u- before -i.

This pattern is quite rare and is commonly restricted to loanwords from Norwegian or Swedish. Examples include the following.

belko	block of wood
reŋko	stool
ruvtto	square, box, screen

viessu 'house'

	Singular	Plural
Nom	**viessu**	**viesu-t**
Acc/Gen	**viesu**	**viesu-id**
Ill	**vissu-i**	**viesu-ide**
Loc	**viesu-s**	**viesu-in**
Com	**viesu-in**	**viesu-iguin**
Ess		**viessu-n**

Point to note:

- Diphthongs in the first syllable of nouns ending in -u are simplified in the illative, as in **viessu** : **vissui**.

3 Nouns

Here is a list of some other commonly used nouns that follow this pattern.

biebmu	food
biergu	meat
diibmu	clock, watch
gáhkku	cake
geaidnu	road
gilvu	competition
guovlu	area
lávvu	Sámi tent
luondu	nature
mánnu	moon, month
muohtu	cheek
siidu	page
stállu	troll
stuollu	chair

lihkuheapme 'unhappy'

	Singular	Plural
Nom	**lihkuheapme**	**lihkuheami-t**
Acc/Gen	**lihkuheami**	**lihkuhemi-id**
Ill	**lihkuheapmá-i**	**lihkuhemi-ide**
Loc	**lihkuheami-s**	**lihkuhemi-in**
Com	**lihkuhemi-in**	**lihkuhemi-iguin**
Ess		**lihkuheapmi-n**

Point to note:

- Negative nominals generally follow the same pattern as **lihkuheapme** 'unhappy', e.g. **bargguheapme** 'unemployed'.

sápmelaš 'Sámi'

	Singular	Plural
Nom	**sápmelaš**	**sápmelačča-t**
Acc/Gen	**sápmelačča**	**sápmelačča-id**
Ill	**sápmelažži-i**	**sápmelačča-ide**
Loc	**sápmelačča-s**	**sápmelačča-in**
Com	**sápmelačča-in**	**sápmelačča-iguin**
Ess	**sápmelažža-n**	

Here is a list of some other commonly used nouns that follow this pattern. Note that many of these end in the suffix **-laš**, which is commonly used to indicate nationality.

ruottelaš	Swede, Swedish
suopmelaš	Finn, Finnish
ruoššalaš	Russian
amerihkálaš	American
risttalaš	Christian
ofelaš	guide

3 Nouns

muitalus 'story'

	Singular	Plural
Nom	muitalus	muitalusa-t
Acc/Gen	muitalusa	muitalusa-id
Ill	muitalussi-i	muitalusa-ide
Loc	muitalusa-s	muitalusa-in
Com	muitalusa-in	muitalusa-iguin
Ess	muitalussa-n	

Here is a list of some other commonly used nouns that follow this pattern.

borramuš	food
čilgehus	explanation
erohus	difference
gáibádus	demand
vástádus	answer

bearjadat 'Friday'

	Singular	Plural
Nom	bearjadat	bearjadaga-t
Acc/Gen	bearjadaga	bearjadaga-id
Ill	bearjadahki-i	bearjadaga-ide
Loc	bearjadaga-s	bearjadaga-in
Com	bearjadaga-in	bearjadaga-iguin
Ess	bearjadahka-n	

Here is a list of some other commonly used nouns that follow this pattern. Note that many of these denote days of the week.

mánnodat	Monday
disdat	Tuesday
duorastat	Thursday
lávvardat/lávvordat	Saturday
sihkaldat	towel
gažaldat	question

Points to note:

- The nominative of nouns like **sápmelaš**, **muitalus**, and **bearjadat** has three syllables, but the accusative-genitive has an even number of syllables.
- Certain even-syllable nouns do not undergo consonant gradation when inflected, e.g. **moarsi** : **moarsi** 'girlfriend, fiancée', **dorski** : **dorski** 'cod'. Agent nouns, e.g. **oahppi** : **oahppi** 'pupil, learner', all fall under this category. (See section 13.1 for details of agent nouns.)
- **Buorre** 'good' and **guokte** 'two' are irregular in that their final vowel is -e in the nominative but -i in all other cases.

3.1.2 Odd-syllable

There are many different patterns of odd-syllable nouns, which are illustrated here. Note also the following general points about these types of nouns.

- Odd-syllable nouns have an odd number of syllables in the accusative-genitive.
- Odd-syllable nouns end in a consonant or a vowel in the nominative singular.
- Other endings are added to an oblique (i.e. non-nominative) stem, except for the essive, which is added to the nominative (though note that the final consonant of the nominative often differs from the final consonant before the essive suffix because Sámi only allows a limited number of consonants to appear at the end of a word).
- The nominative singular and the essive are in the weak grade, and all other cases are in the strong grade.

- Many adjectives form their plurals on analogy with odd-syllable noun patterns and therefore feature in these lists. See chapter 4 for further details about North Sámi adjectives.

beana 'dog'

	Singular	Plural
Nom	**beana**	**beatnag-at**
Acc/Gen	**beatnag-a**	**beatnag-iid**
Ill	**beatnag-ii**	**beatnag-iidda**
Loc	**beatnag-is**	**beatnag-iin**
Com	**beatnag-iin**	**beatnag-iiguin**
Ess		**beana-n**

Here is a list of some other commonly used nouns that follow this pattern. The accusative-genitive forms have been provided in the following table to help illustrate the oblique stem.

gáma, gápmaga	boot
muohta, muohttaga	snow
cealkka, cealkaga	sentence
čotta, čoddaga	throat
čoavdda, čoavdaga	key

skibir 'friend, pal'

	Singular	Plural
Nom	**skibir**	**skihpár-at**
Acc/Gen	**skihpár-a**	**skihpár-iid**
Ill	**skihpár-ii**	**skihpár-iidda**

Loc	**skihpár-is**	**skihpár-iin**
Com	**skihpár-iin**	**skihpár-iiguin**
Ess		**skibir-in**

Here is a list of some other commonly used nouns and adjectives that follow this pattern. The accusative-genitive forms have been provided in the following table to help illustrate the oblique stem.

oahpis, oahppása	acquaintance
ráhkis, ráhkkása	beloved
doavttir, doaktára	doctor
mális, mállása	meal
jeagil, jeahkála	lichen
váttis, váddása	difficult
boaris, boarrása	old

Note that some nouns in this group ending in **-ir** do not undergo a vowel change when inflected, e.g.:

veažir, veahčira	hammer
bábir, báhpira	paper

isit 'husband'

	Singular	Plural
Nom	**isit**	**isid-at**
Acc/Gen	**isid-a**	**isid-iid**
Ill	**isid-ii**	**isid-iidda**

3 Nouns

Loc	**isid-is**	**isid-iin**
Com	**isid-iin**	**isid-iiguin**
Ess		**isid-in**

Here is a list of some other commonly used nouns and adjectives that follow this pattern. Note that all ordinal numerals belong to this group; see section 6.2 for details. The accusative-genitive forms have been provided in the following table to help illustrate the oblique stem.

eamit, eamida	wife
eahket, eahkeda	evening
iđit, iđida	morning
vielgat, vielgada	white
hilbat, hilbada	naughty
viđat, viđada	fifth

čearpmat 'one-year-old reindeer calf'

	Singular	Plural
Nom	**čearpmat**	**čearpmah-at**
Acc/Gen	**čearpmah-a**	**čearpmah-iid**
Ill	**čearpmah-ii**	**čearpmah-iidda**
Loc	**čearpmah-is**	**čearpmah-iin**
Com	**čearpmah-iin**	**čearpmah-iiguin**
Ess		**čearpmah-in**

Here is a list of some other commonly used nouns and adjectives that follow this pattern. The accusative-genitive forms have been provided in the following table to help illustrate the oblique stem.

návet, náveha	barn
alit, aliha	blue
duhát, duháha	thousand
duhpát, duhpáha	tobacco
rievssat, rievssaha	ptarmigan (*Lagopus muta*)
sabet, sabeha	ski
buđet, buđeha	potato

gávpot 'city'

	Singular	Plural
Nom	**gávpot**	**gávpog-at**
Acc/Gen	**gávpog-a**	**gávpog-iid**
Ill	**gávpog-ii**	**gávpog-iidda**
Loc	**gávpog-is**	**gávpog-iin**
Com	**gávpog-iin**	**gávpog-iiguin**
Ess		**gávpog-in**

Below is a list of some other commonly used nouns and adjectives that follow this pattern. The accusative-genitive forms have been provided in the following table to help illustrate the oblique stem.

hivsset, hivssega	toilet
sámegielat, sámegielaga	Sámi-speaking
mádjit, mádjiga	beaver

3 Nouns

heittot, heittoga   bad, weak

álbmot, álbmoga   people, nation

vuoivvas 'liver'

	Singular	Plural
Nom	**vuoivvas**	**vuoivas-at**
Acc/Gen	**vuoivas-a**	**vuoivas-iid**
Ill	**vuoivas-ii**	**vuoivas-iidda**
Loc	**vuoivas-is**	**vuoivas-iin**
Com	**vuoivas-iin**	**vuoivas-iiguin**
Ess	**vuoivvas-in**	

Here is a list of some other commonly used nouns and adjectives that follow this pattern. The accusative-genitive forms have been provided in the following table to help illustrate the oblique stem.

dálkkas, dálkasa	medicine
bivttas, biktasa	item of clothing
fanas, fatnasa	boat
imaš, ipmaša	wonder
buolaš, buollaša	cold spell
rumaš, rupmaša	body
galmmas, galbmasa	cold
duottar, duoddara	tundra, fell
suohtas, suohttasa	fun

skohter 'snowmobile'

	Singular	Plural
Nom	**skohter**	**skohter-at**
Acc/Gen	**skohter-a**	**skohter-iid**
Ill	**skohter-ii**	**skohter-iidda**
Loc	**skohter-is**	**skohter-iin**
Com	**skohter-iin**	**skohter-iiguin**
Ess	**skohter-in**	

Here is a list of some other commonly used nouns that follow this pattern. Note that loanwords often belong to this group (e.g. **gáffal** 'fork', from Norwegian and Swedish **gaffel**, and **teáhter** 'theatre'). The accusative-genitive forms have been provided in the following table to help illustrate the oblique stem.

Ipmil, Ipmila	God
oaivil, oaivila	opinion
suopman, suopmana	dialect
gáffal, gáffala	fork
márkan, márkana	town centre
gievkkan, gievkkana	kitchen
rieban, riebana	fox
dihtor, dihtor	computer
teáhter, teáhtera	theatre

3 Nouns

mánáš 'little child'

	Singular	Plural
Nom	**mánáš**	**mánáž-at**
Acc/Gen	**mánáž-a**	**mánáž-iid**
Ill	**mánáž-ii**	**mánáž-iidda**
Loc	**mánáž-is**	**mánáž-iin**
Com	**mánáž-iin**	**mánáž-iiguin**
Ess	**mánáž-in**	

Here is a list of some other commonly used nouns and adjectives that follow this pattern. Note that diminutive nouns always belong to this group; see section 13.1.2.2. The accusative-genitive forms have been provided in the following table to help illustrate the oblique stem.

bártnáš, bártnáža	little boy, little son
beaivváš, beaivváža	sun
dološ, doloža	ancient

čoahkkin 'meeting'

	Singular	Plural
Nom	**čoahkkin**	**čoahkkim-at**
Acc/Gen	**čoahkkim-a**	**čoahkkim-iid**
Ill	**čoahkkim-ii**	**čoahkkim-iidda**
Loc	**čoahkkim-is**	**čoahkkim-iin**
Com	**čoahkkim-iin**	**čoahkkim-iiguin**
Ess	**čoahkkim-in**	

Here is a list of some other commonly used nominals that follow this pattern. Note that verbal nouns often belong to this group; see section 7.4.2 for further details. The accusative-genitive forms have been provided in the following table to help illustrate the oblique stem.

eallin, eallima	life
muhtun, muhtuma	some
čohkun, čohkuma	comb
ohcan, ohcama	application (form), search
čuoigan, čuoigama	skiing

njuovčča 'tongue'

	Singular	Plural
Nom	**njuovčča**	**njuokčam-at**
Acc/Gen	**njuokčam-a**	**njuokčam-iid**
Ill	**njuokčam-ii**	**njuokčam-iidda**
Loc	**njuokčam-is**	**njuokčam-iin**
Com	**njuokčam-iin**	**njuokčam-iiguin**
Ess		**njuovčča-n**

There are also a number of rarer odd-syllable patterns, shown here.

Here is a list of some other commonly used nouns that follow this pattern. Note that **eana** 'earth, land' has a variant nominative form (used in the West) ending in -**n**. The accusative-genitive forms have been provided in the following table to help illustrate the oblique stem.

ađa, ađđama	marrowbone
eana/eanan, eatnama	earth

The noun **vuoni** 'mother-in-law' inflects the same way, but the final -**i** changes to -**á** in the oblique cases, e.g. accusative-genitive **vuotnáma**.

biđus 'meat stew'

	Singular	Plural
Nom	biđus	biđđos-at
Acc/Gen	biđđos-a	biđđos-iid
Ill	biđđos-ii	biđđos-iidda
Loc	biđđos-is	biđđos-iin
Com	biđđos-iin	biđđos-iiguin
Ess		biđus-in

Here is a list of some other nouns that follow this pattern. The accusative-genitive forms have been provided in the following table to help illustrate the oblique stem.

boađus, bohtosa	result
vuoluš, vulloša	lower part, underside
maŋuš, maŋŋoša	back of a group or flock
njunuš, njunnoša	front of a group or flock

luomi 'cloudberry'

	Singular	Plural
Nom	luomi	luopmán-at
Acc/Gen	luopmán-a	luopmán-iid
Ill	luopmán-ii	luopmán-iidda
Loc	luopmán-is	luopmán-iin
Com	luopmán-iin	luopmán-iiguin
Ess		luomi-n

Point to note:

- Final -i changes to -á in the oblique cases.

The following commonly used noun inflects similarly. Note that the final -u in the nominative becomes -o in the oblique cases; this noun also has a variant nominative form resembling the accusative-genitive. The accusative-genitive form has been provided in the following table to help illustrate the oblique stem.

nisu/nisson, nissona   woman

ustit 'friend'

	Singular	Plural
Nom	**ustit**	**ustib-at**
Acc/Gen	**ustib-a**	**ustib-iid**
Ill	**ustib-ii**	**ustib-iidda**
Loc	**ustib-is**	**ustib-iin**
Com	**ustib-iin**	**ustib-iiguin**
Ess	**ustibi-n**	

3.1.3 Contracted

Contracted nouns have two syllables and end in -u or -is in the nominative singular. The nominative singular and the essive are in the weak grade. All the other cases are in the extra strong grade.

boazu 'reindeer'

	Singular	Plural
Nom	**boazu**	**bohcco-t**
Acc/Gen	**bohcco**	**bohccu-id**

Ill	**bohccu-i**	**bohccu-ide**
Loc	**bohcco-s**	**bohccu-in**
Com	**bohccu-in**	**bohccu-iguin**
Ess	**boazu-n**	

Points to note:

- Nominals ending in -**u** undergo diphthong simplification in the first syllable in all other cases apart from the nominative singular and the essive.
- The final vowel -**u** changes to -**o** in the accusative-genitive and locative singular and in the nominative plural.
- The final vowel -**a** changes to -**á** in all oblique cases.
- This noun type is relatively rare.

Here is a list of some other nouns that follow this pattern. The accusative-genitive forms have been provided in the following table to help illustrate the oblique stem.

eanu, edno	uncle (mother's brother)
suolu, sullo	island
gistta, gistá	mitten
nuorvvu, nurvo	cold, flu

bálggis 'path'

	Singular	Plural
Nom	**bálggis**	**bálgá-t**
Acc/Gen	**bálgá**	**bálgá-id**
Ill	**bálgá-i**	**bálgá-ide**

Loc	**bálgá-s**	**bálgá-in**
Com	**bálgá-in**	**bálgá-iguin**
Ess		**bálggis-in**

Points to note:

- The **-is** ending is replaced by **-á** in all cases apart from the nominative singular and the essive.
- The essive takes the ending normally associated with odd-syllable nouns.
- Note that the nominative singular of this type of contracted noun looks identical to that of odd-syllable nouns and adjectives ending in **-is** (such as **mális** 'meal', **boaris** 'old'). In such instances, one must learn the accusative-genitive form in order to determine the correct noun type.

Here is a list of some other commonly used nouns and adjectives that follow this pattern. The accusative-genitive forms have been provided in the following table to help illustrate the oblique stem.

vievssis, vieksá	bee
stuoris, stuorrá	big
rikkis, riggá	rich
njálggis, njálgá	sweet (noun and adjective)
vielppis, vielpá	puppy
fális, fállá	whale

There are also two slightly irregular contracted nouns, **olmmoš** 'person' and **olmmái** 'friend, pal; man' in the West and 'man' in the East, illustrated here.

olmmoš 'person'

	Singular	Plural
Nom	**olmmoš**	**olbmo-t**
Acc/Gen	**olbmo**	**olbmu-id**
Ill	**olbmu-i**	**olbmu-ide**
Loc	**olbmo-s**	**olbmu-in**
Com	**olbmu-in**	**olbmu-iguin**
Ess		**olmmož-in**

olmmái 'friend, pal; man'

	Singular	Plural
Nom	**olmmái**	**olbmá-t**
Acc/Gen	**olbmá**	**olbmá-id**
Ill	**olbmá-i**	**olbmá-ide**
Loc	**olbmá-s**	**olbmá-in**
Com	**olbmá-in**	**olbmá-iguin**
Ess		**olmmáj-in**

Point to note:

- In the East **almmái** is used as a variant of **olmmái**.

3.2 Cases

3.2.1 Nominative

The nominative is the basic (dictionary) form of a noun. The nominative singular has no ending. The nominative plural ending is -t. The nominative is used for the subject of a sentence, as illustrated in the following examples.

Mu **namma** lea Máhtte.	My name is Máhtte.
Eadni bargá gávppis.	Mum works in a shop.
Mus leat ođđa **sabehat**.	I have new skis.
Jođiheaddjit fitnet Kárášjogas.	The leaders are visiting Karasjok.

The nominative is also used for the predicate of a clause.

Mu namma lea **Máhtte**.	My name is Máhtte.
Biret lea **oahpaheaddji**.	Biret is a teacher.
Sii leat **mánát**.	They are children.

3.2.2 Accusative

The accusative is the form of the direct object.

Mun oasttán **láibbi**.	I am going to buy bread.
Son čállá **divtta**.	S/he is writing a poem.
Oahppit lohket ollu **girjjiid**.	Students read a lot of books.
Iŋgá lea oahppán váldit **govaid**.	Iŋgá has learned how to take photos.

The accusative is also used to indicate a length of time in cases where English would use the preposition 'for'.

Mun ledjen doppe **vahku**.	I was there for a week.
Elle orui Suomas **jagi**.	Elle lived in Finland for a year.

The accusative is also used to indicate the subject of impersonal verbs denoting emotional and physical states.

Máná čaimmaha.   The child feels like laughing (lit: it makes the child feel like laughing).

Finally, the accusative is used in certain greetings and exclamations with an implied object.

Buorre **beaivvi**!   Hello (lit: good day)!

Vuoi **dán dálkki**!   What awful weather (lit: Oh, this weather)!

Vuoi **dán** njálgga **gáhku**!   What a delicious cake (lit: Oh, this delicious cake)!

3.2.3 Genitive

The genitive (which has the same form as the accusative) is used to indicate the possessor, equivalent to the English 's.

Beatnaga namma lea Čáhppe.   The dog's name is Čáhppe.

Helsset lea **Suoma** oaivegávpot.   Helsinki is Finland's capital.

Studeanttaid sihkkelat leat olgun.   The students' bikes are outside.

The genitive is also the form used after prepositions and before postpositions (see chapter 9).

*Muitalus **sámiid** birra*   'An Account of the Sámi'

Máret orru vánhemiid **luhtte**.   Máret lives with her parents.

Mari Boine dovdet miehtá **máilmmi**.   Mari Boine is known around the world.

The genitive is used as the subject of non-finite verb forms (see 7.4).

Áhči vuoššan gáffe lea buoremus.   The coffee made by father is the best.

Son ođii **Máhte** humadettiin.   S/he slept while Máhtte was talking.

The first part of compound nouns (see 13.2.1) is also often in the genitive.

bohccobiergu	reindeer meat
eatnigiella	mother tongue
mánáidgárdi	kindergarten

The genitive can also be used when making comparisons (see 4.3) instead of the conjunction **go** 'than' + nominative.

Biila lea **skohtera** ođđaseabbo.	The car is newer than the snowmobile.
Geasit dáppe leat **dálvviid** ollu lieggaseappot.	Summers here are much warmer than winters.

The genitive plural can also be used to single out an individual from a larger group of the same category.

Mii **mašiinnaid** dát lea?	Which machine is this?
Mii **láibbiid** dát lea?	Which sandwich/bread is this?

3.2.4 Illative

The primary function of the illative is to indicate direction towards, equivalent to the English 'to' or 'towards'.

Mánná viegai **gávpái**.	The child ran to the shop.
Ollu olbmot vulget **mearragáddái** geassit.	Many people go to the seaside in summer.
Mun manan **Guovdageidnui** ihttin.	I'm going to Kautokeino tomorrow.

The movement can be more abstract, e.g.:

Mun liikon mannat **feasttaide**.	I like going to parties.
Goas don vuolggát **lupmui**?	When are you going on holiday?

It is also used as a type of dative, equivalent to the English 'for' or 'to'.

Mun adden **beatnagii** dávtti.	I gave a bone to the dog.
Oahpaheaddji čálii e-boastta **ohppiide**.	The teacher wrote an email to the students.
Elle osttii girjji iežas **oambeallái**.	Elle bought a book for her cousin.

The illative can also be used to indicate purpose, equivalent to the English 'for', as in the following example:

Mun mannen gávpái **mielkái**.	I went to the shop for milk.

It can also be used to indicate a duration of time, equivalent to the English 'for', or a time limit, equivalent to the English 'until', as in the following two examples, respectively.

Ánne boahtá deike golmma **vahkkui**.	Ánne is coming here for three weeks.
Mun ledjen doppe **bearjadahkii**.	I was there until Friday.

Certain verbs take the illative, for example **liikot** 'to like', **oahpásmuvvat** 'to get to know', **gullat** 'to belong to', **bidjat** 'to put', **guođđit** 'to leave (something somewhere)', **báhcit** 'to stay', **hukset** 'to build (something somewhere)', **suhttat** 'to get angry', **álgit** 'to begin', **láhppit** 'to lose (something somewhere)', **heivet** 'to suit', and **vajálduhttit/vajáldahttit** 'to forget'.

Máret liiko **rock-musihkkii**.	Máret likes rock music.
Son oahpásmuvai iežas **irgái** universiteahtas.	She met her boyfriend in university.
Dat biila gullá mu **oabbái**.	That car belongs to my sister.
Mun lean dan bidjan **skáhppii**.	I've put it in the cupboard.
Moai letne guođđán ruđaid **latnjii**.	We left the money in the room.

Joavnna fertii báhcit **Ruttii**.	Joavnna had to stay in Sweden.
Manne suhttet **Márjái**?	Why did you get angry at Márjá?
Mun álggán ođđa **bargui**.	I'm starting a new job.
Dat báidi heive **dutnje**.	That shirt suits you.
Son vajálduhtii iežas giehtatelefovnna **bussii**.	He forgot his mobile on the bus.
Stáhta **huksii** dattetge gymnása Kárášjohkii.	Nevertheless, the state built a high school in Karasjok.

The illative is used with names of languages.

Dat lea čállojuvvon **sámegillii**.	It's written in Sámi.
Su blogga lea **dárogillii**.	His/her blog is in Norwegian.

Finally, the illative is used in certain idiomatic expressions, e.g.:

Boađe min **guossái**.	Come and visit us.
Mun osten dan **guovttečuohtái**.	I bought it for two hundred kroner.

3.2.5 Locative

The locative is used to express location and is equivalent to the English prepositions 'in', 'at', and 'on'.

Mun orun **Mázes**.	I live in Masi.
Turisttat leat Beaivváš Sámi **Našunálateáhteris**.	The tourists are at the Beaivváš Sámi National Theatre.
Bussá čohkká **stuolus**.	The cat is sitting on a chair.

The locative is also used to express movement away from and is equivalent to the English preposition 'from'.

3 Nouns

Iŋgá boahtá **Suomas**.	Iŋgá comes from Finland.
Bussá njuike **stuolus** láhttái.	The cat jumps from the chair onto the floor.
Mun lean ožžon e-boastta **Ristenis**.	I've received an email from Risten.

The use of the locative can be more abstract, e.g.:

Ii oktage jápmán **bárttis**.	Nobody died in the accident.
Son bođii ruovttoluotta **luomus**.	S/he came back from holiday.

The locative is used in the habitive construction (see 12.5) to refer to a person or thing that has something, e.g.:

Nieiddas lea ođđa irgi.	The girl has a new boyfriend.
Bargiin lea dál borranboddu.	The workers have a lunch break now.

The locative is used to denote the length of time within which something is completed and the starting point of an activity.

Son logai olles girjji guovtti **beaivvis**.	S/he read the whole book in two days.
Gursa bistá **mánnodagas** bearjadahkii.	The course lasts from Monday to Friday.

The locative is used in a way that corresponds to the English 'per' in expressions with **geardi** 'time, occasion' and other units.

Studeanta manná girjerádjui golmma geardde **vahkus**.	The student goes to the library three times a week.
Man ollu buđehat mákset **kilos**?	How much do the potatoes cost per kilo?

Some verbs take the locative, for example **fitnat** 'to visit, to go and come back', **heaitit** 'to stop', **jearrat** 'to ask', **beroštit** 'to be interested in, to care about', **dolkat** 'to get sick of', and **ballat** 'to be scared of, to fear'.

Eadni finai **Romssas** mannan vahkus.	Mum went to Tromsø last week.	**3 Nouns**
Heaitte **čierrumis!**	Stop crying!	
Risten jearrá **oahpaheaddjis**.	Risten is going to ask the teacher.	
Mun in beroštan **skuvllas**.	I didn't care about school.	
Son lea dolkan **barggus**.	S/he is sick of work.	
Mu unnavieljaš ballá **stáluin**.	My little brother is scared of trolls.	

The locative is used to indicate the material out of which something is made, e.g.:

Beavdi lea ráhkaduvvon **muoras**.	The table is made out of wood.

The locative can also be used in a partitive sense, equivalent to the English 'of', 'out of', e.g.:

Mun in leat máistán dan **goikebierggus**.	I haven't tasted any of that dried meat.
Dušše okta mu **skihpáriin** bođii festii.	Only one of my friends came to the party.

The locative is used in some idiomatic expressions, e.g.:

Mu **mielas** dat lea hui buorre.	In my opinion it's really good.
Mu oambealli lea mu **agis**.	My cousin is my age.

3.2.6 Comitative

The comitative often corresponds to the English preposition 'with'.

Mun human **Elliin**.	I'm talking with Elle.
Máhtte orru iežas **vánhemiiguin**.	Máhtte lives with his parents.
Norggas lea eananrádji **Ruoŧain**, **Suomain** ja maid **Ruoššain**.	Norway has a border with Sweden, Finland, and also Russia.

It is also frequently used in an instrumental sense, equivalent to the English 'with' or 'by'.

Mun in liiko čállit **beannain**.	I don't like to write with a pen.
Neahttabuvddas sáhtát máksit **goarttain**.	You can pay by card in the online shop.
Son boahtá **skohteriin**.	He's coming by snowmobile.
Son lávlu čáppa **jienain**.	S/he sings with a beautiful voice.

Certain verbs take the comitative, for example **biehkut** 'to complain', **bártidit** 'to get into difficulties', **riidalit** 'to argue'.

Eadni biehku **oaivebákčasiin**.	Mum is complaining of a headache.
Sii bártidedje **bohccuiguin**.	They got into difficulties with the reindeer.
Mun riidalin **oappáin** ikte.	I argued with my sister yesterday.

The comitative also has a few idiomatic uses.

Moai **Iŋggáin** manaime gilvui ovttas.	Iŋgá and I (lit: the two of us with Iŋgá) went to the competition together.
Sáhtát dan dahkat **dáinna lágiin**.	You can do it in this way.

3.2.7 Essive

The essive is used to describe a state or function, which may often be temporary. It often corresponds to the English preposition 'as'.

Heaika bargá **oahpaheaddjin** Álaheajus.	Heaika is working as a teacher in Alta.
Son vulggii ruoktot **buohccin**.	S/he went home sick.
Mun geavahan mobiilla **boktindiibmun**.	I use my mobile as an alarm clock.

Biret lei hui čeahppi lávlut **nuorran**.	Biret was very good at singing in her youth (lit: as a young person).	
Mun dovddan iežan du **unnaoappážin**.	I regard (lit: feel) myself as your little sister.	

It is also used when something enters a new state or becomes something. This usage is commonly found after the verbs **šaddat** 'to become' and **dahkat** 'to make'.

Son šattai **noaidin**.	He became a shaman.
Mun dahken dan **gárvvisin**.	I made it ready.

Verbs of perceiving, regarding, believing, and maintaining also take the essive.

Mun jáhkken Máhte **ruottelažžan**.	I thought that Máhtte was Swedish.
Doalat go dan **čiegusin**?	Are you keeping it a secret?

The essive is also used with reference to natural conditions and the points of the compass.

Mun in liiko vuodjit ná heajos **dálkin**.	I don't like to drive in such bad weather.
Okta oabbá orru **davvin** ja nubbi **lullin**.	One sister lives in the north and the other in the south.

Chapter 4
Adjectives

Adjectives have two different forms depending on whether they are being used predicatively (i.e. following a verb such as **leat** 'to be' or **šaddat** 'to become', e.g. **nieida lea čeahppi** 'the girl is clever') or attributively (i.e. in a noun phrase, e.g. **čeahpes nieida** 'clever girl'). North Sámi attributive adjectives always precede their associated noun.

4.1 Predicative adjective types

Predicative adjectives have the same inflectional patterns as nouns, as illustrated in the following tables. The accusative-genitive forms have been provided in the tables to help illustrate the oblique stem.

Even-syllable

nuorra, nuora	young
guhkki, guhki	long
oanehaš, oanehačča	short

Odd-syllable

ruoksat, ruoksada	red
ráhkis, ráhkkása	dear, beloved

Contracted

njálggis, njálgá	sweet
fiinnis, fiidná	fancy

Predicative adjectives agree in number with their associated noun, e.g.:

> Biila lea **ruoksat**.   The car is red.
>
> Biillat leat **ruoksadat**.   The cars are red.

Predicative adjectives typically appear in the nominative case, as in the previous examples, but may be found in the essive after a verb requiring this case, e.g.:

> Mii dahká olbmo **lihkolažžan**?   What makes a person happy?

A predicative adjective can be used in place of a noun, corresponding to the English construction 'a red one', 'a good one', etc. In such cases the adjective can appear in other cases, e.g.:

> Mun válddán **ruoksada**.   I'll take the red one.
>
> Guđe viesus son orru? — **Ruoksadis**.   Which house does s/he live in? In the red one.

4.2 Attributive adjective types

The attributive form of adjectives is usually different from the predicative form. Unfortunately, there are no set rules governing the formation of attributive adjectives, so each form needs to be learned individually. However, there are only four attributive adjective patterns to choose from, as shown in the following table. The first two patterns are the most common. Note that some attributive forms have a different consonant grade from their predicative counterparts.

Ending in -es

Predicative	Attributive	Translation
guhkki	**guhkes**	long
boaris	**boares**	old
čeahppi	**čeahpes**	clever

4 Adjectives

Ending in -a

Predicative	Attributive	Translation
čáppat	**čáppa**	beautiful
galmmas	**galbma**	cold
ođas	**ođđa**	new

Ending in -is

Predicative	Attributive	Translation
bastil	**bastilis**	sharp
dárkil	**dárkilis**	precise
oanehaš	**oanehis**	short
asehaš	**asehis**	thin
bealjeheapmi	**bealjehis**	deaf

Ending in -s (limited to adjectives ending in -ái)

Predicative	Attributive	Translation
guollái	**guollás**	rich in fish
assái	**assás**	thick

In addition, certain adjectives have the same form in both the attributive and predicative. This applies to many odd-syllable adjectives with consonant gradation, excluding the ones whose predicative form ends in -is.

Predicative	Attributive	Translation
amas	**amas**	strange
bahča	**bahča**	bitter, bad-tasting

4 Adjectives

čiegus	**čiegus**	hidden, secret
dearvas	**dearvas**	healthy, fit
dievas	**dievas**	full
guohca	**guohca**	rotten, spoiled
rabas	**rabas**	open
suohtas	**suohtas**	pleasant, fun
varas	**varas**	fresh

This pattern also applies to some even-syllable adjectives.

Predicative	Attributive	Translation
buorre	**buorre**	good
duohta	**duohta**	true
nuorra	**nuorra**	young

In addition, the following types of adjectives follow this pattern.

Category	Example	Translation
End in **-laš**	**váralaš**	dangerous
End in **-as**	**issoras**	terrible, horrible
End in **-meahttun**	**oaidnemeahttun**	invisible
End in **-t** denoting body part	**alitčalmmat**	blue-eyed
Comparative	**čábbásit/čábbát**	more beautiful
Superlative	**čábbámus**	the most beautiful

4 Adjectives

Attributive adjectives do not inflect for case or person, e.g.:

Dát lea **odda** girji.	This is a new book.
Mun háliidan **odda** girjji.	I want the new book.
Odda girjjis leat ollu govat.	The new book has a lot of pictures.
Máret ii liiko **odda** girjái.	Máret doesn't like the new book.
Gávppis eai leat **odda** girjjit.	The shop doesn't have new books.

4.3 Comparative

All North Sámi adjectives have a special comparative form. There are two different comparative patterns, one for even-syllable and contracted adjectives and one for odd-syllable adjectives. These are illustrated in the following tables. Note that the forms given here are predicatives; the attributive is the same as the nominative singular predicative.

Even-syllable and contracted

nuorra 'young' > **nuorat** 'younger'

	Singular comparative	Plural comparative
Nom	**nuorat**	**nuorabu-t**
Acc/Gen	**nuorabu**	**nuorabu-id**
Ill	**nuorabu-i**	**nuorabu-idda**
Loc	**nuorabu-s**	**nuorabu-in**
Com	**nuorabu-in**	**nuorabu-iguin**
Ess		**nuorabu-n**

Points to note:

- The nominative singular comparative form of even-syllable adjectives is identical to the nominative plural of their positive counterparts.
- Even-syllable adjectives ending in -**laš** have a number of variant comparative forms, e.g. **dábálaš** 'ordinary' > **dábálat, dábálet,**

dábáleabbo, dábálabbo 'more ordinary' in addition to the expected form **dábálaččat**.
- The comparatives of contracted adjectives inflect in the same way as the comparative of even-syllable adjectives, except that in the nominative singular the final consonant is replaced by the comparative ending -t, e.g. **stuoris** 'big' > **stuorit/stuorát** 'bigger'.

Odd-syllable

divrras 'expensive' > **divraseabbo** 'more expensive'

	Singular comparative	Plural comparative
Nom	divraseabbo	divraseappo-t
Acc/Gen	divraseappo	divraseappu-id
Ill	divrasebbu-i	divraseappu-ide
Loc	divraseappo-s	divraseappu-in
Com	divraseappu-in	divraseappu-iguin
Ess	divraseabbo-n	

Point to note:

- Odd-syllable comparative adjectives can have shorter variants, e.g. **divrasat, divraset, divrasut** 'more expensive' instead of **divraseabbo**. There is also a variant with –abbo, e.g. **divrasabbo** instead of **divraseabbo**.

The following examples illustrate the use of comparative adjectives in both predicative and attributive positions:

Máret lea **boarráseabbo** go Biret.	Máret is older than Biret.
Ealggat leat **stuoribut** go bohccot.	Elks are bigger than reindeer.
Nuorat viellja vázzá skuvlla Guovdageainnus.	The younger brother goes to school in Kautokeino.
Máhtte orru **divraset** viesus go iežas oabbá.	Máhtte lives in a more expensive house than his sister.

4
Adjectives

4.4 Superlative

Sámi adjectives all have a special superlative form. There are two different superlative patterns – one for even-syllable and contracted adjectives and one for odd-syllable adjectives. These are illustrated in the following tables. Note that the forms given here are predicatives; the attributive form is the same as the nominative singular predicative.

Even-syllable and contracted

nuorra 'young' > **nuoramus** 'youngest'

	Singular superlative	Plural superlative
Nom	**nuoramus**	**nuoramusa-t**
Acc/Gen	**nuoramusa**	**nuoramusa-id**
Ill	**nuoramussi-i**	**nuoramusa-ide**
Loc	**nuoramusa-s**	**nuoramusa-in**
Com	**nuoramusa-in**	**nuoramusa-iguin**
Ess	**nuoramussa-n**	

Points to note:

- The superlatives of contracted adjectives inflect in the same way as the superlatives of even-syllable adjectives, except that in the nominative singular the final consonant is replaced by the superlative ending, e.g. **stuoris** 'big' > **stuorimus/stuorámus** 'biggest'.
- Even-syllable adjectives ending in -**laš** have two variant superlative forms, ending in -**eamos** and -**amos**, e.g. **dábálaš** 'ordinary' > **dábáleamos, dábálamos** 'most ordinary' in addition to the expected form **dábálaččamus**.

Odd-syllable

divrras 'expensive' > **divraseamos** 'most expensive'

	Singular superlative	Plural superlative
Nom	**divraseamos**	**divrasepmos-at**
Acc/Gen	**divrasepmos-a**	**divrasepmos-iid**
Ill	**divrasepmos-ii**	**divrasepmos-iidda**
Loc	**divrasepmos-is**	**divrasepmos-iin**
Com	**divrasepmos-iin**	**divrasepmos-iiguin**
Ess	**divraseamos-in**	

Point to note:

- There is a variant form with **-amos**, e.g. **divrasamos** 'most expensive' instead of **divraseamos**. Forms in **-amos** do not display consonant gradation, e.g. Acc/Gen **divrasamosa**.

The following examples illustrate the use of superlative adjectives in both predicative and attributive positions:

Mun lean **boarráseamos**.	I'm the oldest.
Mánáidgárddi **nuoramusat** stohke olgun.	The youngest in the nursery played outside.
Iŋgá lea máilmmi **čeahpimus** nieida.	Iŋgá is the cleverest girl in the world.
Giella lea min **divraseamos** árbi.	Language is our most precious inheritance.
Son liiko **čábbámus bárdnái** skuvllas.	S/he likes the best-looking boy in the school.

4.5 Demonstrative

North Sámi has a set of demonstrative adjectives, which are derived from the demonstrative pronouns (see section 5.3). The demonstrative adjectives are listed here.

dákkár(aš)	this kind of
diekkár(aš)	that kind of (near the addressee)
duokkár(aš)	that kind of (far away)
dokkár(aš)	that kind of (even farther away)
dakkár(aš)	that kind of (nonspecific)

The use of these adjectives is illustrated here.

In mun dál láve leat nu čeahppi **dakkár** gilvvuin.	I'm not usually so good at those kinds of competitions.
Ii go dus oba leat ge **diekkár** ođđaáigágaš telefovdna?	Don't you even have that kind of modern phone?

Chapter 5
Pronouns

5.1 Personal

North Sámi personal pronouns inflect in the same cases as nouns, as shown in the following table.

	Singular		
	First person	Second person	Third person
Nom	mun/mon	don	son
Acc/Gen	mu	du	su
Ill	munnje	dutnje	sutnje
Loc	mus	dus	sus
Com	muinna	duinna	suinna
Ess	munin	dunin	sunin

	Dual		
	First person	Second person	Third person
Nom	moai	doai	soai

5 Pronouns

	First person	Second person	Third person
Acc/Gen	munno	du	sudno
Ill	munnuide	dudnuide	sudnuide
Loc	munnos	dudnos	sudnos
Com	munnuin	dudnuin	sudnuin
Ess	munnon	dudnon	sudnon

	Plural		
	First person	Second person	Third person
Nom	mii	dii	sii
Acc/Gen	min	din	sin
Ill	midjiide	didjiide	sidjiide
Loc	mis	dis	sis
Com	minguin	dinguin	singuin
Ess	minin	dinin	sinin

North Sámi personal pronouns function like nouns. Here are some examples of their use.

Mun orun Guovdageainnus.   I live in Kautokeino.

Sus lea ođđa biila.   S/he has a new car.

Mun attán dan **dudnuide**.   I'm giving it to you two.

Boađe **minguin**!   Come with us!

5.2 Possessive

5.2.1 Pronouns

North Sámi has a set of possessive pronouns that are identical in form to the accusative-genitive of the personal pronouns listed in section 5.1. These are illustrated in the following examples:

Dat lea **mu** beana.	That's my dog.
Dovddat go **su** vánhemiid?	Do you know his/her parents?
Lea go dat **dudno** viessu?	Is that your (dual) house?

5.2.2 Suffixes

In addition to the possessive pronouns, North Sámi has a set of possessive suffixes that can be attached to nouns. The suffixes are as follows. Note that they have two different forms; one attaches to a vowel and the other attaches to a consonant.

	Singular		Dual		Plural	
	After vowel	After consonant	After vowel	After consonant	After vowel	After consonant
First	-n	-an	-me	-eame	-met	-eamet
Second	-t	-at	-de	-eatte	-det	-eattet
Third	-s	-is	-ska	-easkka	-set	-easet

Some case endings take slightly different forms when used in conjunction with possessive suffixes, as follows:

	Singular		Plural	
	After vowel	After consonant	After vowel	After consonant
Acc/Gen	—	—	-id-	-iiddá-/-iiddi-

	III	-s-	-asa-	-idasa-	-iiddás-
	Loc	-st-	-isttá-/-istti-	-in-	-iinná-/-iinni-
	Com	-in-	-iinná-/-iinni-	-id- possessive -guin	-iiddá-/-iddi- possessive-**guin**
	Ess			-n-	

Point to note:

- When two variants are listed, the one with -á- is used with the first and second person suffixes, whereas the one with -i- is used with the third person suffixes. See the following tables for full details.

The following tables illustrate the forms of the possessive suffixes when attached to the different noun types in all cases. The nouns chosen are **oabbá** 'sister', **áhčči** 'father', and **eallu** 'reindeer herd' (even-syllable); **vieljaš** 'little brother' (odd-syllable); and **boazu** 'reindeer' (contracted).

Nominative singular

Even-syllable

oabbá 'sister'

	Singular	Dual	Plural
First	**oabbán** 'my sister'	**oabbáme** 'our sister'	**oabbámet** 'our sister'
Second	**oabbát** 'your sister'	**oabbáde** 'your sister'	**oabbádet** 'your sister'
Third	**oabbás** 'his/her sister'	**oabbáska** 'their sister'	**oabbáset** 'their sister'

5 Pronouns

áhčči 'father'

	Singular	Dual	Plural
First	**áhččán** 'my father'	**áhččáme** 'our father'	**áhččámet** 'our father'
Second	**áhččát** 'your father'	**áhččáde** 'your father'	**áhččádet** 'your father'
Third	**áhččis** 'his/her father'	**áhččiska** 'their father'	**áhččiset** 'their father'

Point to note:

- Word-final -**i** changes to -**á** before the first and second person suffixes.

eallu 'reindeer herd'

	Singular	Dual	Plural
First	**ellon** 'my reindeer herd'	**ellome** 'our reindeer herd'	**ellomet** 'our reindeer herd'
Second	**ellot** 'your reindeer herd'	**ellode** 'your reindeer herd'	**ellodet** 'your reindeer herd'
Third	**eallus** 'his/her reindeer herd'	**ealluska** 'their reindeer herd'	**ealluset** 'their reindeer herd'

Points to note:

- Word-final -**u** changes to -**o** before the first and second person possessive suffixes.
- Diphthongs simplify before -**o**.

5 Pronouns

Odd-syllable

vieljaš 'little brother'

	Singular	Dual	Plural
First	**vieljažan** 'my little brother'	**vieljažeame** 'our little brother'	**vieljažeamet** 'our little brother'
Second	**vieljažat** 'your little brother'	**vieljažeatte** 'your little brother'	**vieljažeattet** 'your little brother'
Third	**vieljažis** 'his/her little brother'	**vieljažeaskka** 'their little brother'	**vieljažeaset** 'their little brother'

Point to note:

- The possessive suffixes are attached to the accusative-genitive form of the noun.

Contracted

boazu 'reindeer'

	Singular	Dual	Plural
First	**bohccon** 'my reindeer'	**bohccome** 'our reindeer'	**bohccomet** 'our reindeer'
Second	**bohccot** 'your reindeer'	**bohccode** 'your reindeer'	**bohccodet** 'your reindeer'
Third	**bohccos** 'his/her reindeer'	**bohccoska** 'their reindeer'	**bohccoset** 'their reindeer'

Point to note:

- The possessive suffixes are attached to the accusative-genitive form of the noun.

Accusative-genitive singular

Even-syllable

oabbá 'sister'

	Singular	Dual	Plural
First	**oabbán** 'my sister'	**oabbáme** 'our sister'	**oabbámet** 'our sister'
Second	**oappát** 'your sister'	**oappáde** 'your sister'	**oappádet** 'your sister'
Third	**oappás** 'his/her sister'	**oappáska** 'their sister'	**oappáset** 'their sister'

Point to note:

- The accusative-genitive is identical with the nominative (i.e. it remains in the strong grade) in conjunction with the first person possessive suffixes.

áhčči 'father'

	Singular	Dual	Plural
First	**áhččán** 'my father'	**áhččáme** 'our father'	**áhččámet** 'our father'
Second	**áhčát** 'your father'	**áhčáde** 'your father'	**áhčádet** 'your father'
Third	**áhčis** 'his/her father'	**áhčiska** 'their father'	**áhčiset** 'their father'

Points to note:

- Word-final -i changes to -á before the first and second person suffixes.
- The accusative-genitive is identical with the nominative (i.e. it remains in the strong grade) in conjunction with the first person possessive suffixes.

eallu 'reindeer herd'

	Singular	Dual	Plural
First	**ellon** 'my reindeer herd'	**ellome** 'our reindeer herd'	**ellomet** 'our reindeer herd'
Second	**elot** 'your reindeer herd'	**elode** 'your reindeer herd'	**elodet** 'your reindeer herd'
Third	**ealus** 'his/her reindeer herd'	**ealuska** 'their reindeer herd'	**ealuset** 'their reindeer herd'

Points to note:

- Word-final -u changes to -o before the first and second person possessive suffixes.
- Diphthongs simplify before -o.
- The accusative-genitive is identical with the nominative (i.e. it remains in the strong grade) in conjunction with the first person possessive suffixes.

Odd-syllable and contracted

The accusative-genitive form of suffixed odd-syllable and contracted nouns is identical to the nominative.

Illative singular

Even-syllable

oabbá 'sister'

	Singular	Dual	Plural
First	**oabbásan** 'to my sister'	**oabbáseame** 'to our sister'	**oabbáseamet** 'to our sister'

5 Pronouns

	Singular	Dual	Plural
Second	**oabbásat** 'to your sister'	**oabbáseatte** 'to your sister'	**oabbáseattet** 'to your sister'
Third	**oabbásis** 'to his/her sister'	**oabbáseaskka** 'to their sister'	**oabbáseaset** 'to their sister'

áhčči 'father'

	Singular	Dual	Plural
First	**áhččásan** 'to my father'	**áhččáseame** 'to our father'	**áhččáseamet** 'to our father'
Second	**áhččásat** 'to your father'	**áhččáseatte** 'to your father'	**áhččáseattet** 'to your father'
Third	**áhččásis** 'to his/her father'	**áhččáseaskka** 'to their father'	**áhččáseaset** 'to their father'

Point to note:

- Word-final -i changes to -á before all suffixes.

eallu 'reindeer herd'

	Singular	Dual	Plural
First	**ellosan** 'to my reindeer herd'	**elloseame** 'to our reindeer herd'	**elloseamet** 'to our reindeer herd'
Second	**ellosat** 'to your reindeer herd'	**elloseatte** 'to your reindeer herd'	**elloseattet** 'to your reindeer herd'
Third	**ellosis** 'to his/her reindeer herd'	**elloseaskka** 'to their reindeer herd'	**elloseaset** 'to their reindeer herd'

Points to note:

- Word-final -**u** changes to -**o** before all suffixes.
- Diphthongs simplify before -**o**.

Odd-syllable

vieljaš 'little brother'

	Singular	Dual	Plural
First	**vieljažasan** 'to my little brother'	**vieljažasame** 'to our little brother'	**vieljažasamet** 'to our little brother'
Second	**vieljažasat** 'to your little brother'	**vieljažasade** 'to your little brother'	**vieljažasadet** 'to your little brother'
Third	**vieljažasas** 'to his/her little brother'	**vieljažasaska** 'to their little brother'	**vieljažasaset** 'to their little brother'

Contracted

boazu 'reindeer'

	Singular	Dual	Plural
First	**bohccosan** 'to my reindeer'	**bohccoseame** 'to our reindeer'	**bohccoseamet** 'to our reindeer'
Second	**bohccosat** 'to your reindeer'	**bohccoseatte** 'to your reindeer'	**bohccoseattet** 'to your reindeer'
Third	**bohccosis** 'to his/her reindeer'	**bohccoseaskka** 'to their reindeer'	**bohccoseaset** 'to their reindeer'

Point to note:

- The possessive suffixes are attached to the accusative-genitive form of the noun.

Locative singular

Even-syllable

oabbá 'sister'

	Singular	Dual	Plural
First	**oappástan** 'at/from my sister'	**oappásteame** 'at/from our sister'	**oappásteamet** 'at/from our sister'
Second	**oappástat** 'at/from your sister'	**oappásteatte** 'at/from your sister'	**oappásteattet** 'at/from your sister'
Third	**oappástis** 'at/from his/her sister'	**oappásteaskka** 'at/from their sister'	**oappásteaset** 'at/from their sister'

áhčči 'father'

	Singular	Dual	Plural
First	**áhčistan** 'at/from my father'	**áhčisteame** 'at/from our father'	**áhčisteamet** 'at/from our father'
Second	**áhčistat** 'at/from your father'	**áhčisteatte** 'at/from your father'	**áhčisteattet** 'at/from your father'
Third	**áhčistis** 'at/from his/her father'	**áhčisteaskka** 'at/from their father'	**áhčisteaset** 'at/from their father'

eallu 'reindeer herd'

	Singular	Dual	Plural
First	**ealustan** 'at/from my reindeer herd'	**ealusteame** 'at/from our reindeer herd'	**ealusteamet** 'at/from our reindeer herd'

5 Pronouns

Second	**ealustat** 'at/from your reindeer herd'	**ealusteatte** 'at/from your reindeer herd'	**ealusteattet** 'at/from your reindeer herd'
Third	**ealustis** 'at/from his/her reindeer herd'	**ealusteaskka** 'at/from their reindeer herd'	**ealusteaset** 'to their reindeer herd'

Odd-syllable

vieljaš 'little brother'

	Singular	Dual	Plural
First	**vieljažisttán** 'at/from my little brother'	**vieljažisttáme** 'at/from our little brother'	**vieljažisttámet** 'at/from our little brother'
Second	**vieljažisttát** 'at/from your little brother'	**vieljažisttáde** 'at/from your little brother'	**vieljažisttádet** 'at/from your little brother'
Third	**vieljažisttis** 'at/from his/her little brother'	**vieljažisttiska** 'at/from their little brother'	**vieljažisttiset** 'at/from their little brother'

Contracted

boazu 'reindeer'

	Singular	Dual	Plural
First	**bohccostan** 'at/from my reindeer'	**bohccosteame** 'at/from our reindeer'	**bohccosteamet** 'at/from our reindeer'
Second	**bohccostat** 'at/from your reindeer'	**bohccosteatte** 'at/from your reindeer'	**bohccosteattet** 'at/from your reindeer'

| Third | bohccostis 'at/from his/her reindeer' | bohccosteaskka 'at/from their reindeer' | bohccosteaset 'at/from their reindeer' |

Comitative singular

Even-syllable

oabbá 'sister'

	Singular	Dual	Plural
First	oappáinan 'with my sister'	oappáineame 'with our sister'	oappáineamet 'with our sister'
Second	oappáinat 'with your sister'	oappáineatte 'with your sister'	oappáineattet 'with your sister'
Third	oappáinis 'with his/her sister'	oappáineaskka 'with their sister'	oappáineaset 'with their sister'

áhčči 'father'

	Singular	Dual	Plural
First	áhčiinan 'with my father'	áhčiineame 'with our father'	áhčiineamet 'with our father'
Second	áhčiinat 'with your father'	áhčiineatte 'with your father'	áhčiineattet 'with your father'
Third	áhčiinis 'with his/her father'	áhčiineaskka 'with their father'	áhčiineaset 'with their father'

5 Pronouns

eallu 'reindeer herd'

	Singular	Dual	Plural
First	**ealuinan** 'with my reindeer herd'	**ealuineame** 'with our reindeer herd'	**ealuineamet** 'with our reindeer herd'
Second	**ealuinat** 'with your reindeer herd'	**ealuineatte** 'with your reindeer herd'	**ealuineattet** 'with your reindeer herd'
Third	**ealuinis** 'with his/her reindeer herd'	**ealuineaskka** 'with their reindeer herd'	**ealuineaset** 'with their reindeer herd'

Odd-syllable

vieljaš 'little brother'

	Singular	Dual	Plural
First	**vieljažiinnán** 'with my little brother'	**vieljažiinnáme** 'with our little brother'	**vieljažiinnámet** 'with our little brother'
Second	**vieljažiinnát** 'with your little brother'	**vieljažiinnáde** 'with your little brother'	**vieljažiinnádet** 'with your little brother'
Third	**vieljažiinnis** 'with his/her little brother'	**vieljažiinniska** 'with their little brother'	**vieljažiinniset** 'with their little brother'

Contracted

boazu 'reindeer'

	Singular	Dual	Plural
First	**bohccuinan** 'with my reindeer'	**bohccuineame** 'with our reindeer'	**bohccuineamet** 'with our reindeer'
Second	**bohccuinat** 'with your reindeer'	**bohccuineatte** 'with your reindeer'	**bohccuineattet** 'with your reindeer'
Third	**bohccuinis** 'with his/her reindeer'	**bohccuineaskka** 'with their reindeer'	**bohccuineaset** 'with their reindeer'

Essive

Even-syllable

oabbá 'sister'

	Singular	Dual	Plural
First	**oabbánan** 'as my sister(s)'	**oabbáneame** 'as our sister(s)'	**oabbáneamet** 'as our sister(s)'
Second	**oabbánat** 'as your sister(s)'	**oabbáneatte** 'as your sister(s)'	**oabbáneattet** 'as your sister(s)'
Third	**oabbánis** 'as his/her sister(s)'	**oabbáneaskka** 'as their sister(s)'	**oabbáneaset** 'as their sister(s)'

áhčči 'father'

	Singular	Dual	Plural
First	**áhččinan** 'as my father(s)'	**áhččineame** 'as our father(s)'	**áhččineamet** 'as our father(s)'

5 Pronouns

	Singular	Dual	Plural
Second	**áhččinat** 'as your father(s)'	**áhččineatte** 'as your father(s)'	**áhččineattet** 'as your father(s)'
Third	**áhččinis** 'as his/her father(s)'	**áhččineaskka** 'as their father(s)'	**áhččineaset** 'as their father(s)'

eallu 'reindeer herd'

	Singular	Dual	Plural
First	**eallunan** 'as my reindeer herd(s)'	**ealluneame** 'as our reindeer herd(s)'	**ealluneamet** 'as our reindeer herd(s)'
Second	**eallunat** 'as your reindeer herd(s)'	**ealluneatte** 'as your reindeer herd(s)'	**ealluneattet** 'as your reindeer herd(s)'
Third	**eallunis** 'as his/her reindeer herd(s)'	**ealluneaskka** 'as their reindeer herd(s)'	**ealluneaset** 'as their reindeer herd(s)'

Odd-syllable

Odd-syllable nouns do not occur at all with possessive suffixes in the essive case.

Contracted

boazu 'reindeer'

	Singular	Dual	Plural
First	**boazunan** 'as my reindeer'	**boazuneame** 'as our reindeer'	**boazuneamet** 'as our reindeer'

Second	**boazunat** 'as your reindeer'	**boazuneatte** 'as your reindeer'	**boazuneattet** 'as your reindeer'
Third	**boazunis** 'as his/her reindeer'	**boazuneaskka** 'as their reindeer'	**boazuneaset** 'as their reindeer'

Points to note:

- Possessive suffixes are relatively rarely used with nouns in the essive case.
- Contracted nouns ending in -is do not occur at all with possessive suffixes in the essive case.

Nominative plural

The possessive suffixes are not used in conjunction with nominative plural nouns.

Accusative-genitive plural

Even-syllable

oabbá 'sister'

	Singular	Dual	Plural
First	**oappáidan** 'my sisters'	**oappáideame** 'our sisters'	**oappáideamet** 'our sisters'
Second	**oappáidat** 'your sisters'	**oappáideatte** 'your sisters'	**oappáideattet** 'your sisters'
Third	**oappáidis** 'his/her sisters'	**oappáideaskka** 'their sisters'	**oappáideaset** 'their sisters'

5 Pronouns

áhčči 'father'

	Singular	Dual	Plural
First	**áhčiidan** 'my fathers'	**áhčiideame** 'our fathers'	**áhčiideamet** 'our fathers'
Second	**áhčiidat** 'your fathers'	**áhčiideatte** 'your fathers'	**áhčiideattet** 'your fathers'
Third	**áhčiidis** 'his/her fathers'	**áhčiideaskka** 'their fathers'	**áhčiideaset** 'their fathers'

eallu 'reindeer herd'

	Singular	Dual	Plural
First	**ealuidan** 'my reindeer herds'	**ealuideame** 'our reindeer herds'	**ealuideamet** 'our reindeer herds'
Second	**ealuidat** 'your reindeer herds'	**ealuideatte** 'your reindeer herds'	**ealuideattet** 'your reindeer herds'
Third	**ealuidis** 'his/her reindeer herds'	**ealuideaskka** 'their reindeer herds'	**ealuideaset** 'their reindeer herds'

Odd-syllable

vieljaš 'little brother'

	Singular	Dual	Plural
First	**vieljažiiddán** 'my little brothers'	**vieljažiiddáme** 'our little brothers'	**vieljažiiddámet** 'our little brothers'

	Second	**vieljažiiddát** 'your little brothers'	**vieljažiiddáde** 'your little brothers'	**vieljažiiddádet** 'your little brothers'
	Third	**vieljažiiddis** 'his/her little brothers'	**vieljažiiddiska** 'their little brothers'	**vieljažiiddiset** 'their little brothers'

Contracted

boazu 'reindeer'

	Singular	Dual	Plural
First	**bohccuidan** 'my reindeer'	**bohccuideame** 'our reindeer'	**bohccuideamet** 'our reindeer'
Second	**bohccuidat** 'your reindeer'	**bohccuideatte** 'your reindeer'	**bohccuideattet** 'your reindeer'
Third	**bohccuidis** 'his/her reindeer'	**bohccuideaskka** 'their reindeer'	**bohccuideaset** 'their reindeer'

Illative plural

Even-syllable

oabbá 'sister'

	Singular	Dual	Plural
First	**oappáidasan** 'to my sisters'	**oappáidasame** 'to our sisters'	**oappáidasamet** 'to our sisters'
Second	**oappáidasat** 'to your sisters'	**oappáidasade** 'to your sisters'	**oappáidasadet** 'to your sisters'
Third	**oappáidasas** 'to his/her sisters'	**oappáidasaska** 'to their sisters'	**oappáidasaset** 'to their sisters'

5 Pronouns

áhčči 'father'

	Singular	Dual	Plural
First	áhčiidasan 'to my fathers'	áhčiidasame 'to our fathers'	áhčiidasamet 'to our fathers'
Second	áhčiidasat 'to your fathers'	áhčiidasade 'to your fathers'	áhčiidasadet 'to your fathers'
Third	áhčiidasas 'to his/her fathers'	áhčiidasaska 'to their fathers'	áhčiidasaset 'to their fathers'

eallu 'reindeer herd'

	Singular	Dual	Plural
First	eluidasan 'to my reindeer herds'	ealuidasame 'to our reindeer herds'	ealuidasamet 'to our reindeer herds'
Second	ealuidasat 'to your reindeer herds'	ealuidasade 'to your reindeer herds'	ealuidasadet 'to your reindeer herds'
Third	ealuidasas 'to his/her reindeer herds'	ealuidasaska 'to their reindeer herds'	ealuidasaset 'to their reindeer herds'

Odd-syllable

vieljaš 'little brother'

	Singular	Dual	Plural
First	vieljažiiddásan 'to my little brothers'	vieljažiiddáseame 'to our little brothers'	vieljažiiddáseamet 'to our little brothers'

Second	**vieljažiiddásat** 'to your little brothers'	**vieljažiiddáseatte** 'to your little brothers'	**vieljažiiddáseattet** 'to your little brothers'
Third	**vieljažiiddásis** 'to his/her little brothers'	**vieljažiiddáseaskka** 'to their little brothers'	**vieljažiiddáseaset** 'to their little brothers'

Contracted

boazu 'reindeer'

	Singular	Dual	Plural
First	**bohccuidasan** 'to my reindeer'	**bohccuidasame** 'to our reindeer'	**bohccuidasamet** 'to our reindeer'
Second	**bohccuidasat** 'to your reindeer'	**bohccuidasade** 'to your reindeer'	**bohccuidasadet** 'to your reindeer'
Third	**bohccuidasas** 'to his/her reindeer'	**bohccuidasaska** 'to their reindeer'	**bohccuidasaset** 'to their reindeer'

Locative plural

Even-syllable

oabbá 'sister'

	Singular	Dual	Plural
First	**oappáinan** 'at/from my sisters'	**oappáineame** 'at/from our sisters'	**oappáineamet** 'at/from our sisters'

5 Pronouns

Second	**oappáinat** 'at/from your sisters'	**oappáineatte** 'at/from your sisters'	**oappáineattet** 'at/from your sisters'
Third	**oappáinis** 'at/from his/her sisters'	**oappáineaskka** 'at/from their sisters'	**oappáineaset** 'at/from their sisters'

áhčči 'father'

	Singular	Dual	Plural
First	**áhčiinan** 'at/from my fathers'	**áhčiineame** 'at/from our fathers'	**áhčiineamet** 'at/from our fathers'
Second	**áhčiinat** 'at/from your fathers'	**áhčiineatte** 'at/from your fathers'	**áhčiineattet** 'at/from your fathers'
Third	**áhčiinis** 'at/from his/her fathers'	**áhčiineaskka** 'at/from their fathers'	**áhčiineaset** 'at/from their fathers'

eallu 'reindeer herd'

	Singular	Dual	Plural
First	**ealuinan** 'at/from my reindeer herds'	**ealuineame** 'at/from our reindeer herds'	**ealuineamet** 'at/from our reindeer herds'
Second	**ealuinat** 'at/from your reindeer herds'	**ealuineatte** 'at/from your reindeer herds'	**ealuineattet** 'at/from your reindeer herds'

				5 Pronouns
Third	ealuinis 'at/from his/her reindeer herds'	ealuineaskka 'at/from their reindeer herds'	ealuineaset 'at/from their reindeer herds'	

Odd-syllable

vieljaš 'little brother'

	Singular	Dual	Plural
First	**vieljažiinnán** 'at/from my little brothers'	**vieljažiinnáme** 'at/from our little brothers'	**vieljažiinnámet** 'at/from our little brothers'
Second	**vieljažiinnát** 'at/from your little brothers'	**vieljažiinnáde** 'at/from your little brothers'	**vieljažiinnádet** 'at/from your little brothers'
Third	**vieljažiinnis** 'at/from his/her little brothers'	**vieljažiinniska** 'at/from their little brothers'	**vieljažiinniset** 'at/from their little brothers'

Contracted

boazu 'reindeer'

	Singular	Dual	Plural
First	**bohccuinan** 'at/from my reindeer'	**bohccuineame** 'at/from our reindeer'	**bohccuineamet** 'at/from our reindeer'
Second	**bohccuinat** 'at/from your reindeer'	**bohccuineatte** 'at/from your reindeer'	**bohccuineattet** 'at/from your reindeer'
Third	**bohccuinis** 'at/from his/her reindeer'	**bohccuineaskka** 'at/from their reindeer'	**bohccuineaset** 'at/from their reindeer'

5 Pronouns

Comitative plural

Even-syllable

oabbá 'sister'

	Singular	Dual	Plural
First	**oappáidanguin** 'with my sisters'	**oappáideameguin** 'with our sisters'	**oappáideametguin** 'with our sisters'
Second	**oappáidatguin** 'with your sisters'	**oappáideatteguin** 'with your sisters'	**oappáideattetguin** 'with your sisters'
Third	**oappáidisguin** 'with his/her sisters'	**oappáideaskkaguin** 'with their sisters'	**oappáideasetguin** 'with their sisters'

áhčči 'father'

	Singular	Dual	Plural
First	**áhčiidanguin** 'with my fathers'	**áhčiideameguin** 'with our fathers'	**áhčiideametguin** 'with our fathers'
Second	**áhčiidatguin** 'with your fathers'	**áhčiideatteguin** 'with your fathers'	**áhčiideattetguin** 'with your fathers'
Third	**áhčiidisguin** 'with his/her fathers'	**áhčiideaskkaguin** 'with their fathers'	**áhčiideasetguin** 'with their fathers'

eallu 'reindeer herd'

	Singular	Dual	Plural
First	**ealuidanguin** 'with my reindeer herds'	**ealuideameguin** 'with our reindeer herds'	**ealuideametguin** 'with our reindeer herds'

Second	ealuidatguin 'with your reindeer herds'	ealuideatteguin 'with your reindeer herds'	ealuideattetguin 'with your reindeer herds'
Third	ealuidisguin 'with his/her reindeer herds'	ealuideaskkaguin 'with their reindeer herds'	ealuideasetguin 'with their reindeer herds'

5 Pronouns

Odd-syllable

vieljaš 'little brother'

	Singular	Dual	Plural
First	vieljažiiddánguin 'with my little brothers'	vieljažiiddámeguin 'with our little brothers'	vieljažiiddámetguin 'with our little brothers'
Second	vieljažiiddátguin 'with your little brothers'	vieljažiiddádeguin 'with your little brothers'	vieljažiiddádetguin 'with your little brothers'
Third	vieljažiiddisguin 'with his/her little brothers'	vieljažiiddiskaguin 'with their little brothers'	vieljažiiddisetguin 'with their little brothers'

Contracted

boazu 'reindeer'

	Singular	Dual	Plural
First	bohccuidanguin 'with my reindeer'	bohccuideameguin 'with our reindeer'	bohccuideametguin 'with our reindeer'

Second	**bohccuidat-guin** 'with your reindeer'	**bohccuideatte-guin** 'with your reindeer'	**bohccuideat-tetguin** 'with your reindeer'
Third	**bohccuidis-guin** 'with his/her reindeer'	**bohccuideaskka-guin** 'with their reindeer'	**bohccuidea-setguin** 'with their reindeer'

Point to note:

- The comitative plural possessive element is infixed between the two parts of the case ending.

The possessive suffixes are not very widely used in everyday speech, but are sometimes found attached to oblique nouns (often kinship terms) referring back to the subject of the sentence, e.g.:

Mun ožžon skeaŋkka **eatnistan**.	I got a present from my mother.
Son riŋgii **muottásis**.	S/he phoned his/her mother's younger sister.
Atte munnje **ruđaidan**!	Give me my money!
Mun lávejin dárostit **oappáidanguin** ja **vieljainan**.	I used to speak Norwegian with my sisters and my brother.
Dalle veahkehin **váhnemiiddán** šibitdoaluin.	Then I helped my parents with the cattle.
Mu eatnibeali máttarvánhemat ledje badjeolbmot geat bohte mearragáddái **bohccuideasetguin**.	My ancestors on my mother's side were nomadic reindeer herders who came to the seaside with their reindeer.

5.3 Demonstrative

The demonstrative pronouns in Sámi are as follows

- **dát**   this/these (near the speaker)
- **diet**   that/those (near the addressee)
- **duot**   that/those (near neither the speaker nor the addressee)
- **dot**   that/those (far away)
- **dat**   that/those (nonspecific, previously mentioned)

Dát inflects as follows:

Nom	**dát**	**dát**
Acc/Gen	**dán**	**dáid**
Ill	**dása**	**dáidda**
Loc	**dás**	**dáin**
Com	**dáinna**	**dáiguin**
Ess	**dánin**	

Dat, diet, duot, and **dot** all inflect in the same way, e.g. **dan, dasa; dien, diesa; duon, duosa,** etc.

When appearing directly before a noun, the demonstratives are inflected in the same case as the noun, e.g.:

Oainnát go **duoid lottiid**?   Do you see those birds?

However, the illative and locative singular take the form of the accusative-genitive, e.g.:

Liikot go **dán** čuvlii?   Do you like this dress?

Son orru **duon** viesus.   S/he lives in that house.

The following examples illustrate the use of the demonstrative pronouns.

Maid **dát** mearkkaša dutnje?   What does this mean to you?

Lea bat **diet** duohta?   Is that true?

Váldde **dien** stuolu.	Take that chair.
Oainnát go **duon** gappa?	Do you see that white reindeer?
Dat viessu lei ovdal geavahuvvon boarrásiidsiidan.	That house had previously been used as an old people's home.
Leat go oaidnán **dan** filmma?	Have you seen that film?

Note that **dat** is often used as a third person singular pronoun, e.g.:

| **Dat** máhttá hupmat sámegiela. | S/he can speak Sámi. |

The illative and locative forms of the demonstratives can be used as adverbs of place, e.g.:

| Mun orun **dás**. | I live here. |

5.4 Interrogative

The North Sámi interrogative pronouns are as follows:

mii	what
gii	who
goabbá	which (out of two)
guhte	which (out of a specific group; out of many)
guhtemuš	which (out of many)
makkár(aš)	what kind of

Mii inflects as follows:

Nom	**mii**	**mat**
Acc	**man, maid**	**maid**
Gen	**man**	**maid**
Ill	**masa**	**maidda**
Loc	**mas**	**main**

Com	**mainna**	**maiguin**
Ess	**manin**	

The following examples illustrate the use of the various forms of **mii** 'what'.

Mii sámi álbmotbeaivi lea? — What is the Sámi National Day?

Maid Johan Turi muitala sámi identitehta birra? — What does Johan Turi say about Sámi identity?

Masa son liiko? — What does s/he like?

Mainna barggaidet? — What did you work with?

Gii inflects as follows.

Nom	gii	geat
Acc/Gen	gean	geaid
Ill	geasa	geaidda
Loc	geas	geain
Com	geainna	geaiguin
Ess	geanin	

The following examples illustrate the use of the various forms of **gii** 'who'.

Gii lea boahtán? — Who has come?

Geasa don addet dan skeaŋkka? — Who did you give that present to?

Geainna Máret manai? — Who did Máret go with?

Geat barget dáppe? — Who (pl.) works here?

Geaiguin Sámi Radio lea háleštan? — Who (pl.) has the Sámi Radio spoken with?

Guhte inflects as follows:

Nom	guhte	guđet
Acc/Gen	guđe	guđiid
Ill	guhtii	guđiide
Loc	guđes	guđiin
Com	guđiin	guđiiguin
Ess		guhten

Goabbá, guhte, and **guhtemuš** inflect like nouns. Here are some examples of their use:

Goabbái don liikot buorebut?	Which (out of two) do you like better?
Guhtemuš lávlu vuittii Sámi Grand Prix?	Which singer won the Sámi Grand Prix?

When appearing directly before a noun, **mii, guhte,** and **goabbá** inflect in the same case as the noun. However, the illative and locative singular take the form of the accusative-genitive, e.g.:

Man skohterii don liikot?	Which snowmobile do you like?
Guđe lanjas dat lea?	Which room is it in?

5.5 Relative

The most common North Sámi relative pronouns are as follows. Note that these are identical to the interrogative pronouns. See section 5.3 for inflection of these forms.

mii	which, that
gii	who, which, that
goabbá	who, which, that (out of two)
guhte	who, which, that

Here are some examples of relative pronoun use:

Gánda **gii** bođii festii lea Iŋggá viellja.	The boy who came to the party is Iŋgá's brother.
Mun liikon sidjiide **geat** sihke máhttet jurddašit iehčaneaset ja doibmat joavkobarggus.	I like those who can both think for themselves and work as a team (lit: function in groupwork).
Dat lea balddonasmuitalus **mii** lea muitaluvvon Nuorta-Finnmárkkus.	It's a ghost story which has been told in East Finnmark.
Leat go dus dehálaš báikkit **maid** birra háliidivččet diehtit eambbo?	Do you have important places that you would like to know more about?
Dállu, **mas** Biret-Elle orru, lea unni.	The house in which Biret-Elle lives is small.
Doppe ledje ollu girjjit. Girji **guđe** mun válden ii lean nu buorre.	There were a lot of books there. The book that I took wasn't so good.

5.6 Indefinite

North Sámi has a number of indefinite pronouns. The most common ones are shown here.

buohkat	everyone
buot	everything
juohke	every
juohkehaš	each
eanas, eanaš	most
eatnagat	many
ollugat	many

5 Pronouns

eará	other
soames	a few, some
muhtin, muhtun	someone, something, some
juoga	something

Points to note:

- **Buohkat, juohkehaš, eatnagat,** and **ollugat** are used independently, not attributively, and inflect like nouns.
- **Buot, eará, soames,** and **muhtin/muhtun** can be used either independently or attributively.
- **Juohke** can only be used attributively.
- **Eará, soames,** and **muhtin/muhtun** do not inflect when used attributively and inflect like nouns when used independently. Note that **muhtin/muhtun** does not undergo consonant gradation.
- **Buot** and **juohke** do not inflect.
- **Juoga** is used independently and has an irregular inflection.

Nom	**juoga**
Acc	**juoga, juoidá, juoidáid**
Gen	**juoga**
Ill	**juosát**
Loc	**juostá**
Com	**juoidáin**
Ess	**juonin**

The following examples illustrate the use of these pronouns:

Mun in dieđe **buot**.	I don't know everything.
Sii fitne **buot** báikkiin.	They visited all the places.
Buori sámi álbmotbeaivvi **buohkaide**!	Happy Sámi National Day to everyone!

Oahpa veahá sámegiela **juohke** beaivvi.	Learn a bit of Sámi every day.	**5** **Pronouns**
Juohkehaččas lea riekti mearridit.	Each one has the right to decide.	
Eanas olbmot ballet das.	Most people are afraid of that.	
Eatnagat liikojit dasa.	Some people like it.	
Mun bovdejin **ollugiid** festii.	I invited many people to the party.	
Lea go dus **eará** ivdni?	Do you have another colour?	
Dušše **hárvásat** besse dohko.	Only a few got to go there.	
Son bođii ruoktot **muhtun** jagiid geažes.	S/he came home some years later.	
Muhtimat jurdiledje nu.	Some people thought like that.	
Mun oidnen **juoidá** seavdnjadasas.	I saw something in the dark.	

In addition, North Sámi has a number of indefinite pronominal constructions made up of a combination of an interrogative pronoun and a particle. Each construction is outlined here.

Interrogative pronoun + ge

(ii) **giige**	no one, anyone
(ii) **miige, mihkkege**	nothing, anything
(ii) **guhtege**	none of them, any of them (out of a group)
(ii) **goabbáge**	neither, either
(ii) **oktage**	no one, anyone
(ii) **makkárge**	no such, any such

5 Pronouns

These are all typically used in negative sentences and inflect like the corresponding interrogative pronouns (**okta** inflects like the corresponding numeral), e.g.:

In leat hupman **geainnage**.	I haven't talked with anyone.
Mii eat oastán **maidege**.	We didn't buy anything.
Ii **guhtege** oaččo eanet go beali.	None of them gets more than half.
It go liiko **goabbáige**?	Don't you like either of them?
Ii **oktage** boahtán festii.	No one came to the party.
Mun in háliit **makkárge** váivvi.	I don't want any kind of trouble.

Vaikko/feara + interrogative pronoun

vaikko/feara gii	whoever, anyone
vaikko/feara mii	whatever, anything
vaikko/feara guhte	whichever, anyone (out of a group)
vaikko/feara goabbá	whichever, either (of two)
vaikko/feara makkár	whatever kind, any kind

The following examples illustrate the use of these constructions.

Vaikko gii sáhttá dan dahkat.	Anyone can do it.
Don sáhtát čállit **feara maid**.	You can write anything.

Interrogative pronoun + fal/beare/ihkinassii

gii fal/beare/ihkinassii	whoever, anyone
mii fal/beare/ihkinassii	whatever, anything
guhte fal/beare/ihkinassii	whichever (out of a group)
goabbá fal/beare/ihkinassii	whichever (out of two)

Note that **ihkinassii** has a variant, **ihkenassii**.

The following examples illustrate the use of these constructions.

Gii beare sáhttá vástidit interneahtas.	Anyone can answer on the internet.
Gii ihkinassii galggašii sáhttit oažžut oahpahusa sámegielas.	Anyone should be able to receive instruction in Sámi.
Atte munnje **goappá fal**.	Give me either one.

Interrogative pronoun + **nu**

gii nu	something
mii nu	someone
guhte nu	someone (out of a group)
goabbá nu	either (of two)
makkár nu	some kind of
gos nu	somewhere

Note that **nu** can be found in conjunction with other interrogatives in addition to the ones listed.

The following example illustrates the use of this construction:

Son orru **gos nu** Suomas.	S/he lives somewhere in Finland.
Lea go dus **makkár nu** muitalus midjiide?	Do you have some kind of story for us?

5.7 Distributive

North Sámi possesses a number of distributive pronouns. They inflect in the same way as the equivalent interrogative pronouns.

(ieš)guhtege, (ieš)guhtenai	each one (out of a group)
goabbáge, goabbánai	each one (of two)

The following example illustrates the use of these forms.

Ožžot go **goappásge** nummára?   Did you get each one's
                                 (of two) number?

5.8 Reflexive

The forms of the North Sámi reflexive pronoun (corresponding to English 'self') are as follows:

Case	Person	Singular	Dual	Plural
Nom		**ieš**	**ieža**	**ieža**
Acc/Gen	1	**iežan/ iehčan**	**iežame**	**iežamet**
	2	**iežat**	**iežade**	**iežadet**
	3	**iežas**	**iežaska**	**iežaset**
Ill	1	**alccesan/ alccen**	**alcceseame/ alcceme**	**alcceseamet/ alccemet**
	2	**alccesat/ alccet**	**alcceseatte/ alccede**	**alcceseattet/ alccedet**
	3	**alccesis/ alcces**	**alcceseaskka/ alccseska**	**alcceseaset/ alccseset**
Loc	1	**alddán**	**alddáme**	**alddámet**
	2	**alddát**	**alddáde**	**alddádet**
	3	**alddis**	**alddiska**	**alddiset**
Com	1	**iežainan**	**iežaineame**	**iežaineamet**
	2	**iežainat**	**iežaineatte**	**iežaineattet**
	3	**iežainis**	**iežaineaskka**	**iežaineaset**

Ess	1	iehčanan	iehčaneame	iehčaneamet
	2	iehčanat	iehčaneatte	iehčaneattet
	3	iehčanis	iehčaneaskka	iehčaneaset

Points to note:

- There are dialectal variations on some of these forms.
- The essive forms can all be replaced by **iehčanassii**.

The following examples illustrate the use of the reflexive pronoun:

Mun lean **ieš** dan dahkan.	I've done it myself.
Mo sáhtán oahpásmuvvat **iežainan** buorebut?	How can I get to know myself better?
Sii vigge dan **ieža** ráhkadit.	They tried to make it themselves.
Váldde dan **alccesat**.	Take it for yourself.
Nuorat ordnejedje **alcceseaset** guhkit juovlaluomu.	The young people arranged a longer Christmas holiday for themselves.
Mii galgat beroštit **alddámet**.	We have to look after ourselves.

5.9 Reciprocal

North Sámi possesses the following three reciprocal constructions (equivalent to English 'each other'), each consisting of two parts:

- **nubbi nuppi** 'each other' (dual or plural)
- **goabbat guoibmi** + possessive suffix 'each other' (dual)
- **guhtet + guoibmi** + possessive suffix 'each other' (plural)

For each construction, the first word is always in the nominative, whereas the second word inflects like a noun in the relevant case. Details of each construction are given here.

Nubbi nuppi

This construction can appear in the singular or plural. As the following table and examples show, the singular forms are used with dual subjects and the plural forms with plural subjects.

	Dual	Plural
Acc/Gen	**nubbi nuppi**	**nuppit nuppiid**
Ill	**nubbi nubbái**	**nuppit nuppiide**
Loc	**nubbi nuppis**	**nuppit nuppiin**
Com	**nubbi nuppiin**	**nuppit nuppiiguin**
Ess	**nubbi nubbin**	**nuppit nubbin**

The following examples illustrate the use of these forms.

Soai liikoba **nubbi nubbái**.	They (two) like each other.
Sii eai huma **nuppit nuppiiguin**.	They (more than two) don't speak to each other.
Máret ja Elle oinniiga **nubbi nuppi**.	Máret and Elle saw each other.
Dii galgabehtet veahkehit **nuppit nuppiid**.	You (more than two) have to help each other.

Goabbat guoibmi

This construction is used with dual subjects. As the following table and examples show, the second word always has a possessive suffix.

	First person
Acc/Gen	**goabbat guoibmáme**
Ill	**goabbat guoibmáseame**

Loc	**goabbat guoimmisteame**
Com	**goabbat guimmiineame**

Second person	
Acc/Gen	**goabbat guoimmáde**
Ill	**goabbat guoibmáseatte**
Loc	**goabbat guoimmisteatte**
Com	**goabbat guimmiineatte**

Third person	
Acc/Gen	**goabbat guoimmiska**
Ill	**goabbat guoibmáseaskka**
Loc	**goabbat guoimmisteaskka**
Com	**goabbat guimmiineaskka**

The following examples illustrate the use of these forms.

Soai fitnaba **goabbat guoimmiska** luhtte.	They visit each other.
Moai láviime čállit **goabbat guoibmáseame**.	We used to write to each other.

Guhtet guoibmi

This construction is used with plural subjects. As in the case of **goabbat guoibmi**, the second word always has a possessive suffix. Note that the second word has two variants (one inflecting like a singular noun and one like a plural), which are used interchangeably.

5 Pronouns

First person

Acc/Gen	**guhtet guoibmámet/guimmiideamet**
Ill	**guhtet guoibmáseamet/ guimmiidasamet**
Loc	**guhtet guoimmisteamet/ guimmiineamet**
Com	**guhtet guimmiineamet/ guimmiideametguin**

Second person

Acc/Gen	**guhtet guoimmádet/guimmiideattet**
Ill	**guhtet guoibmáseattet/ guimmiidasadet**
Loc	**guhtet guoimmisteattet/ guimmiineattet**
Com	**guhtet guimmiineattet/ guimmiideattetguin**

Third person

Acc/Gen	**guhtet guoimmiset/ guimmiideaset**
Ill	**guhtet guoibmáseaset/ guimmiidasaset**
Loc	**guhtet guoimmisteaset/ guimmiineaset**
Com	**guhtet guimmiineaset/ guimmiideasetguin**

The following examples illustrate the use of these forms.

Sii hupmet **guhtet guoimmiset** birra.   They talk about each other.

Mii attiimet skeaŋkkaid **guhtet guoibmáseamet**.   We gave each other presents.

Chapter 6
Numerals

6.1 Cardinal

The nominal forms of the cardinal numerals 0–10 are as follows:

0 **nolla, nulla**

1 **okta**

2 **guokte**

3 **golbma**

4 **njeallje**

5 **vihtta**

6 **guhtta**

7 **čieža**

8 **gávcci**

9 **ovcci**

10 **logi**

Numerals from 11 to 19 are formed by adding **-nuppelohkái** (lit: to the second ten) to the units 1–9:

11 **oktanuppelohkái**

12 **guoktenuppelohkái**

13 **golbmanuppelohkái**

14	njealljenuppelohkái
15	vihttanuppelohkái
16	guhttanuppelohkái
17	čiežanuppelohkái
18	gávccinuppelohkái
19	ovccinuppelohkái

6 Numerals

When used attributively, -**nuppelohkái** shortens to -**nuppelot**:

vihttanuppelot studeantta   fifteen students

The tens are formed by adding -**logi** to the units 1–9:

20	guoktelogi
30	golbmalogi
40	njealljelogi
50	vihttalogi
60	guhttalogi
70	čiežalogi
80	gávccilogi
90	ovccilogi

When used attributively, -**logi** shortens to -**lot**:

guoktelot kilomehtera   twenty kilometres

100 is **čuođi,** and the hundreds are formed by adding -**čuođi** to the units 1–9:

100	čuođi
200	guoktečuođi

6 Numerals

300	**golbmačuođi**
400	**njeallječuođi**
500	**vihttačuođi**
600	**guhttačuođi**
700	**čiežačuođi**
800	**gávccičuođi**
900	**ovccičuođi**

1,000 is **duhát**, and the thousands are formed by adding **-duhát** to the units 1–9:

1,000	**duhát**
2,000	**guokteduhát**
3,000	**golbmaduhát**
4,000	**njealljeduhát**
1,000,000	**millijovdna, miljon**

These numerals are combined predictably, e.g.:

25	**guoktelogivihtta**
38	**golbmalogiovcci**
167	**čuođiguhttalogičieža**
2,054	**guokteduhátvihttaloginjeallje**

In a numeral phrase the noun follows the numeral and appears in the accusative-genitive singular, e.g.:

golbma girjji	three books
vihtta beatnaga	five dogs
guoktečuođi ruvnno	200 kroner

6 Numerals

The cardinal numbers are inflected in all the cases like other nouns. Take note of the following points:

- The accusative of the numerals is the same as the nominative, apart from **okta**, **nolla/nulla**, and **millijovdna**.
- **Vihtta** and **guhtta** change -htt- to -đ- instead of the expected change from -htt- to -ht-.
- The final vowel of **guokte** and **njeallje** is -i in all cases except the nominative/accusative.

The inflected forms are used on their own or with adpositions (discussed in chapter 9). This is particularly common in expressions of time:

Doaimmahusčoahkkimat dollojuvvojit dábálaččat **guovttis njealljái**.	The office meetings are usually held from two to four.
Sii vulge **viđas**.	They left at five.
Mun boađán ovdal **guđa**.	I'll come before six.
Muhto mii fertet bargat gitta **golmma** rádjái.	But we have to work up until three.

They can also be used in conjunction with nouns in inflected form. In such cases the numeral is inflected like **dat** (see section 5.3), i.e. when the noun is in the illative or the locative, the numeral is in the genitive. This also applies to inflected compound numerals, where the final unit is treated like the head noun.

Sápmelaččat orrot **njealji** riikkas.	The Sámi live in four countries.
Mun liikon **guovtti** bárdnái.	I like two boys.
Son bargá **guvttiin** ustibiin.	S/he works with two friends.
Mun osten dan **guovttečuohtái**.	I bought it for 200 kroner.

If the noun is plural but refers to one item (e.g. **buvssat** 'trousers') the plural of the numeral is used.

Mus leat **golmmat** ođđa buvssat.	I have three pairs of new trousers.

113

6.2 Ordinal

The ordinal numerals are as follows. Most are formed by adding -át to the accusative-genitive form of the corresponding cardinal. The ordinals first, second, and seventh are irregular.

first	**vuosttaš**
second	**nubbi**
third	**goalmmát**
fourth	**njealját**
fifth	**viđát**
sixth	**guđát**
seventh	**čihččet**
eighth	**gávccát**
ninth	**ovccát**
tenth	**logát**
eleventh	**oktanuppelogát**
twentieth	**guoktelogát**
hundredth	**čuođát**

The ordinal numerals function like adjectives. When used attributively they do not change their form. **Nubbi** 'second' inflects like **dat** (see section 5.3).

Dát lea mu **vuosttaš** mátki olgoriikii.	This is my first trip abroad.
Mii fitnat áhku luhtte juohke **nuppi** beaivve.	We visit grandma every other day.
Guovtti teavsttas lea eará ortografiija go **goalmmádis**.	Two texts have a different orthography than the third one.
Lohket **viđat** siiddus **ovccát** siidui.	Read from the fifth page to the ninth page.

When used substantively the ordinals inflect like odd-syllable nouns:

Vuosttaža namma lea Birjá, **nuppi** namma lea Mirjá.	The first one's name is Birjá; the second one's name is Mirjá.
Dan **goalmmáda** gal in oba gávdnange.	I didn't even find the third one.

6.3 Derived

The suffix -**ii** added to the strong grade of numerals is used to indicate a number of times. The resulting form often resembles, but is not identical to, the illative singular. Note that when the suffix -**ii** is added, the diphthong in the first syllable of **guokte** and **njeallje** is simplified.

Mun lean juo **guktii** dan filmma oaidnán.	I've already seen that film twice.
Son lea **golbmii** vuoitán Sámi Grand Prix.	S/he has won the Sámi Grand Prix three times.
Čoahkkimat dollojit **njelljii** jagis.	The meetings are held four times a year.

The suffix -**s** can be added to the genitive singular of the cardinal numerals to form collective numerals, designating a number of people. The resulting forms look identical to the locative singular.

Golmmas ožžo stipeandda dán jagi.	Three people received a stipend this year.
Mii leimmet **njealjis**.	There were four of us.
Viđas ledje mielde gilvvus.	There were five people in the competition.

The collective forms inflect like odd-syllable nouns, e.g.:

Máhtte oinnii dan **golbmasa** ikte.	Máhtte saw the three of them yesterday.

The suffix -eš can be added to the weak grade of numerals to make them into nouns, such as 'number one', 'a fiver', etc. When the suffix is added diphthongs simplify.

Dat árvvoštallojuvvo skálain 1–5 – mas **viđeš** lea buoremus.	It is assessed on a scale of 1 to 5 – where 'five' is the best.
Biret oaččui **logeža** tenttes.	Biret got a 'ten' on the exam.
Gávdnen **čuđeža** geainnu alde.	I found a hundred-kroner note on the road.

The following are common fractions. Note that there is a special word for 'one and a half'.

bealli	half
goalmmadas or **goalmmatoassi**	a third
njealjádas or **njealjátoassi**	a fourth
viđadas or **viđatoassi**	a fifth
beannot or **okta ja bealli**	one and a half

The following examples illustrate the use of fractions.

Son barggai **beannot** jagi Sámi Teáhteris.	S/he worked for half a year at the Sámi Theatre.
Riika gokčá measta **goalmmatoasi** eurásialaš kontineanttas.	The country covers almost a third of the Eurasian continent.

Chapter 7
Verbs

7.1 Tense

7.1.1 Present

7.1.1.1 Form

Like nouns, verbs can be divided into three different types: even-syllable, odd-syllable, and contracted.

Even-syllable

mannat 'to go'

	Singular	Dual	Plural
First	manan 'I go'	manne	mannat
Second	manat	mannabeahtti	mannabehtet
Third	manná	mannaba	mannet

boahtit 'to come'

	Singular	Dual	Plural
First	boađán 'I come'	bohte	boahtit
Second	boađát	boahtibeahtti	boahtibehtet
Third	boahtá	boahtiba	bohtet

orrut 'to live'

	Singular	Dual	Plural
First	**orun** 'I live'	**orro**	**orrut**
Second	**orut**	**orrubeahtti**	**orrubehtet**
Third	**orru**	**orruba**	**orrot**

Points to note:

- First and second person singular are in the weak grade.
- In the third person singular final -a- and -i- become -á.
- In the first person dual and third person plural the following vowel changes take place at the end of the word: **a** > **e**, **i** > **e**, and **u** > **o**
- The first person dual and third person plural undergo diphthong simplification.

Odd-syllable

muitalit 'to tell'

	Singular	Dual	Plural
First	**muitalan** 'I tell'	**muitaletne**	**muitalit**
Second	**muitalat**	**muitaleahppi**	**muitalehpet**
Third	**muitala**	**muitaleaba**	**muitalit**

Point to note:

- Odd-syllable verbs do not have consonant gradation.

Contracted

čohkkát 'to sit'

	Singular	Dual	Plural
First	čohkkán 'I sit'	čohkkájetne	čohkkát
Second	čohkkát	čohkkábeahtti	čohkkábehtet
Third	čohkká	čohkkába	čohkkájit

čilget 'to explain'

	Singular	Dual	Plural
First	čilgen 'I explain'	čilgejetne	čilget
Second	čilget	čilgebeahtti	čilgebehtet
Third	čilge	čilgeba	čilgejit

liikot 'to like'

	Singular	Dual	Plural
First	liikon 'I like'	liikojetne	liikot
Second	liikot	liikobeahtti	liikobehtet
Third	liiko	liikoba	liikojit

Points to note:

- Contracted verbs do not have consonant gradation.
- In the first person dual and third person plural a -j- appears before the person suffix.

The verb 'to be'

The verb 'to be' could be classified as an odd-syllable verb, but it is somewhat irregular. The present tense paradigm is shown here.

7 Verbs

leat 'to be'

	Singular	Dual	Plural
First	**lean** 'I am'	**letne**	**leat**
Second	**leat**	**leahppi**	**lehpet**
Third	**lea**	**leaba**	**leat**

7.1.1.2 Usage

The North Sámi present tense can be used to express present (both non-progressive and progressive) and future actions, as illustrated in the following examples.

Son **čuoigá** bures.	He skis well.
Mun **orun** Ohcejogas.	I live in Utsjoki.
Mun **goban** dál guvssi.	I'm carving a cup now.
Vuoššat go gáfe?	Are you making coffee?
Mun **vuolggán** Ruttii ihttin.	I'm going to Sweden tomorrow.
Goas don **manat** heargevuodjimiidda?	When are you going to the reindeer races?

7.1.2 Past

7.1.2.1 Form

Even-syllable

mannat 'to go'

	Singular	Dual	Plural
First	**mannen** 'I went'	**manaime**	**manaimet**
Second	**mannet**	**manaide**	**manaidet**
Third	**manai**	**manaiga**	**manne**

boahtit 'to come'

	Singular	Dual	Plural
First	bohten 'I came'	bođiime	bođiimet
Second	bohtet	bođiide	bođiidet
Third	bođii	bođiiga	bohte

orrut 'to live'

	Singular	Dual	Plural
First	orron 'I lived'	oruime	oruimet
Second	orrot	oruide	oruidet
Third	orui	oruiga	orro

Points to note:

- The first and second person singular and third person plural are in the strong grade.
- In the first and second person singular and third person plural the following vowel changes take place at the end of the word: a > e, i > e, and u > o
- The first and second person singular and third person plural undergo diphthong simplification.
- Throughout the entire paradigm -it verbs exhibit diphthong simplification.

Odd-syllable

muitalit 'to tell'

	Singular	Dual	Plural
First	muitalin 'I told'	muitaleimme	muitaleimmet
Second	muitalit	muitaleidde	muitaleiddet
Third	muitalii	muitaleigga	muitaledje

Point to note:

- Odd-syllable verbs do not have consonant gradation.

Contracted

čohkkát 'to sit'

	Singular	Dual	Plural
First	**čohkkájin** 'I sat'	**čohkkáime**	**čohkkáimet**
Second	**čohkkájit**	**čohkkáide**	**čohkkáidet**
Third	**čohkkái**	**čohkkáiga**	**čohkkájedje**

čilget 'to explain'

	Singular	Dual	Plural
First	**čilgejin** 'I explained'	**čilgiime**	**čilgiimet**
Second	**čilgejit**	**čilgiide**	**čilgiidet**
Third	**čilgii**	**čilgiiga**	**čilgejedje**

liikot 'to like'

	Singular	Dual	Plural
First	**liikojin** 'I liked'	**liikuime**	**liikuimet**
Second	**liikojit**	**liikuide**	**liikuidet**
Third	**liikui**	**liikuiga**	**liikojedje**

Points to note:

- Contracted verbs do not have consonant gradation.
- In the first and second person singular and third person plural a -j- appears before the person suffix.
- In -et and -ot verbs, the final vowel of the stem becomes -i- in all persons except the first and second person singular and third person plural.

The verb 'to be'

As in the present, the past tense of the verb 'to be' is slightly irregular:

leat 'to be'

	Singular	Dual	Plural
First	**ledjen** 'I was'	**leimme**	**leimmet**
Second	**ledjet**	**leidde**	**leiddet**
Third	**lei**	**leigga**	**ledje**

7.1.2.2 Usage

The past tense is typically used for simple past actions, e.g.:

Áhkku **goarui** mu nje ođđa gávtti.	Grandma sewed a new gákti for me.
Máret **bođii** ruoktot ikte.	Máret came home yesterday.
Sii **orro** Oslos vihtta jagi.	They lived in Oslo for five years.
Mii **finaimet** mearragáttis mannan vahkus.	We visited the coast last week.

7.1.3 Perfect

7.1.3.1 Form

The North Sámi perfect tense consists of a conjugated present tense form of the verb 'to be' followed by the past participle of the main verb. The past participle is formed by replacing the infinitive suffix -t with -n, as follows:

Even-syllable	Odd-syllable	Contracted
mannan 'gone'	**muitalan** 'told'	**čohkkán** 'sat'
boahtán 'come'	**leamaš** 'been'	**čilgen** 'explained'
orron 'lived'		**liikon** 'liked'

Points to note:

- In even-syllable verbs stem-final -i- becomes -á-.
- In odd-syllable verbs stem-final -i- becomes -a-.
- In even-syllable verbs stem-final -u- becomes -o-.
- The past participle of the verb **leat** 'to be' is irregular.

The entire perfect paradigm of the verb **mannat** 'to go' is given below for illustration.

	Singular	Dual	Plural
First	**lean mannan** 'I have gone'	**letne mannan**	**leat mannan**
Second	**leat mannan**	**leahppi mannan**	**lehpet mannan**
Third	**lea mannan**	**leaba mannan**	**leat mannan**

7.1.3.2 Usage

The North Sámi perfect tense corresponds in meaning to the English perfect, i.e. it is used with reference to past actions with present relevance, past experiences that took place at an unspecified time, and future actions that precede another future action. In addition, it corresponds to the English perfect progressive (typically in conjunction with temporal expressions). These uses are illustrated below:

Lean geahččalan su veahkehit.	I've tried to help him/her.
Son **lea** olles eallima **bargan** boazodoaluš.	He has worked in reindeer herding his whole life.
Leat go **borran** bohccobierggu? De **lean**, dieđusge.	Have you eaten reindeer meat? I have, of course.
Mun boađán du lusa go **lean geargan** barggus.	I'll come to yours when I've finished work.
Eanandoallo- ja biebmodepartemeanta **lea sádden** reivve Boazodoallostivrii.	The Agriculture and Food Department has sent a letter to the Reindeer Herding Authority.
Mun **lean lávlon** ja **čuojahan** sámi musihka mánnávuođa rájes.	I've been singing and playing Sámi music since childhood.

7.1.4 Pluperfect

7.1.4.1 Form

The pluperfect is constructed from a conjugated past form of the verb **leat** 'to be' and the same past participle as the perfect (see section 7.1.3.1). The entire pluperfect paradigm of the verb **mannat** 'to go' is given for illustration.

	Singular	Dual	Plural
First	**ledjen mannan** 'I had gone'	**leimme** **mannan**	**leimmet** **mannan**
Second	**ledjet mannan**	**leidde** **mannan**	**leiddet** **mannan**
Third	**lei mannan**	**leigga** **mannan**	**ledje** **mannan**

7.1.4.2 Usage

The North Sámi pluperfect corresponds in meaning to its English counterpart, i.e. it denotes a past action that was already complete by the time of the main past action in the clause. This is illustrated below:

Áddjá **lei** juo **vuolgán** go Biret lihkai.	Grandpa had already left when Biret got up.
Mun **ledjen** juo **oahppan** veahá sámegiela ovdalgo bohten Sápmái.	I had already learned a bit of Sámi before I came to Sápmi.

7.1.5 Progressive

7.1.5.1 Form

In addition to the tenses discussed earlier, North Sámi possesses a compound construction used to denote progressive actions in each tense (and mood; see section 7.2 for details of moods in North Sámi). Each progressive tense is composed of a form of the verb **leat** 'to be' conjugated for person, tense, and mood, followed by the main verb in a form called the actio essive, which is constructed as follows:

1. For even-syllable and contracted verbs, the infinitive ending is replaced with -**min** (in the East) or -**me** (in the West), e.g. **mannamin/manname, boahtimin/boahtime, čohkkámin/čohkkáme**.

2. For odd-syllable verbs, the infinitive ending is replaced with -**eamen** (in the East) or -**eame** (in the West), e.g. **muitaleamen/muitaleame**.

The progressive construction is illustrated below with the verb **mannat** 'to go' in the first person singular in various tenses and moods:

Present progressive	**lean mannamin**	I'm going
Past progressive	**ledjen mannamin**	I was going
Perfect progressive	**lean leamaš mannamin**	I have been going
Pluperfect progressive	**ledjen leamaš mannamin**	I had been going
Conditional progressive	**livččen mannamin**	I would be going
Conditional perfect progressive	**livččen leamaš mannamin**	I would have been going
Potential progressive	**leaččan mannamin**	I might be going
Potential perfect progressive	**leaččan leamaš mannamin**	I might have been going

7.1.5.2 Usage

In general, the use of the North Sámi progressive constructions corresponds very closely to that of their English counterparts. However, use of the present progressive is optional in North Sámi, in contrast to English. For example, the North Sámi equivalent of the English sentence 'I am reading a book' could be either the present simple **mun logan girjji** or the present progressive **mun lean lohkamin girjji**.

Use of the progressive construction in various tenses and moods is illustrated here.

Iŋgá **lea vuoššamin** aḍḍamiid.	Iŋgá is cooking bone marrow.
Mun **ledjen oaḍḍime** go bohtet ruoktot.	I was sleeping when you got home.

Mun **lean leamaš lohkamin** ollu sámi historjjá birra.	I've been reading a lot about Sámi history.
Mii havssiimet ahte son **lei leamaš suovasteame** guliid.	We smelled that he had been smoking fish.

7.1.6 Alternative ways of expressing tense

In addition to the present tense, North Sámi can also convey future actions by means of the following modal verbs plus an infinitive (discussed in 7.4.1).

áigut	to intend to, to be going to
boahtit	to be going to

The following examples illustrate the use of these constructions.

Mun **áiggun** dainna **geargat** ihttin.	I'm going to finish it tomorrow.
Dat **boahtá leat** váttis.	It'll be difficult.

North Sámi also has a verb, **lávet**, which is used to convey habitual actions. This can be used in the present, e.g.:

Mun **láven vázzit** bargui.	I usually walk to work.

The past tense of **lávet** is used to convey habitual past actions, corresponding to English 'used to', e.g.:

Mun **lávejin** ollu **čuoigat** go orron Sámis.	I used to ski a lot when I lived in Sápmi.

7.1.7 Tense in reported speech

Theoretically North Sámi does not have sequence of tense, meaning that verbs in reported speech keep the same tense as in direct speech (in contrast to English, Norwegian, and Swedish). The following examples illustrate this.

Máhtte logai ahte son **ii boađe**.	Máhtte said that he wasn't coming.
Son fuobmái ahte **ii** duođaid **dárbbaš** nu ollu.	S/he noticed that s/he didn't really need so much.
Mun oidnen ahte son **lea** juo **čollon** daid guliid.	I saw that he had already gutted the fish.

However, due to the fact that North Sámi speakers in Norway and Sweden are bilingual, sequence of tense is also attested.

7.2 Mood

7.2.1 Indicative

See section 7.1 for discussion of the indicative mood (i.e. the standard present, past, perfect, etc.) in North Sámi.

7.2.2 Potential

7.2.2.1 Form

The potential marker is -ž- or -žž-. It is suffixed to verbs in the following ways.

Even-syllable

mannat 'to go'

	Singular	Dual	Plural
First	**manažan** 'I might go'	**manažetne**	**manažit**
Second	**manažat**	**manažeahppi**	**manažehpet**
Third	**manaža/manaš**	**manažeaba**	**manažit**

7 Verbs

boahtit 'to come'

	Singular	Dual	Plural
First	**bođežan** 'I might come'	**bođežetne**	**bođežit**
Second	**bođežat**	**bođežeahppi**	**bođežehpet**
Third	**bođeža/bođeš**	**bođežeaba**	**bođežit**

orrut 'to live'

	Singular	Dual	Plural
First	**orožan** 'I might live'	**orožetne**	**orožit**
Second	**orožat**	**orožeahppi**	**orožehpet**
Third	**oroža/oroš**	**orožeaba**	**orožit**

Points to note:

- All forms are in the weak grade.
- In verbs ending in -**it**, the final -**i** becomes -**e**-.
- In verbs ending in -**ut**, the final -**u** becomes -**o**-.
- Verbs ending in -**it** and -**ut** undergo diphthong simplification.
- The third person singular has a short variant form ending in -**š**.

Odd-syllable

muitalit 'to tell'

	Singular	Dual	Plural
First	**muitaleaččan** 'I might tell'	**muitaležže**	**muitaleažžat**

Second	**muitaleaččat**	muita-leažžabeahtti	muita-leažžabehtet
Third	**muitaleažžá/ muitaleaš /muitaleš**	muitaleažžaba	muitaležžet

The verb 'to be' behaves like a regular odd-syllable verb in the potential.

leat 'to be'

	Singular	Dual	Plural
First	**leaččan** 'I might be'	**ležže**	**leažžat**
Second	**leaččat**	**leažžabeahtti**	**leažžabehtet**
Third	**leažžá/leaš/leš**	**leažžaba**	**ležžet**

Points to note:

- The first and second person singular are in the weak grade.
- The third person singular has two short variant forms ending in -š.

Contracted

čohkkát 'to sit'

	Singular	Dual	Plural
First	**čohkkážan** 'I might sit'	**čohkkážetne**	**čohkkážit**
Second	**čohkkážat**	**čohkkážeahppi**	**čohkkážehpet**
Third	**čohkkáža/ čohkkáš**	**čohkkážeaba**	**čohkkážit**

čilget 'to explain'

	Singular	Dual	Plural
First	**čilgežan** 'I might explain'	**čilgežetne**	**čilgežit**
Second	**čilgežat**	**čilgežeahppi**	**čilgežehpet**
Third	**čilgeža/čilgeš**	**čilgežeaba**	**čilgežit**

liikot 'to like'

	Singular	Dual	Plural
First	**liikožan** 'I might like'	**liikožetne**	**liikožit**
Second	**liikožat**	**liikožeahppi**	**liikožehpet**
Third	**liikoža/liikoš**	**liikožeaba**	**liikožit**

Point to note:

- The third person singular has a short variant form ending in -š.

7.2.2.2 Usage

The potential expresses uncertainty and doubt. It is not used very frequently; instead, an indicative form with an adverb is often employed to achieve the same effect. It is most commonly found with the verb **leat** 'to be'. The use of the potential is illustrated here.

Dat lea buot čábbámus maid mun **leaččan** goassige oaidnán.	It's probably the most beautiful [thing] that I've ever seen.
Mun in beroš maid **dagažat**.	I don't care what you might do.

In mun dieđe gos son **oroš**.	I don't know where s/he might live.
Leažžá bat son nu rikkis?	Could s/he really be so rich?

7.2.3 Conditional

7.2.3.1 Form

The conditional marker is -š- (or, in the West, -l-) or -včč-. It is suffixed to verbs in the following ways.

Even-syllable

mannat 'to go'

	Singular	Dual	Plural
First	**manašin** 'I would go'	**manašeimme**	**manašeimmet**
Second	**manašit**	**manašeidde**	**manašeiddet**
Third	**manašii**	**manašeigga**	**manašedje/manaše**

boahtit 'to come'

	Singular	Dual	Plural
First	**boađášin** 'I would come'	**boađášeimme**	**boađášeimmet**
Second	**boađášit**	**boađášeidde**	**boađášeiddet**
Third	**boađášii**	**boađášeigga**	**boađášedje/boađáše**

orrut 'to live'

	Singular	Dual	Plural
First	**orošin** 'I would live'	**orošeimme**	**orošeimmet**

7 Verbs

Second	**orošit**	**orošeidde**	**orošeiddet**
Third	**orošii**	**orošeigga**	**orošedje/oroše**

Points to note:

- All forms are in the weak grade.
- In verbs ending in -**it**, the final -**i**- becomes -**á**-.
- In verbs ending in -**ut**, the final -**u**- becomes -**o**-.
- Verbs ending in -**ut** undergo diphthong simplification.
- The third person plural has two variant forms, ending in -**edje** and -**e**, respectively.
- There is a colloquial variant form ending in -**šivčč**-, e.g. **manašivččer** 'I would go'.
- In the West, -**š**- is replaced by -**l**-, e.g. **manalin** 'I would go', **manalit** 'you would go', **manalii** 's/he would go'.

Odd-syllable

muitalit 'to tell'

	Singular	Dual	Plural
First	**muitalivččen** 'I would tell'	**muitalivččiime**	**muitalivččiimet**
Second	**muitalivččet**	**muitalivččiide**	**muitalivččiidet**
Third	**muitalivččii**	**muitalivččiiga**	**muitalivčče**

The verb **leat** 'to be' behaves like a regular odd-syllable verb in the potential.

leat 'to be'

	Singular	Dual	Plural
First	**livččen** 'I would be'	**livččiime**	**livččiimet**
Second	**livččet**	**livččiide**	**livččiidet**
Third	**livččii**	**livččiiga**	**livčče**

Contracted

čohkkát 'to sit'

	Singular	Dual	Plural
First	**čohkkášin** 'I would sit'	**čohkkášeimme**	**čohkkášeimmet**
Second	**čohkkášit**	**čohkkášeidde**	**čohkkášeiddet**
Third	**čohkkášii**	**čohkkášeigga**	**čohkkášedje/ čohkkáše**

čilget 'to explain'

	Singular	Dual	Plural
First	**čilgešin** 'I would explain'	**čilgešeimme**	**čilgešeimmet**
Second	**čilgešit**	**čilgešeidde**	**čilgešeidde**
Third	**čilgešii**	**čilgešeigga**	**čilgešedje/čilgeše**

liikot 'to like'

	Singular	Dual	Plural
First	**liikošin** 'I would like'	**liikošeimme**	**liikošeimmet**
Second	**liikošit**	**liikošeidde**	**liikošeidde**
Third	**liikošii**	**liikošeigga**	**liikošedje/liikoše**

Points to note:

- The third person plural has two variant forms, ending in -**edje** and -**e**, respectively.
- There is a colloquial variant form ending in -**šivčč**-, e.g. **čohkkášivččen** 'I would sit'.

There is also a perfect conditional, which is formed by a combination of the conditional and the past participle (see section 7.1.3.1 for the formation of the past participle), as illustrated here.

	Singular	Dual	Plural
First	**livččen mannan** 'I would have gone'	**livččiime mannan**	**livččiimet mannan**
Second	**livččet mannan**	**livččiide mannan**	**livččiidet mannan**
Third	**livččii mannan**	**livččiiga mannan**	**livčče mannan**

7.2.3.2 Usage

The North Sámi conditional is used to express hypothetical situations, corresponding to the English conditional construction with 'would'. The conditional form is used in both the main clause and the subordinate (**jus/jos** 'if') clause.

Jos mun **sáhtášin** vuolgit gosa beare, mun **vuolggášin** Londonii.	If I could go anywhere, I would go to London.
Maid **dagašit** jos **livččet** miljoneara?	What would you do if you were a millionaire?
Livččii buorre, jos **oahpahivčče** mánáide sámegiela dán guovllus.	It would be good if they would teach children Sámi in this area.

The conditional may also be used in a main clause without a subordinate clause, e.g.:

Mun **vuorddášin** du, dieđusge.	Of course I would wait for you.
Gos don **livččet** mu haga?	Where would you be without me?

Sometimes the usage corresponds to English constructions beginning with 'as if', e.g.:

Son láhttii dego **ii dovddaše** mu.	S/he acted as if s/he didn't know me.

The perfect conditional is used to express hypothetical situations in the past, e.g.:

Jos mun **livččen diehtán**, in **livčče** gal dan **oastán**.	If I had known, I wouldn't have bought it.
Jos son ii **livčče boahtán**, eat **livčče beassan** dan dahkat.	If s/he hadn't come, we wouldn't have been able to do it.

It is also used to express politeness (typically in requests, offers, and questions), e.g.:

Boađášit go mu mielde?	Would you come with me?
Háliidivččet go gáhku?	Would you like to have some cake?
Mun **áiggošin** dahkat dola.	I'd like to make a fire.

Finally, it is used to express wishes (corresponding to English expressions with 'if only'), e.g.:

Jos mun beare **livččen diehtán**!	If only I had known!
Vare áhkku ain **ealášii**!	If only granny were still alive!

7.2.4 Imperative

North Sámi has first person, second person, and third person imperative forms. The second person imperatives resemble English imperatives. The first and third person imperatives resemble the English constructions 'let me', 'let us', 'let him', etc. In the following tables the singular North Sámi imperative forms have been translated into English in order to illustrate this point.

7.2.4.1 Form

Even-syllable

mannat 'to go'

	Singular	Dual	Plural
First	—	mannu	mannot
Second	**mana** 'go!'	manni	mannet
Third	**mannos** 'let him/her go'	mannoska	mannoset

boahtit 'to come'

	Singular	Dual	Plural
First	—	boahttu	bohtot
Second	**boađe** 'come!'	boahtti	bohtet
Third	**bohtos** 'let him/her come'	bohtoska	bohtoset

orrut 'to live'

	Singular	Dual	Plural
First	—	orru	orrot
Second	**oro** 'live!'	orri	orrot
Third	**orros** 'let him/her live'	orroska	orroset

Points to note:

- The second person singular is in the weak grade.
- The first and second person dual are in the extra strong grade. In the East, the first and second person plural are also in the extra strong grade.
- In the second person singular, stem-final -i- becomes -e and stem-final -u- becomes -o. This does not cause diphthong simplification.
- In all of the third person forms, all of the stem-final vowels become -o-, and there is diphthong simplification.
- Stem-final -i- becomes -e- and final -u- becomes -o- in the first and second person plural forms, e.g. **bohtet** 'come'.

Odd-syllable

muitalit 'to tell'

	Singular	Dual	Plural
First	—	**muitaleadnu**	**muitalehkot**
Second	**muital** 'tell!'	**muitaleahkki**	**muitalehket**
Third	**muitalehkos** 'let him tell'	**muitalehkoska**	**muitalehkoset**

leat 'to be'

	Singular	Dual	Plural
First	—	**leadnu**	**lehkot**
Second	**leage** 'be!'	**leahkki**	**lehket/ leahkket**
Third	**lehkos** 'let him/her be'	**lehkoska**	**lehkoset**

Point to note:

- The second person singular form has no ending.

7 Contracted Verbs

čohkkát 'to sit'

	Singular	Dual	Plural
First	—	čohkkájeadnu/ čohkkájeahkku	čohkkájehkot/ čohkkájeahkkot
Second	čohkká 'sit!'	čohkkájeahkki	čohkkájehket
Third	čohkkájehkos 'let him/her sit'	čohkkájehkoska	čohkkájehkoset

čilget 'to explain'

	Singular	Dual	Plural
First	—	čilgejeadnu/ čilgejeahkku	čilgejehkot/ čilgejeahkkot
Second	čilge 'explain!'	čilgejeahkki	čilgejehket
Third	čilgejehkos 'let him/her explain'	čilgejehkoska	čilgejehkoset

liikot 'to like'

	Singular	Dual	Plural
First	—	liikojeadnu/ liikojeahkku	liikojehkot/ liikojeahkkot
Second	liiko 'like!'	liikojeahkki	liikojehket
Third	liikojehkos 'let him/her like'	liikojehkoska	liikojehkoset

Points to note:

- The second person singular form has no ending.
- The first person plural form is **čohkkájehkot** in the West and **čohkkájeahkkot** in the East.

Note that the second person singular imperative can appear with an -s or -l suffix, e.g. **boađes** 'come', **vuordil** 'wait a second'. These are subitive and diminutive suffixes respectively (see sections 13.1.1.1.2.1 and 13.1.1.1.2.5 for details), which are used for making polite requests.

7.2.4.2 Usage

The second person imperatives are used to give orders and make requests, e.g.:

Atte munnje niibbi.	Give me a knife.
Boađe mu mielde.	Come (singular) with me.
Hupmet sámegiela!	Speak Sámi (plural)!
Manni dearvan!	Goodbye (lit: go in health) (dual)!

Note the use of the imperative ending in -s or -l for polite requests, e.g.:

Buvttes munnje dien girjji.	Please bring me that book.
Vuordil dáppe.	Please wait here.

The first person dual and plural imperatives are used to make suggestions (equivalent to English 'let's').

Na de borrot guoli!	Let's (plural) eat fish!
Vuolgu Mázii!	Let's (dual) go to Masi!

The third person imperatives are used to express a desire for another person to carry out an action. They often appear in religious texts.

Bohtos du riika, **šaddos** du dáhttu.	Thy kingdom come, thy will be done.
Dahkos dat maid háliida.	Let him/her do what s/he wants.
Vulgoset fal.	Let them (plural) go.

7.2.5 Alternative ways of expressing modality

Various modal senses can also be expressed using one of the following verbs, typically preceding an infinitive (see section 7.4.1).

Desire

dáhttut	to want to
háliidit	to want (to)

Necessity

galgat	to have to (subjective view)
fertet	to have to (external obligation)
šaddat	to have to, to end up

Possibility

dáidit	may
sáhttit	can
soaitit	may, to happen to

Possibility/ability

beassat	to be able to, to manage to
oažžut	to get to, to manage to
máhttit	to know how to

The following examples illustrate the function of some of these verbs:

Son **soaitá** boahtit.	S/he may come.
Don **galggat** muitalit maid leat dahkan.	You have to tell what you've done.
Máhtte **beasai** čoahkkimis eret.	Máhtte managed to get away from the meeting.
Dalle mun **šattan** ruovttus čohkkát go sii leat barggus.	Then I'll have to sit at home when they're at work.

7.3 Negation

In North Sámi the negative form of a verb consists of a negation verb that takes person suffixes followed by a lexical verb. The forms of the negation verb are as follows.

	Singular	Dual	Plural
First	**in** 'I don't'	**ean**	**eat**
Second	**it**	**eahppi**	**ehpet**
Third	**ii**	**eaba**	**eai**

The negation verb is used in all tenses and moods except the imperative (see section 7.3.6). The form of the lexical verb varies depending on the tense and mood, as follows.

7.3.1 Indicative present

In the indicative present, the lexical verb (also known as the connegative) takes the following forms.

Negation verb	Lexical verb	Verb type
in	**mana**	Even-syllable
it	**boađe**	
ii	**oro**	
ean	**muital**	Odd-syllable
eahppi	**leat**	
eaba	**čohkká**	Contracted
eat	**čilge**	
ehpet	**liiko**	
eai		

Points to note:

- In even-syllable verbs, the lexical verb is in the weak grade and has no suffix. Stem-final -i- becomes -e and final -u- becomes -o.

7 Verbs

- In odd-syllable verbs, the lexical verb is formed by removing the infinitive ending -it.
- Leat 'to be' has the same form as the infinitive.
- In contracted verbs, the lexical verb is formed by removing the infinitive ending -it.

The following examples illustrate the function of some of these verbs:

In mun šat **muitte**.	I don't remember any more.
It go don **liiko** goikebirgui?	Don't you like dried meat?
Sámiid juovlastállu **ii juoge** skeaŋkkaid muhto lea sámiid mytologiija baháninkkánis sivdnádus.	The Sámi Santa Claus (lit: Christmas troll) doesn't hand out presents but rather is an evil creature of Sámi mythology.
Jus bohccot lihkká **eai guođe** geainnu, de vuoje siivvut.	If the reindeer still don't leave the road, drive carefully.

7.3.2 Indicative past, perfect, and pluperfect

The negative past consists of the negation verb and the past participle form of the lexical verb. See section 7.1.3.1 for the formation of the past participle.

Negation verb	Lexical verb	Verb type
in	mannan	Even-syllable
it	boahtán	
ii	orron	
ean	muitalan	Odd-syllable
eahppi	lean	
eaba	čohkkán	Contracted
eat	čilgen	
ehpet	liikon	
eai		

The following examples illustrate the use of the negated past.

Son **ii boahtán** skohteriin.	S/he didn't come by snowmobile.
Dii **ehpet oaidnán** mu.	You (pl.) didn't see me.
Mánát **eai** šat **háliidan** sámástit.	The children didn't want to speak Sámi any more.

The negative perfect consists of the negation verb followed by the connegative form of **leat** 'to be' and the past participle of the lexical verb, e.g. **in leat mannan** 'I haven't gone'. The following example illustrates the usage:

Mii **eat leat fitnan** Guovdageainnu márkanis guhkes áigái.	We haven't been to the Kautokeino town centre for a long time.

The negative pluperfect consists of the negation verb followed by the past participle of **leat** 'to be' and the past participle of the lexical verb, e.g. **in lean mannan** 'I hadn't gone'. The following example illustrates the usage:

Son logai ahte son **ii lean** dan **oaidnán**.	S/he said that s/he hadn't seen it.

7.3.3 Potential

In the potential, the lexical verb takes the following forms.

Negation verb	Lexical verb	Verb type
in	**manaš**	Even-syllable
it	**bođeš**	
ii	**oroš**	
ean	**muitaleačča, muitaleš**	Odd-syllable
eahppi	**leačča, leaš, leš**	
eaba	**čohkkáš**	Contracted
eat	**čilgeš**	
ehpet	**liikoš**	
eai		

Points to note:

- In even-syllable verbs, the lexical verb is in the weak grade and takes the suffix -š. Stem-final -i- becomes -e-, stem-final -u- becomes -o-, and there is diphthong simplification. Note that this form is identical to the alternative third person singular potential form discussed in section 7.3.3.
- In odd-syllable verbs, the lexical verb is formed by suffixing -**eačča** or -**eš** to the stem. Note that **leat** 'to be' has an additional alternative form.
- In contracted verbs, the lexical verb is formed by adding -š to the stem.

The following example illustrates the usage of this construction.

Jos dás **ii leš** veahkki, de váldde oktavuođa e-boasttain.	If this doesn't help, make contact through email.

7.3.4 Conditional

In the conditional, the lexical verb takes the following forms.

Negation verb	Lexical verb	Verb type
in	manaše	Even-syllable
it	boađáše	
ii	oroše	
ean	muitalivčče	Odd-syllable
eahppi	livčče	
eaba	čohkkáše	Contracted
eat	čilgeše	
ehpet	liikoše	
eai		

Points to note:

- The form of the lexical verb resembles the affirmative potential but ends in -e instead of the person suffix.

- In the West, even-syllable verbs have a variant form with -l- instead of -š-. Even-syllable and contracted verbs also have two other dialectal variants ending in -šii and -šivčče.

The following examples illustrate the use of negative conditionals.

Ii bat sámi teáhter galggašii leat juoidá eará?	Shouldn't Sámi theatre be something different?
Mun bázášin, jos ii livčče nu maŋŋit.	I would stay if it weren't so late.

7.3.5 Progressive

The progressive verbal forms are negated by placing the negation verb before the relevant construction, e.g.:

Iŋgá **ii leat bargame** dáppe odne.	Iŋgá isn't working here today.
Son **ii lean čuohppamin** muoraid, son lei suovasteamen guliid.	He wasn't chopping wood, he was smoking fish.

7.3.6 Imperative

The negation verb has a distinct imperative form, shown here.

	Singular	Dual	Plural
First	—	**allu**	**allot**
Second	**ale**	**alli**	**allet**
Third	**allos**	**alloska**	**alloset**

Point to note:

- In the East, the negative imperative forms all start with á- instead of a-, e.g. **ále, állet**.

The negative imperative is followed by the same form of the lexical verb as in the indicative present, except for **leat** 'to be', which takes the form **leage**, e.g.:

Allot dáros sámegielgurssas.	Let's not speak Norwegian during the Sámi course.
Allet sádde mánáid okto konsertii.	Don't send the children to the concert alone.
Ale dájo!	Don't be silly!

7.4 Non-finite verb forms

7.4.1 Infinitive

7.4.1.1 Form

All North Sámi infinitives end in -t. The infinitive forms of the various verb types are given here.

Even-syllable

The infinitive of even-syllable verbs ends in -at, -it, or -ut, as shown here.

mannat	to go
boahtit	to come
orrut	to live

Odd-syllable

The infinitive of odd-syllable verbs ends in -it, as shown here. Note that **leat** 'to be' is considered to be an odd-syllable verb even though its infinitive is somewhat irregular.

muitalit	to tell
leat	to be

Contracted

čohkkát	to sit
čilget	to explain
liikot	to like

7.4.1.2 Usage

Complement

The infinitive commonly appears following the verbs listed here, which convey various types of modalities. Note that many of these correspond to English modal verbs.

astat	to have time to
áigut	to intend to, to be going to
álgit	to start to
beassat	to manage to, to get to
berret	to have to
boahtit	to end up
dáidit	might, to be likely to
fertet	to have to
galgat	to have to
háliidit	to want to
lávet	to do habitually
máhttit	to know how to
oažžut	to get to, to come to
ollet	to have time to
riepmat	to start to

7 Verbs

sáhttit	to be able to
soaitit	might
šaddat	to end up
veadjit	to be able to
viggat	to try to
viššat	to be bothered to

The following examples illustrate the use of these constructions:

Sotnabeaivve lea fas filbma man áiggun **geahččat**.	On Sunday there's another film that I'm planning to watch.
Jos son bohccuid gávdná, de ii son sáhte daid **guođđit**.	If he finds reindeer, he can't leave them.
Elle-Márjá čájehii mo gámasuinniid galggai **čuohppat**.	Elle-Márjá showed how one was supposed to cut shoe hay (hay used to line Sámi shoes).
It dáidde **máhttit** vástidit.	You might not be able to answer.
In mun ádden maid son vikkai munnje **muitalit**.	I didn't understand what s/he was trying to tell me.
In máhte **vuodjit**.	I don't know how to drive.
Iŋgá ii viššan su **hoahpuhit**.	Iŋgá couldn't be bothered to hurry him/her up.
Stállu sáhtii oaidnemeahttumin **jođašit** olbmuid siste.	A troll could travel among people without being seen.
Našuvdnagirjeráju siiddus beassá **lohkat** girjjiid.	On the National Library's website one can read books.

Beasaimet **diehtit**, ahte dathan lei lihkostuvvan buorebut go mii leimmet jurddašan.	We came to understand that it had succeeded better than we had thought.	
Ollugat háliidit **šaddat** oahpaheaddjin.	Many people want to become teachers.	
Mun ferten **čilgestit** ahte lei su iežas sivva.	I have to explain that it was his/her own fault.	

Verbs of motion such as the following are often found in conjunction with an infinitive, which serves as an optional complement:

čohkkedit, čohkánit	to sit down
čuoččahit, čuoččastit	to stand, to stop
girdit	to fly
mannat	to go
viehkat	to run
vuodjit	to drive
vuolgit	to leave

This type of construction is illustrated in the following examples:

Son vulggii meahccái **murjet**.	He went to the forest to pick berries.
Mii čohkkedeimmet gáfe **juhkat**.	We sat down to drink coffee.
Mii vujiimet gávpogii biepmu **oastit**.	We drove to town to buy food.
Maŋŋel go finaimet skuvllas, mii manaimet gávpogii **boradit** ja **gávppašit**.	After we'd been to the school, we went to town to eat and shop.

7 Verbs

Verbs indicating cause, command, influence, and enabling are also commonly found in conjunction with an infinitive:

bivdit	to ask for
diktit	to let, to allow
gohččut	to order, to call
oahpahit	to teach
oažžut	to get
sihtat	to ask
suovvat	to let, to allow
veahkehit	to help

This type of construction is illustrated in the following examples:

Sámi álbmotbeaivi veahkeha sápmelaččaid **atnit** árvvus iežaset duogáža.	Sámi Independence Day helps Sámi people to appreciate their own background.
Mun divttán mánáid **dárostit** maiddái.	I let the children speak Norwegian too.
Son siđai isida **lásset** uvssa.	She asked her husband to lock the door.
Sápmelaš oažžu **sámástit** juos dáčča suovvá.	Sámis are permitted to speak Sámi if Norwegians allow.
Skuvllas galggaše oahpahit **bivdit**.	In school they should teach [the kids] to hunt.
Ádde go mánná jus gohčut **dahkat** juoidá?	Does the child understand if you order [him/her] to do something?

Finally, the infinitive can also be used as a replacement for complement clauses following verbs of utterance (e.g. **dadjat** 'to say', **muitalit** 'to tell'), volition (e.g. **dáhttut** 'to want'), and cognition (e.g. **diehtit** 'to know', **jáhkkit** 'to believe', **muitit** 'to remember'), as well as the verbs **gierdat** 'to endure' and **vuordit** 'to wait for'. In such cases the infinitive denotes a present or future action. The infinitive takes its own nominal or pronominal subject, which appears in the accusative-genitive. If the subject of the infinitive is the same as that of the finite verb, the reflexive pronoun **ieš** 'oneself' is used. This usage is illustrated here.

Ontario provinssa álgoálbmogat dáhttot Canada oaiveministara **nammadit** historjjá vuosttaš álgoálbmotlahtu duopmárin.	The indigenous people of Ontario Province want Canada's Prime Minister to appoint the first indigenous judge in history.
Lea váttis einnostit mo máilmmi-meašttirgilvvuin manná, muhto jáhkán su **birget**.	It's difficult to predict how it will go in the World Cup, but I think that s/he will manage.
EU čuoččuhii sin **leat** nana demokratiija ja olmmošvuoigatvuođaid doarju.	The EU claimed that they were a strong democracy and champion of human rights.
Sii vurdet skuvlla **nannet** mánáid sámegiela dáiddu ja oahpahit mánáide sámekultuvrra.	They expect the school to strengthen the children's Sámi language skills and to teach the children Sámi culture.
Jovnna logai iežas **diehtit** máilmmi buoremus hávgareseaptta.	Jovnna said that he knows the world's best pike recipe.

Subject

Infinitives can serve as the subject of a sentence, e.g.:

Lea hávski **dolastit** ja **stoahkat** olgun meahcis.	To make a fire and play outside in the wilderness is fun.
Noiddiide lei váttis **guođđit** dološ oskku ja **guorrasit** báhpaid oskui.	For the shamans to abandon the old belief and to conform to the priests' belief was difficult.

7 Verbs

Modifying nouns, adjectives, and pronouns

Infinitives can be used to modify nouns, as in the following examples.

Dákkár barggus čuožžila dárbu **ásahit** čilgehusaid.	With this kind of work there arises a need to put explanations in place.
Mus ii leat miella **fárret** gosage.	I don't feel like moving anywhere.
Mus ledje plánat **álgit** joatkkaskuvlii.	I had plans to start high school.
Njeallje bohcco jápme ja ovcci lei bággu **goddit**.	Four reindeer died and it was necessary to kill eight.
Mis sámi servodagas lea vel veaháš bargu **dahkat** ovdal go mis lea dievas ovttaveardásašvuohta.	We in Sámi society still have a bit of work to do before we have full equality.

Likewise, they can be used to modify adjectives, e.g.:

Son lea maid viššal **govvet**.	S/he is also keen to take photos.
Áhkku lea hui čeahppi **muitalit** iežas duogáža birra.	Grandma is very good at talking about her background.
Mii leat gergosat **ráhkadit** sámi historjjá.	We're ready to make Sámi history.

Finally, they can be used to modify pronouns, e.g.:

Ii leat oktage geainna **hupmat**.	There's no one to talk to.

7.4.2 Verbal nouns

A verbal noun is a noun that is derived from a verb and describes an action, e.g. 'sleeping', 'walking', etc. North Sámi verbal nouns are described here.

7.4.2.1 Form

North Sámi verbal nouns are formed by attaching the suffix **-n** to the strong grade of even-syllable verbs and to contracted verbs, and the suffix **-eapmi** to odd-syllable verbs. The formation of verbal nouns is illustrated in the following table (note that **leat** 'to be' is irregular).

Even-syllable	Odd-syllable	Contracted
mannan 'going'	**muitaleapmi** 'telling'	**čohkkán** 'sitting'
boahtin 'coming'	**leahkin** 'being'	**čilgen** 'explaining'
orrun 'living'		**liikon** 'liking'

7.4.2.2 Usage

Verbal nouns function like nouns in that they can be used as a subject or object and take nominal inflections. The following examples illustrate their use.

Stoahkan lea **oahppan**.	Playing is learning.
Mii sáhttit mánáidasamet čájehit ahte **lohkan** lea suohtas.	We can show our children that reading is fun.
Daga **lohkamis** ja **muitaleamis** beaivválaš dábi.	Make reading and [story]telling a daily habit.
Ollugiid mielas dat dagaha giddagasas **čohkkáma** losibun.	In many people's opinion, that makes serving time (lit: sitting) in jail tougher.
Dieđán bures iežan máná sámegiela **ovdáneami** birra.	I know well about my own child's progress (lit. progressing) in the Sámi language.
5. ja 8. luohká oahppit leat dán čavčča dahkan riikkalaš **geahččalemiid lohkamis**.	Pupils in Year 5 and Year 8 have undertaken state exams in reading this autumn.
Mii leat dolkan ja váiban **doarrumis**.	We are fed up and tired of fighting.

7.4.3 Actio essive

7.4.3.1 Form

The actio essive is formed by attaching the suffix -**min**/-**me** to the strong grade of even-syllable verbs and to contracted verbs, and the suffix -**eamen**/-**eame** to odd-syllable verbs. The variants -**min** and -**eamen** are typically used in the East, while -**me** and -**eame** are typically used in the West. This is illustrated here.

Even-syllable	Odd-syllable	Contracted
mannamin/ manname 'going'	**muitaleamen/ muitaleame** 'telling'	**čohkkámin/ čohkkáme** 'sitting'
boahtimin/ boahtime 'coming'	**leamen/ leame** 'being'	**čilgemin/ čilgeme** 'explaining'
orrumin/ orrume 'living'		**liikomin/ liikome** 'liking'

7.4.3.2 Usage

The actio essive is used in the formation of the progressive tenses following the auxiliary **leat** 'to be', as in the following example. See section 7.3.5 for further details of the progressive tenses.

| Son lea **mannamin** ruoktot. | S/he is going home. |

The actio essive can also appear after the verb **orrut** 'to live' used in the sense of 'to seem', e.g.:

| Son **orui leame** joavkku násti. | S/he seemed to be the star of the group. |
| Soai **oruiga bargamin** hui viššalit. | The two of them seemed to be working very diligently. |

The actio essive is also used with a verb of motion, most commonly **fitnat** 'to go somewhere and back, to stop by', to indicate that the subject has gone somewhere to perform the action of the actio essive and then returned. This usage is illustrated here.

Son maiddái láve goarrut singuin ja **fitnat** vaikkoba **murjemin**.	S/he also regularly sews with them and even goes berry-picking.
Mii **mannat** maid meahcis **viežžame** ávdnasiid.	We also go to the wilderness to fetch materials.

Finally, it is used with verbs of perception (e.g. **oaidnit** 'to see', **gullat** 'to hear', **dovdat** 'to feel'), cognition (e.g. **diehtit** 'to know', **doaivut** 'think', **jáhkkit** 'to believe'), and utterance (e.g. **lohkat** 'to say') to indicate simultaneous action. The subject of the actio essive in this type of simultaneous action appears in the accusative-genitive. If the subject of the actio essive is the same as that of the finite verb, the reflexive pronoun **ieš** 'oneself' is used. This usage is illustrated in the following examples:

Sámediggepresideanta **oidnui** **murjemin** iežas isidiin.	The president of the Sámi Parliament was seen picking berries with her husband.
Mun **gulan** su **čorgeme** gievkkanis.	I hear him/her cleaning in the kitchen.
Nisu **oinnii** čuđiid **boahtimin** vári mielde.	The woman saw the Chudes coming along the mountain.
Son **muitalii** eatnis **leamen** buohccin.	S/he said that his/her mother was sick.
Mun **jáhkán** su **boahtime** dál.	I think that s/he is coming now.
Dan áigge guldalin ollu Mari Boine musihka ja **govahallen** su **lávlume** mearragáttis.	At that time I listened to a lot of Mari Boine music and imagined her singing on the seashore.
Áilu manná olggos, muhto boahtá fas ja **lohká** iežas **vuolgimin** áhčis mielde.	Áilu goes outside, but comes back and says that he is going with his father.

7.4.4 Actio locative

7.4.4.1 Form

The actio locative is the locative form of the verbal noun, e.g. **mannamis** 'in/from going'. As such, it is formed by attaching the suffix **-mis** to the strong grade of even-syllable verbs and to contracted verbs, and the suffix **-eamis/-eames** to odd-syllable verbs. The following table illustrates this.

Even-syllable	Odd-syllable	Contracted
mannamis	**muitaleamis/ muitaleames**	**čohkkámis**
boahtimis	**leames**	**čilgemis**
orrumis		**liikomis**

7.4.4.2 Usage

The actio locative is used as the complement of certain verbs. These verbs are listed here.

ádjánit	to linger
ballat	to be afraid
beassat	to get away from
biehttalit	to refuse
dolkat	to get sick of
geargat	to finish
gieldit	to forbid
heaitit	to stop
hehttet	to prevent
vajálduhttit	to forget
váibat	to get tired from

The use of the actio locative in conjunction with these verbs is illustrated here.

Dál it šat dárbbaš **ballat vázzimis** skuvlla gili olggobealde.	Now you don't need to be afraid of going to school outside the village anymore.
Sii **biehttalit hupmamis** muhtun áššiid birra.	They refuse to talk about certain issues.
Dus lea ovddasvástádus bidjat rusttegiid sadjái go leat **geargan** daid **geavaheames**.	You have the responsibility to put the equipment in [its] place when you've finished using it.
'Mun **gielddán** du agibeaivvis šat **deaivvadeames** suinna,' áhčči šikkui.	'I forbid you from ever meeting him/her again,' scolded father.
Oahpaheaddjiskuvla **heittii oahpaheames** sámegiela.	The teacher [training] school stopped teaching Sámi.
Buolaš ii **hehtte** su **govvideames**.	The cold weather doesn't prevent him/her from filming.
Norgga Sámedikki várrepresideanta lea **dolkan čilgemis** eiseválddiide buot vuođđodieđuid sápmelaččaid birra.	The Norwegian Sámi Parliament's vice president has grown tired of explaining all the basic facts about the Sámi to the authorities.

The actio locative can also be used in conjunction with the verb **leat** 'to be' or **gávdnot** 'to be found' to indicate that a given action is possible and that the subject of the sentence is available or obtainable. This usage is most commonly found with verbs such as **oastit** 'to buy', **oažžut** 'to get, to receive', **oaidnit** 'to see', **deaivat** 'to meet', and **vuordit** 'to expect'. Examples include the following:

Kaleanddar máksá 100 ruvnno, ja dat lea **oastimis** kioskkas.	The calendar costs 100 kroner and is available for purchase in the kiosk.
Vearuhusdieđáhusaid ofelaš lea **oažžumis** dál maiddái golmma sámegillii.	A tax information guide is now also available (to get) in three Sámi languages.

7 Verbs

Geatki lea **oaidnimis** ee. Kristiansand elliidgárddis.	Wolverines (lit: a wolverine) can be seen, among other places, at the Kristiansand Zoo.
Doppe leat maid SáB [Sámeálbmotbellodat] fylkadiggekandidáhtat **deaivamis**.	Candidates for County Representative from the Sámi People's Party are also available to meet there.
Makkár sámepolitihkka lea **vuordimis**, go Guovddáš vuittii?	What kind of Sámi politics can be expected, since the Centre won?

The actio locative can also be used to convey the meaning of 'since' in conjunction with a main verb, as in the following example. In this temporal sense the actio locative is equivalent to a finite clause introduced by the conjunction **dan rájes go** 'since' (see section 10.2.2).

Dien gova **váldimis** lea gollan jo guhkes áigi.	A long time has passed since that picture was taken.

7.4.5 Actio comitative

7.4.5.1 Form

The actio comitative is the comitative form of the verbal noun. As such, it is formed by attaching the suffix -**miin** to the strong grade of even-syllable verbs and to contracted verbs, and the suffix -**emiin** to odd-syllable verbs, as follows:

Even-syllable	Odd-syllable	Contracted
mannamiin 'by going'	**muitalemiin** 'by telling'	**čohkkámiin** 'by sitting'
boahtimiin 'by coming'		**čilgemiin** 'by explaining'
orrumiin 'by living'		**liikomiin** 'by liking'

7.4.5.2 Usage

The actio comitative functions as an adverbial instrumental construction, conveying the means by which the action of the main verb happens, e.g.:

Sii ealihedje iežaset **bivdimiin**, **guolástemiin** ja **murjemiin**.	They sustained themselves by hunting, fishing, and berry-picking.
Sámi duojáriid searvi oassálastá dáhpáhussii **ovdanbuktimiin** ja **vuovdimiin** sámemusihka, girjjiid ja dujiid.	The Sámi artisans' society is taking part in the event by presenting and selling Sámi music, books, and duodji.

7.4.6 Gerund

7.4.6.1 Form

The gerund is formed by adding the suffix **-dettiin** to the weak grade of even-syllable verbs and to contracted verbs, and the suffix **-ettiin** to odd-syllable verbs. This is illustrated here.

Even-syllable	Odd-syllable	Contracted
manadettiin 'while/when going'	**muitalettiin** 'while/when telling'	**čohkkádettiin** 'while/when sitting'
boađedettiin 'while/when coming'		**čilgedettiin** 'while/when explaining'
orodettiin 'while/when living'		**liikodettiin** 'while/when liking'

Points to note:

- The alternative endings **-diin** and **-din** are also used.
- Even-syllable verbs may show vowel changes i > e and u > o, e.g. **boađedettiin** 'while coming', **orodettiin** 'while living'.
- The gerund of the irregular verb **leat** 'to be' is not used.

7.4.6.2 Usage

The gerund is used to express an action that occurs at the same time as the action of a finite verb in the same sentence. It is equivalent to a finite subordinate clause introduced by the temporal conjunctions **go** 'when' or **dan botta go** 'while' (discussed in section 10.2.2). It corresponds to the English construction 'while . . .ing'. As a rule, the subject of the gerund is the same as that of the finite verb. Like other non-finite verbs, the gerund can take its own arguments (e.g. objects and adverbials). The use of the gerund is illustrated in the following examples.

Siidii **manadettiin** mii bisáneimmet Buktamo kroas boradit.	While going to the Sámi village, we stopped at the Buktamo roadside canteen to have a meal.
Ruoktot **čuoiggadettiin** jurddašin Máreha birra.	While skiing home, I thought about Máret.
Barggadettiin prošeavttas lean geavahan ollu girjjiid ja čilgehusaid mat leat interneahtas.	While working on the project, I've made use of a lot of books and explanations that are on the internet.
Dat boagustedje **viegadettiin**.	They laughed while running.

Note that the subject of the gerund can be indicated by possessive suffixes, e.g.:

Oainnestin su bargui **manadettiinan**.	I saw him/her while I was going to work.
Son barggai giddagasas **čohkkádettiinis**.	S/he worked while s/he was serving time (lit: sitting) in jail.

Note that while the subject of the gerund is usually the same as that of the finite verb (as above), in some cases a gerund may have a different subject. In such cases the subject of the gerund will be clear from the context, even if it is not explicitly mentioned. The following example illustrates this.

Du jierbmi bargá ollu eambbo **oađedettiin** go TV **geahčadettiin**.	Your mind works much more while you're sleeping than while you're watching TV.

Similarly, if the gerund is based on an impersonal verb, the subject of the finite verb will be different, e.g.:

Arvvedettiin mii stoagaimet siste.   While it was raining we played inside.

Finally, in some cases the subject of the gerund is in the accusative-genitive. This is illustrated in the following examples (in which the accusative-genitive subject is in bold).

Lottiid oaidná ja gullá buoremusat **jieŋaid suttadettiin** miessemánu loahpas ja geassemánu álggus.   One can see and hear (lit: one sees and hears) birds best when the ice is melting at the end of May and beginning of June.

Odne lea dát čála ollašuvvan **din guladettiin**.   Today this scripture is fulfilled in your hearing. (Luke 4:21)

7.4.7 Verbal genitive

7.4.7.1 Form

The verbal genitive is formed by removing the infinitive ending, as illustrated here.

Even-syllable	Odd-syllable	Contracted
viega 'running'	**veahket** 'helping'	**čohkká** 'sitting'
vuoji 'driving'		**riide** 'riding'
čuorvvu 'shouting'		**diŋgo** 'ordering'

Points to note:

- The stem of even-syllable verbs is in the weak grade.
- Odd-syllable verbs whose stem ends in a consonant cluster or in a consonant other than **l, n, r, s, š, t** undergo the sound changes discussed at the end of section 2.4, e.g. **veahkehit** 'to help' : **veahket** 'helping'.

7.4.7.2 Usage

The verbal genitive is used to indicate the manner in which an action happens or an action that takes place concurrently with that of the main verb of the sentence. It is largely restricted to verbs of motion, sound, and position. This is illustrated here.

Hoahpus son viehkalii olggos ja manai **viega** daid stuorra jekkiid mielde.	S/he hastily ran outside and went running along those big bogs.
Eanahearrát bohtet **vuoji** ja eanabargit fertejit čáhkket saji.	The landlords come driving and the land workers have to make room.
Daga juoidá; son boahtá **čuorvvu** min maŋis.	Do something; she is coming crying out after us. (Matthew 15:23)
Mu mielas mii galgat **vácci** johtit.	I think we have to move on foot.

The verbal genitive of even-syllable verbs may appear following the prepositions **gaskan** 'in the middle of' and **lahka** 'close to', e.g.:

Dát dutkamuš lei **gaskan daga**.	This research was in progress (lit: in the middle of doing).
Son veallái nu buohccin, ahte lei **lahka jámi**.	S/he lay so ill that s/he was close to dying.

Finally, the verbal genitive can be doubled to indicate that the action is about to happen, e.g.:

Mielleravddas lea ovtta sajis boares lavdnjegáhtot stohpu – **gahča gahča** gáhtu deattu geažil.	At the edge of the sandy bank in a certain place there is an old turf-roofed house – about to fall under the weight of the roof.
Ođđa sátnegirji lea **boađi-boađi**.	A new dictionary is on its way.

7.4.8 Verbal abessive

7.4.8.1 Form

The verbal abessive is formed by attaching the suffix **-keahttá** or **-haga** 'without' to the stem of the verb, e.g.:

Even-syllable	Odd-syllable	Contracted
manakeahttá, manahaga 'without going'	**muitalkeahttá, muitalhaga** 'without telling'	**čohkkákeahttá, čohkkáhaga** 'without sitting'
boađekeahttá, boađihaga 'without coming'		**čilgekeahttá, čilgehaga** 'without explaining'
orokeahttá, oruhaga 'without living'		**liikokeahttá, liikohaga** 'without liking'

Points to note:

- The verbal abessive suffixes are attached to the weak grade of even-syllable verbs.
- You may see final -i- and -u- in even-syllable verbs with -**keahttá**, e.g. **boađikeahttá** 'without coming', **orukeahttá** 'without living'.

7.4.8.2 Usage

The verbal abessive is used to denote actions that do not take place. It is equivalent to the English construction 'without . . .ing'. This is illustrated in the following examples.

Ollu sámegielat mánát álge skuvlii **humakeahttá** dárogiela.	Many Sámi-speaking children started school without speaking Norwegian.
Boazoguođoheaddjit sáhtte čuoigat máŋga beaivvi unnán nisttiin ja beanta **oađekeahttá**.	Reindeer herders could ski for many days with little food and almost without sleeping.

	Maŋŋá muitalusa son manai olggos **dajakeahttá** sánige.	After the story s/he went out without saying even a word.
	Buot oahppit čállet golbma siva manne leat **jugakeahttá** alkohola.	All pupils will write three reasons not to drink alcohol.

The subject of the verbal abessive is typically the same as that of the main verb in the sentence, as in these examples. However, on occasion the subjects of the verbal abessive and the finite verb may be different. In such cases, the subject of the verbal abessive appears in the accusative-genitive, e.g.:

Álkit lea ságastallat váttes áššiid birra **mánáid gulakeahttá**.	It's easier to talk about difficult issues without the children hearing.

The verbal abessive may optionally be preceded by the preposition **almmá** 'without', which does not change the meaning of the construction. This is illustrated in the following examples.

Ii leat lobi ohcat diamánttaid Finnmárkkus **almmá jearakeahttá** Sámedikkis.	It is not allowed to look for diamonds in Finnmark without asking the Sámi Parliament.
Dus lea vejolašvuohta háleštit bolesiin **almmá váiddekeahttá** ášši.	You have the opportunity to talk to the police without reporting the incident.
Ahte bárdni lea čohkkán njeallje diimmu dihtora ovddas **almmá** maidege **dajakeahttá**, **almmá** unnaoappážiin **diggokeahttá**, ii leat gusto doarvái.	[The fact] that the boy has sat for four hours in front of the computer without saying anything, without arguing with [his] little sister, apparently isn't enough.

In some cases the verbal abessive can be used to indicate that an action remains undone, corresponding to English negative passive participles beginning in 'un-'. Verbal abessives with this sense are usually found in conjunction with verbs such as **leat** 'to be', **báhcit** 'to remain', **vajálduhttit** 'to forget', and others of similar meaning, as illustrated here.

		7 Verbs

Jos stohpu lea **čorgekeahttá** go don boađát, de váldde dalán oktavuođa stobu fuolaheddjiin.

If the house is uncleaned when you arrive, make contact immediately with the caretaker of the house.

Musihkas mii oaidnit ahte sátni "rock" lea sajáiduvvan **rievddakeahttá** sihke dárogillii ja sámegillii.

In music we see that the word 'rock' has been adopted (lit: settled) unchanged into both Norwegian and Sámi.

Jos bileahtat leat báhcán **vuovddekeahttá**, de daid sáhttá oastit vel uvssas.

If the tickets remain unsold, you can still buy them at the door.

Olmmoš vástida das, maid son lea dahkan dahje guođđán **dagakeahttá**.

A person is responsible for that which s/he has done or left undone.

In a few cases the verbal abessive has become grammaticalised as an adposition in conjunction with the accusative-genitive or locative, corresponding to English prepositions such as 'regardless of', 'irrespective of', and 'in spite of'. This usage is illustrated here.

Mii buohkat, riikkarájáin **beroškeahttá**, galgat fuomášit sin heađi.

We all, regardless of national borders, must take notice of their predicament.

Gilvvut čuigojuvvojit Anáris heittogis muohtadilis **fuolakeahttá**.

The [skiing] competition will take place (lit: be skied) in Inari regardless of the bad snow conditions.

Finally, in some cases the verbal abessive has become lexicalised as an adverb, as here.

Doppe orudettiin barggai Ruvdnaprinseassa **váibbakeahttá** Norgga beroštumiid ovddas.

While living there the Crown Princess worked tirelessly for Norwegian interests.

Dát **eahpitkeahttá** šaddá erenoamáš musihkkavásáhus.

This will undoubtedly be a special musical experience.

7.4.9 Purposive (supine)

7.4.9.1 Positive

North Sámi possesses a purposive (supine) form, which can be used instead of the infinitive in the sense of 'in order to'. The purposive is only used in a few Western dialects and therefore is not very commonly seen. It is formed as follows:

Even-syllable

The ending -žit is added to the weak grade of the verbal stem, e.g. **manažit** 'in order to go'.

Odd-syllable

The ending -eažžat is added to the verbal stem, e.g. **muitaleažžat** 'in order to tell'.

Contracted

The ending -žit is added to the verbal stem, e.g. **čilgežit** 'in order to explain'.

The following examples illustrate the use of the purposive.

Mun mannen olggos muoraid **vieččažit**.	I went outside in order to fetch some wood.
Turisttat bohtet Sápmái guovssahasaid **geahčažit**.	Tourists come to Sápmi in order to see the Northern Lights.

7.4.9.2 Negative

The negative purposive (supine) functions as a negative infinitive, equivalent to the English 'not to', 'in order not to', or 'so that X won't/wouldn't'. It is composed of the following inflected form followed by an infinitive

	Singular	Dual	Plural
First	**aman** 'in order for me not to'	**amame** 'in order for us not to'	**amamet** 'in order for us not to'

Second	**amat** 'in order for you not to'	**amade** 'in order for you not to'	**amadet** 'in order for you not to'
Third	**amas** 'in order for him/her not to'	**amaska** 'in order for them not to'	**amaset** 'in order for them not to'

The following examples illustrate the use of the negative purposive.

Mun geardduhin daid sániid **aman** vajálduhttit.	I repeated those words so that I wouldn't forget.
Skuvlenbáikkiid ferte fállat doppe gos nuorat ásset **amaset** sii dárbbašit vuolgit nuppe beallái Suoma studeret.	School places must be offered where the young people live, so that they don't need to go to the other side of Finland to study.

7.4.10 Participles

7.4.10.1 Present participle

7.4.10.1.1 Form

Even-syllable	Odd-syllable	Contracted
manni 'going'	**muitaleaddji** 'telling'	**čohkkájeaddji** 'sitting'
boahtti 'coming'	**leahkki** 'being'	**čilgejeaddji** 'explaining'
orru 'living'		**liikojeaddji** 'liking'

Points to note:

- Even-syllable verbs are in the extra strong grade in the present participle.
- Present participles do not undergo consonant gradation (e.g. nominative **boahtti** 'coming'; accusative-genitive **boahtti**).
- The present participle of **leat** 'to be' is slightly irregular.

7.4.10.1.2 Usage

The present participle is used to indicate an action in progress. It functions adjectivally, modifying a directly following noun. The following examples illustrate this.

Mun háliidivččen **veahkeheaddji** eŋgela gii čorgestivččii min eallima vai visot gillámušat jávkkaše.	I would like a helping angel who would sort out our lives (lit: life) so that all suffering would disappear.
Makkár lea mánnu, **šaddi** vai **nuossi** mánnu?	Which moon is it, a waxing or waning moon?

In some cases, particularly among Finnish North Sámi speakers, the present participle can function verbally, taking its own arguments (subject, object, adverbial, etc.). The arguments are placed before the participle. In such instances the participle phrase corresponds to a relative clause in English, as illustrated here.

Bállás-Ylläsduoddara álbmotmeahccái **vuolgi** vánddardeaddji galgá vuohččan rasttildit Ovnnesjávrri.	A hiker going to the Pallas-Yllästunturi National Park has to first cross Ounasjärvi.
Dáiddadáhpáhussii bovdejuvvojit buot sámegielat oahpahusas **leahkki** mánát ja nuorat.	All children and youths who are in Sámi-language education will be brought to the art event.
Boahtteáiggis sámegiela eatnigiellan **hubmi** mánáid mearri geahppána unnán muhto stuorru de fas dáláš dássái.	In future the number of children speaking Sámi as [their] mother tongue will reduce slightly, but will then increase again to the current level.
Vázzima **govvideaddji** vearbbaid semantihkka	The semantics of verbs describing walking

Present participles can also serve as agent nouns, as in the following examples. Note that the same participle can often function either adjectivally/verbally or as an agent noun depending on the context; for example, in the last example above, **govvideaddji** is a participle meaning 'describing', whereas in the next set of examples, the same word functions as an agent noun meaning 'photographer'.

Dalle čužžo mánát olgun 40 buolašis ja vuorddašedje **oahpaheaddji** gii ii boahtán.	Then the children stood outside in -40° weather and waited for a teacher who didn't come.	
Lappii vurdet badjelaš 1500 olgoriikkalaš **murjejeaddji**.	They expect over 1,500 foreign berry-pickers [to come] to Lapland.	
Bállás-Ylläsduoddara álbmotmeahccái vuolgi **vánddardeaddji** galgá vuohččan rasttildit Ovnnesjávrri.	A hiker going to the Pallas-Yllästunturi National Park has to first cross Ounasjärvi.	
Govvideaddji bargui gullá dábálaččat govvidit olbmuid, buktagiid, luonddu ja dáhpáhusaid.	A photographer's work usually includes taking photos of people, products, nature, and events.	

In some cases, present participles have become lexicalised as adjectives. For example, in the sentence below the present participle **boahtti** 'coming' is being used in the sense of the adjective 'future'. (Note that the synonymous adjective **boahttevaš** 'future' is more commonly used in this context.)

Jagi 1953 Amerihká ovttastuvvan stáhtaid **boahtti** presideanta John F. Kennedy ja Jacqueline Bouvier náitaleigga.	In 1953 the future president of the United States of America John F. Kennedy and Jacqueline Bouvier got married.

7.4.10.2 Past participle

7.4.10.2.1 Form

The past participle is formed by replacing the infinitive suffix -**t** with -**n**, as follows:

Even-syllable	Odd-syllable	Contracted
mannan 'gone'	**muitalan** 'told'	**čohkkán** 'sat'

7 Verbs

boahtán 'come'   **leamaš** 'been'   **čilgen** 'explained'

orron 'lived'   **liikon** 'liked'

Points to note:

- In even-syllable verbs stem-final -i- becomes -á-.
- In odd-syllable verbs stem-final -i- becomes -a-.
- In even-syllable verbs stem-final -u- becomes -o-.
- The past participle of the verb **leat** 'to be' is irregular.

7.4.10.2.2 Usage

The main use of the past participle is in the construction of the perfect, the pluperfect, and the negative past. See sections 7.1.3, 7.1.4, and 7.3.2 for discussion of these constructions.

The past participle is also used as a replacement for complement clauses following verbs of utterance (e.g. **dadjat** 'to say', **muitalit** 'to tell'), perception (e.g. **oaidnit** 'to see', **gullat** 'to hear'), and cognition (e.g. **diehtit** 'to know', **jáhkkit** 'to believe', **muitit** 'to remember'). In such cases the past participle denotes an action that has already taken place; this can be contrasted with a similar construction involving the infinitive and actio essive, which is used to indicate an ongoing or future action (see sections 7.4.1.2 and 7.4.3 for details of these constructions, respectively). The past participle takes its own nominal or pronominal subject, which appears in the accusative-genitive. If the subject of the past participle is the same as that of the finite verb, the reflexive pronoun **ieš** 'oneself' is used. This usage is illustrated in the following examples.

Ávviris čuožžu mu **vuoitán** iPad-mini!	In Ávvir [North Sámi newspaper] it says that I have won an iPad-mini!
Son muitalii iežas **gullan** ahte Máret ii lean šiega iežas ustibiiguin.	S/he wrote and said that s/he had heard that Máret wasn't nice to her own friends.
Boazodoalli navdá fuođarfitnodagaid **vuovdán** billašuvvan fuođđariid elliid biebmun.	A reindeer herder suspects fodder companies of having sold spoiled fodder as animals' food.

Gullen su **fárren** Ruŧŧii.	I heard that s/he had moved to Sweden.
Muittán oahpaheaddji **váldán** muhtin oahppi olggos.	I remember how a teacher took some pupil outside.

The past participle can also be used adjectivally in conjunction with a directly following noun. In this type of setting the North Sámi past participle corresponds to the English past participle, as illustrated here.

Dál almmuhit Nuorta-Finnmárkku politiijat ahte galgá sidjiide cavgilit, jos ležžet dieđut **suoláduvvon** skohtera birra.	The East Finnmark police are now announcing that people should tip them off if they have information about the stolen snowmobile.
Dieđit jus fuomášat **bieđganan** ja **billašuvvan** boazoáiddiid.	Let us know if you notice scattered and ruined reindeer fences.
Ođđa fitnodat álgá buvttadit **sáltejuvvon** guoli.	A new company is starting to import salted fish.

As in the case of the present participle discussed in section 7.4.10.1.2, the past participle may take its own arguments (subject, object, adverbial, etc.). The argument precedes the participle. This is illustrated here.

Mun in háliit čuoččuhit, ahte sámiid **dahkan** dutkanbargguin livččii mearkkašupmi dušše beare sámiide.	I don't want to claim that research done by Sámis would be relevant only for the Sámi.

Like the present participle (as discussed in section 7.4.10.1), in some cases the past participle has been lexicalised as an adjective. For example, in the sentence below the past participle **mannan** 'gone' is being used in the sense of the adjective 'last'.

Mun álgen **mannan** jagi oahpahallat sámegiela.	I started learning Sámi last year.

Chapter 8
Adverbs

North Sámi adverbs can be formed in a variety of ways. Some are indeclinable, others are derived from demonstrative pronouns, some are nouns with case suffixes, and some are formed with derivative suffixes. The following endings are commonly associated with adverbs. Note that adverbs sometimes appear in cases not seen on nouns.

Suffix	Case	Function
-t	prolative	by way of; also generic adverb suffix
-l	ablative	movement away from
-s	translative	movement towards
-n, -na	essive	state, location in

In addition, many adverbs of time, place, and degree can take comparative and superlative suffixes, as illustrated in the following two examples. Note that the comparative and superlative forms of adverbs often have more than one variant. The comparative and superlative adverbs are typically formed regularly on analogy with comparative and superlative adjectives (see sections 4.3 and 4.4); occasional exceptions include the final example here, which has a suppletive paradigm.

Base adverb	Comparative	Superlative
dávjá 'often'	**dávjjit** or **dávjjibut** 'more often'	**dávjjimus, dávjjimusat, dávjjimustá** 'most often'

lahka 'close'	lagat, lagabut 'closer'	lagamus 'the closest'
ollu 'much, a lot'	eamb(b)o 'more'	eanemus 'most'

8.1 Manner

North Sámi has a group of adverbs of manner formed on analogy with the demonstrative pronouns (see section 5.3). These are shown here.

ná, návt	in this way
nie, nievt	in that way (related to the addressee)
nu, nuvt	in that way (general)
nuo	in that way (not related to the speaker or addressee; previously mentioned)
no	in that way (distant)

The following examples illustrate the use of these adverbs.

Ná galget sápmelaččaid boarásmanbeaivvit šaddat buorebun.	In this way the Sámis' twilight years will become better.
Sárggas diekko **nie** ja čuohpat.	Draw [a line] over there like that, and cut.
Nu fuomášin ahte gávdnojit maid mánát, geat eai máhte sámegiela.	In that way I realised that there are also children who can't speak Sámi.

North Sámi also has an array of adverbs of manner lacking any specific ending. The most common adverbs of this type are listed here. Note that some of these adverbs, such as **rabas** 'open', do not have a distinct form from the corresponding adjective.

almmatge	anyway
aŋkke	anyway

8 Adverbs

bahás	evilly, wickedly
báljo	hardly
bures	well
duođas	truthfully, in truth, seriously
dušše	only
fas	conversely, by contrast
gitta	closed
goit(ge)	anyway
gusto	evidently, apparently
jur	just
lihkká	anyway
maiddái	also
nappo	thus, therefore, so, consequently
njuolgga	directly, straight
okto	alone
rabas (also adjective)	open
riekta	correctly
summal	randomly
suoli	secretly

The use of this type of adverb of manner is illustrated in the following examples.

Sámi giellaláhka lea šaddamin oađđiláhkan, go ii oktage oro váldimin dan **duođas**.

The Sámi language law is becoming a sleeping law, as no one seems to be taking it seriously.

Girjerájus lea **gitta**.

The library is closed.

Don sáhtát maid mannat **njuolgga** dan poliisadállui doppe gos orut.	You can also go directly to the police station where you live.
Mu áhčči jámii go ledjen 7-jahkásaš ja eadni bázii **okto**.	My father died when I was seven years old, and my mother was left alone.
Mii láviimet sámástit gaskaneamet, muhto dan fertiimet dahkat **suoli**, go sihke internáhtas ja skuvllas gilde min sámásteames.	We used to speak Sámi among ourselves, but we had to do it secretly, as both in the boarding school and in the school they forbade us from speaking Sámi.
Ikte lei Sámi álbmotbeaivi ja ollusat ledje coggalan gávtti, **aŋkke** dáppe Romssas.	Yesterday was the Sámi National Day, and many people had put on a gákti, here in Tromsø anyway.

In addition, North Sámi has a productive suffix that can be used to form adverbs of manner. The suffix is -**t** (attached to the accusative-genitive form of even-syllable and contracted adjectives) or -**it** (attached to the accusative-genitive form of odd-syllable adjectives). The formation of this type of adverb is shown here.

Even-syllable adjectives: suffix -**t**

Base adjective (nominative)	Derived adverb
čeahppi 'clever'	**čeahpit**, **čehpet** 'cleverly'
headju 'bad, weak'	**heajut**, **hejot** 'badly, weakly'
garraseappo, **garrasabbo** 'harder'	**garraseappot**, **garrasabbot** 'harder'
buoremus 'the best'	**buoremusat** 'in the best way'
issoras 'terrible'	**issorasat** 'terribly'
čuočču 'standing'	**čuoǯǯut** 'in a standing position'; also has variant **čuoččat**

8
Adverbs

8 Adverbs

Points to note:

- Many adverbs have two variants with the same meaning, e.g. čeahpit, čehpet 'cleverly'.
- The final vowel of some adjectives may change from -i to -e and from -u to -o. This causes diphthong simplification, e.g. čeahppi 'clever' : čehpet 'cleverly'.

Odd-syllable adjectives: suffix -it

Base adjective	Derived adverb
nanus 'firm'	**nannosit** 'firmly'
viššal 'industrious'	**viššalit** 'industriously'
viššaleamos 'the most industrious'	**viššalepmosit** 'in the most industrious way'
buoret 'better'	**buorebut** 'in a better way'

Odd-syllable adjectives ending in -t: no suffix, or suffix -it

Base adjective	Derived adverb
jaskat 'quiet'	**jaska, jaskadit** 'quietly'
čorgat 'tidy'	**čorga, čorgadit** 'tidily'

Point to note:

- This type of adjective has two adverbial variants, one formed by removing the -t suffix from the base adjective and one ending in -it.

Contracted adjectives: suffix -t

Base adjective	Derived adverb
čáppat 'beautiful'	**čábbát** 'beautifully'

8
Adverbs

Points to note:

- Adverbs derived from contracted adjectives are relatively rare.
- The final vowel of the adjective **čáppat** 'beautiful' undergoes an irregular change from **a** to **á** when the adverbial suffix is attached.

The use of this type of derived adverb is illustrated in the following examples.

Ollu mánát vedjet **heajut** cáinna sosiála media geavahemiin.	Many children cope badly using this kind of social media.
Sámegielat báikenamaid botnje **boastut** suomagielat kárttaide.	Sámi-language placenames were wrongly corrupted on Finnish-language maps.
Dábálaččat dat lávlojuvvo **čuoččat**.	Usually they are sung standing up.
Ođđa Statoil-hoavda šaddá Norgga **buoremusat** bálkáhuvvon jođiheaddjin.	The new head of Statoil will become Norway's best paid manager.
Porsáŋggu skohterluottat merkejuvvojit **buorebut**.	Porsanger's snowmobile tracks are going to be better marked.
Sámi giella ja kultuvra leat **nannosit** náiton oktii.	Sámi language and culture are firmly wedded together.
Mii dárkkistit ahte gálvvut lástejuvvojit **čorga** ja **njuolga**.	We make sure that the goods are loaded neatly and straightly.
Gonagas ieš ja su dronnet čuovuiga hui **viššalit** prošeavtta.	The king himself and his queen followed the project very diligently.
Bargga **jaskadit**, nu ahte it ráfehuhte earáid.	Work quietly, so that you don't disturb others.
Lávejin sus nu **issorasat** ballat.	I used to be so terribly afraid of him/her.
Sámegiella čuodjá **čábbát**.	Sámi sounds beautiful.

8 Adverbs

8.2 Time

The most common general North Sámi adverbs of time are listed here. Note that, as in the case of certain adverbs of manner discussed in section 8.1, some of these (e.g. **árrat** 'early') can also be used as adjectives depending on the context.

ain	still
áigá	a long time ago
álggos	at first
álo	always
árrat (also adjective)	early
čađat	always
dábálaččat	usually
dađistaga	gradually
dakkaviđe	immediately
dal	now (without emphasis)
dál	now (emphatic)
dale	then
dassá, dassážii	until then
dasto	then, afterwards
dastožii	until later
dávjá	often
diibmá	last year
dolin	a long time ago, in the past
dovle	a long time ago
duollet dálle	off and on

8 Adverbs

duvle	a while ago
easka, easkka	a little while ago, recently; not until
fargga	soon
fas	the next time
fáhkka, fáhkkestaga	suddenly
gaskkohagaid	from time to time
guhká	for a long time
hárve	rarely
ihttin	tomorrow
ii goassege	never (note that the negative verb conjugates in accordance with the subject)
ii vuos	not yet
ikte	yesterday
jo, juo	already
loahpas	finally, at the end
maŋážassii	finally
maŋŋit	late
maŋŋelaš	later
maŋŋel, maŋŋil	later
muhtumin	sometimes
oanehaš (also adjective 'short')	for a short time
odne	today

8 Adverbs

oktanaga	at the same time
ovdal	earlier, sooner
ovttatmano	immediately
ovtto	always
vuos	first, firstly
vuot	again

The following examples illustrate the use of these adverbs of time.

Váldde oktavuođa midjiide jus don sáhtát álggahit **dakkaviđe**!	Make contact with us if you can start immediately!
Ledje go **dolin** eambo lottit go dán áigge?	Were there more birds in the past than at this time?
Máŋgasat eai soaitte diehtit dan doppe Sámi ávdin duoddariin, muhto **ihttin**, guovvamánu 14. beaivve, lea Valentinabeaivi; ráhkisvuođa beaivi.	Many may not know it there in the distant Sámi tundra, but tomorrow, 14 February, is Valentine's Day, the day of love.
Mánát, geat álget **árrat** mánáidgárdái, leat čeahpibut gielain ja matematihkas go álget skuvlii.	Children who start kindergarten early are better with language and maths when they start school.
Sus lea pedagogalaš oahppu ja son bargá **dál** Sámi allaskuvllas Guovdageainnus.	S/he has pedagogical training and now s/he works at the Sámi University College in Kautokeino.
Easka go lei **oanehaš** čohkohallan, de Biera fuomášii ahte olgun lei oalle čoaskkis.	Not until he had been sitting down for a little while did Biera realise that outside it was quite chilly.

8 Adverbs

Dassážii galggai Christian Frederik jođihit riikka regeantan.
Until then Christian Frederik had to run the country as a regent.

Máttarádját mis leat **dovle** vuoitán vearredahkkiid badjel.
In the distant past our ancestors won over the evildoers.

Diibmá dušše 52 olbmo bargolihkohisvuođain Ruotas.
Last year 52 people died in work accidents in Sweden.

Mii leat **easka** guldalan Sámi giellalávdegotti jođiheaddji muitaleame dan ášši birra.
We have recently heard the director of the Sámi Language Board talking about that issue.

Muhto **ain** leat ollu sámi báikenamat mat eai leat registrerejuvvon.
But there are still a lot of Sámi placenames that have not been registered.

Mari Boine lei okta mu oahpaheddjiin, ja **muhtumin** válddii gitára fárrui ja lávlestii midjiide.
Mari Boine was one of my teachers, and sometimes she took the guitar into her lap and sang a bit to us.

Ovdal ledje máŋgasat geat ieža dáhko niibbiid, muhto **dál hárve** olbmot máhttet dan dáiddu, sihke sámiid ja dážaid gaskkas.
Before there were many people who forged knives themselves, but now people rarely know that craft, among both Sámis and Norwegians.

Mii doallat **dábálaččat** rabas buot árgabeivviid.
We usually stay open on all weekdays.

Anáris **guhká** bargan girkohearrá báhcá ealáhahkii.
The long-serving pastor in Inari is retiring.

Son oassálasttii Sámi Teáhterii **easkka** 1990-logu loahpas.
S/he didn't take part in the Sámi Theatre until the end of the 1990s.

Konsearta odne Álaheajus! **In** leat **goassege** leamaš doppe.
A concert today in Alta! I've never been there.

183

8 Adverbs

Nils Jovnna jámii **fáhkka** juovlamánus.	Nils Jovnna died suddenly in December.
Man **dávjá** jugat alkohola?	How often do you drink alcohol?
Dávjjit ja **dávjjit** oaidnit ahte sámi musihkkajoavkkut hástalit sápmelaččaid čiŋadit gávttiin.	More and more often we see that Sámi music groups call on Sámi people to dress up in the Sámi tunic.

The adverbs based on times of the day are listed below:

iđđes, iđđedis	in the morning
beaivet	during the day
eahkes, eahkedis	in the evening
ihkku	at night

The following examples illustrate the use of these forms:

Ohcan álggahuvvui bearjadaga **iđđes** ovcci áigge.	The search operation was begun on Friday at about nine in the morning.
Ja de lea **ihkku** hui seavdnjat, nu seavdnjat.	And at night it's very dark, so dark.

There are also adverbs based on the four seasons, as follows:

dálvet, dálvit	in the winter
giđđat	in the spring
geasset, giessit	in the summer
čakčat	in the autumn

The following example illustrates the use of these forms:

Geahča makkár oahput mis álget **čakčat** 2014 ja **giđđat** 2015.
Look what kinds of courses (lit: studies) we have starting in autumn 2014 and spring 2015.

Adverbs of frequency from 1 to 9 take the form of a cardinal numeral in the illative case. The same pattern is also used for adverbs denoting an imprecise number of times. These points are shown here.

oktii, okte	once
guktii	twice
golbmii	three times
njelljii	four times
vihttii	five times
guhttii	six times
čihččii, čihčii	seven times
gákcii	eight times
okcii	nine times
máŋgii	many times
moddii	a few times

Alternatively, the same adverbs of frequency may be expressed using a cardinal numeral followed by **geardde** or **háve** 'time, occasion', e.g.:

guovtti geardde, guovtte háve	twice
moatte geardde, moatte háve	a few times

This construction is additionally used to denote adverbs of frequency greater than 10, e.g.:

logi geardde, logi háve	ten times
čuođi geardde, čuođi háve	a hundred times

8 Adverbs

Adverbs of time meaning 'for the second time, third time', etc., are also derived from numerals, as here. Note that there is no adverb denoting 'for the first time'.

nuppádis, nuppes	for the second time
goalmmádis	for the third time
njealjádis	for the fourth time
viđádis	for the fifth time

Similarly, adverbs used when listing points, such as 'firstly', 'secondly', etc., are derived from numerals, e.g.:

vuohččan, vuosttažettiin	firstly, first of all
nuppádassii, nuppádassii	secondly
goalmmádassii, goalmmádassii	thirdly

The use of the adverbs of frequency and other adverbs derived from numerals is illustrated here.

Áviisa bođii olggos **oktii** mánnui.	The newspaper came out once a month.
Ovdal lei Sámi Áigi deadline **guktii** vahkus.	Previously the *Sámi Áigi* [North Sámi newspaper] deadline was twice a week.
Gursalaččat leatge čoahkkanan dán jagi jo **moddii**.	The course participants have already met a few times this year.
Stivrra čoahkkimat dollojuvvojedje **golmma geardde** jagis.	The board meetings were held three times a year.
Lean **máŋgga háve** álggahan blokka čállima.	I have started writing a blog many times.
Son searvá **nuppes** Sámi Grand Prix lávlungilvui.	S/he is taking part in the Sámi Grand Prix song competition for the second time.
Máhtte lea golbmanuppelot jagi ja galgá **vuosttaš geardde** mearkut iežas misiid.	Máhtte is thirteen years old and has to mark his own reindeer calves for the first time.

Prográmma gullo **nuppádassii** vuossárgga diibmu 22.05.
The programme will be broadcast for the second time on Monday at 22:05.

The days of the week are used in the accusative-genitive to indicate when an event takes place, e.g.:

Bearjadaga cokka nala rukses biktasa.
On Friday put on a red piece of clothing.

The months of the year are used in the locative to indicate when an event takes place, e.g.:

Berlinas lea konfereansa vehádagaid ja identitehtaid birra **čakčamánus**.
There is a conference about minorities and identities in Berlin in September.

Finally, certain adjectives denoting time can be used adverbially in the locative and illative to indicate beginning and end points, respectively. This phenomenon is shown in the following table.

Adjective	Illative adverb	Locative adverb
dálaš 'current'	**dálážii** 'until now'	**dálážis** 'from now on'
i(e)vttáš 'yesterday's'	**i(e)vttážii** 'until yesterday'	**i(e)vttážis** 'since yesterday'
ih(t)táš 'tomorrow's'	**ih(t)tážii** 'until tomorrow'	**ih(t)tážis** 'from tomorrow on'
diimmáš 'last year's'	**diimmážii** 'until last year'	**diimmážis** 'since last year'

The use of these forms is illustrated here.

Ja **ievttážii** ledje filmma geahččan sullii golbmaduhát olbmo.
And up to yesterday around 3,000 people had watched the film.

Olgoriikalaččaid oassálastin lea lassánan **diimmážis**.
The participation of foreigners has increased since last year.

8
Adverbs

8.3 Place

North Sámi has a large number of adverbs of place. The following adverbs are derived from the demonstrative pronouns (e.g. **dát** 'this', **diet** 'that'; see section 5.3 for details). These adverbs are inflected for case.

Illative	Locative	Ablative	Prolative	Demonstrative
dohko 'to there' (nonspecific or faraway location in relation to the speaker and addressee)	**doppe** 'there, from there' (nonspecific or faraway location in relation to the speaker and addressee)	**doppil** 'around there, from around there' (nonspecific or faraway location in relation to the speaker and addressee)	**dokko** 'by that way'; 'right there' (nonspecific or faraway location in relation to the speaker and addressee)	**do** 'there' (nonspecific or faraway location in relation to the speaker and addressee)
deike 'to here'	**dáppe** 'here, from here'	**dáppil** 'around here, from around here'	**dákko** 'by this way'; 'right here'	**dá** 'here'
diehko 'to there' (near the addressee)	**dieppe** 'there, from there' (near the addressee)	**dieppil** 'around there, from around there' (near the addressee)	**diekko** 'by that way'; 'right there' (near the addressee)	**die** 'there' (near the addressee)

duohko	duoppe	duoppil	duokko	duo
'to there' (near neither the speaker nor the addressee)	'there, from there' (near neither the speaker nor the addressee)	'around there, from around there' (near neither the speaker nor the addressee)	'by that way'; 'right there' (near neither the speaker nor the addressee)	'there' (near neither the speaker nor the addressee)

Points to note:

- North Sámi has several different words corresponding to English 'there', as it makes a three-way distinction between a nonspecific faraway location, a location close to the addressee, and a location distant from both the speaker and the addressee.
- The ablative form is used to indicate that the location being referred to is a big or imprecise area, corresponding to the English 'around here, around there'.
- The prolative form is used to indicate a) a pathway, like the English 'by' or 'via', or b) a very specific place, like the English 'right here, right there'.
- The prolative forms have a set of variants with the same meaning, namely **daiggo/daigo, dáiggo/dáigo, dieiggo/dieigo,** and **duoiggo/duoigo.**

The use of some of these adverbs is shown here.

Dáppe sáhtát jienastit sámediggeválggas.	You can vote in the Sámi Parliament elections here.
Mii leat váillahan ahte árktalaš eamiálbmogat oidnojit, ja dál máilmmi čalmmit geahččagohtet **deike**.	We have been missing the visibility of Arctic indigenous peoples, and now the world's eyes are starting to look in this direction (lit: to here).
Girjái leat čohkken teavsttaid **duoppil dáppil**.	They have collected texts from here and there for the book.

8 Adverbs

Buot studeanttat ja bargit sáhttet **dákko** bokte dieđihit áššiid maid mii berret čuovvulit.

All students and workers can inform [us] right here of issues which we should follow up.

"**Dá** lea buorre duođaštus," lohká Gaup filmmas birra.

"This (lit: here) is good evidence," says Gaup about his film.

Sápmelaččat leat álo johtán **daiggo** bohccuideasetguin.

The Sámi have always travelled around these parts with their reindeer.

In addition, North Sámi possesses another set of adverbs of place that are used to indicate comparative location, such as 'closer to here, farther that way', etc. These are illustrated here.

Genitive	Illative singular	Illative plural	Locative
dabbil/ dobbil 'farther along that way' (nonspecific location in relation to the speaker and addressee)	**dabbelii/ dobbelii** 'to farther that way' (nonspecific location in relation to the speaker and addressee)	**dabbeliidda/ dobbeliidda** 'to farther that way' (nonspecific location in relation to the speaker and addressee)	**dabbelis/ dobbelis** 'farther that way' (nonspecific location in relation to the speaker and addressee)
dábbil 'farther along this way'	**dábbelii** 'to farther this way'	**dábbeliidda** 'to farther this way'	**dábbelis** 'farther this way'
diebbil 'farther along that way' (near the addressee)	**diebbelii** 'to farther that way' (towards the addressee)	**diebbeliidda** 'to farther that way' (towards the addressee)	**diebbelis** 'farther that way' (towards the addressee)

duobbil	cuobbelii	duobbeliidda	duobbelis
'farther along that way' (near neither the speaker nor the addressee)	'to farther that way' (near neither the speaker nor the addressee)	'to farther that way' (near neither the speaker nor the addressee)	'farther that way' (near neither the speaker nor the addressee)

Points to note:

- The genitive form is used to indicate a pathway, like the English 'along', 'by', or 'via'.
- The illative form has singular and plural variants. The plural variants are used to indicate a larger or more nonspecific area.

The use of these comparative forms is illustrated here.

Jos háliida gávdnat vástádusa dán áššái, de gánnáha vuolgit vehá **dobbelii**.	If one wants to find an answer to this issue, it is worth going a bit farther that way.
Eatnašat geat bohte lustamátkeskiippain johte Levdnjii bussiin, muhto muhtimat maid háliidedje finadit **dobbelis**.	Most of those who came with the cruise ship went to Lakselv by bus, but some also wanted to visit [places] farther away.

These forms also have a diminutive variant, which is used to indicate that the location is only a little bit removed.

Genitive	Illative	Locative
dabbelačča/ dobbelačča, dabbelaš/dobbelaš 'a bit farther along that way' (nonspecific location in relation to the speaker and addressee)	**dabbelažžii/ dobbelažžii** 'to a bit farther that way'	**dabbelaččas/ dobbelaččas** 'in/from a little bit closer to there'

8 Adverbs

	(nonspecific location in relation to the speaker and addressee)	(nonspecific location in relation to the speaker and addressee)
dábbelačča/dábbelaš 'a bit farther along this way'	**dábbelažžii** 'to a bit farther this way'	**dábbelaččas** 'in/from a little bit closer to here'
diebbelačča/diebbelaš 'a bit farther along that way' (near the addressee)	**diebbelažžii** 'to a bit farther that way' (near the addressee)	**diebbelaččas** 'in/from a little bit closer to there' (near the addressee)
duobbelačča/duobbelaš 'a bit farther along that way' (far away from the speaker and addressee)	**duobbelažžii** 'to a bit farther that way' (far away from the speaker and addressee)	**duobbelaččas** 'in/from a little bit closer to there' (far away from the speaker and addressee)

The following examples illustrate this type of form.

Nieida ásai **dobbelaččas** go Trond.

The girl lived a little bit farther that way than Trond.

Johtolat manná muhtun mátkki Geavvoroggeravdda ja de fas jorggiha johkarokkis **dobbelažžii**.

The migration route goes a stretch along Geavvoroggeravda and then turns at the river valley a bit farther that way.

The points of the compass can function as adverbs of place and are inflected for case, as follows:

Base noun	Compound form	Illative	Essive	Ablative
davvi 'north'	**davá-**	**davás** 'to the north'	**davvin** 'in, from the north'	**davil** 'in, from the general area of the north'
lulli, **máddi** 'south'	**lulá-**, **mátta-**	**lulás**, **luksa**, **máttás** 'to the south'	**lullin**, **máddin** 'in, from the south'	**lulil**, **máttil** 'in, from the general area of the south'
nuorta, **nuorti** 'east'	**nuortta-**	**nuorttas** 'to the east'	**nuortan**, **nuortin** 'in, from the east'	**nuorttal**, **nuorttil** 'in, from the general area of the east'
oarji 'west'	**oarjjá-**	**oarjjás** 'to the west'	**oarjin** 'in, from the west'	**oarjjil** 'in, from the general area of the west'

Points to note:

- There are two variant words for 'south', **lulli** and **máddi**.
- There are two variant forms of the word for 'east', **nuorta** and **nuorti**.
- The essive functions in a locative sense, equivalent to 'in' or 'from'.
- The ablative likewise functions in a locative sense but denotes a bigger or more imprecise area than the essive, equivalent to 'in or from the general area of'.
- The compound form can be used in conjunction with a noun, typically -**bealli** '-side' or -**geahči** 'end', e.g. **lulábeallái** 'to the southern side', **lulágeažis** 'on/from the southern end'.

8 Adverbs

The use of these adverbs is illustrated in the following sentences.

Davvin lea siseatnandálkkádat, **lullin** lea mearra lagabus.	In the north there is an inland climate; in the south, it's a bit closer to the sea.
Stuorámus oassi olbmuin orrot **oarjjábealde** Urála ja Kaukasusa.	The majority of the people live on the western side of the Urals and Caucasus [mountains].
Eai buohkat sáhttán vuolgit **davás** dakka maŋŋel go Norga beasai eret Duiskkas.	Not everyone could leave for the north after Norway escaped from [the control of] Germany.
Oarjjil leat vuollegis várit go fas **nuorttal** eanan lea badjeleappos.	In the western area there are low mountains, whereas by contast in the eastern area the land is higher.

Like the adverbs of place meaning 'here' and 'there' discussed earlier, the points of the compass have comparative forms meaning 'farther north/south/east/west', shown here.

Genitive	Illative singular	Illative plural	Locative
davvil 'farther along the northern side'	**davvelii** 'to farther north'	**davveliidda** 'to farther north'	**davvelis** 'farther north, from farther north'
lullil, máddil 'farther along the southern side'	**lullelii, máddelii** 'to farther south'	**lulleliidda, máddeliidda** 'to farther south'	**lullelis, máddelis** 'farther south, from farther south'

nuortal, nuortil 'farther along the eastern side'	**nuortalii, nuortelii** 'to farther east'	**nuortaliidda, nuorteliidda** 'to farther east'	**nuortalis, nuortelis** 'farther east, from farther east'
oarjil 'farther along the western side'	**oarjelii** 'to farther west'	**oarjeliidda** 'to farther west'	**oarjelis** 'farther west, from farther west'

Points to note:

- The genitive form is used to indicate a pathway, like the English 'along', 'by', or 'via'.
- The illative form has singular and plural variants. The plural variants are used to indicate a larger or more nonspecific area.

Examples of these comparative adverbs of place are shown here.

70 bearraša ja 50.0000 bohcco johte **máddelii**.	Seventy families and 50,000 reindeer travelled farther to the south.
Ruota bealde rájá manná guovlu **davvil** Árjepluovi.	On the Swedish side of the border the region goes farther along the northern side of Arjeplog.

Adpositions of place (discussed in section 9.1) can also be used adverbially, and inflect for case in a similar way to the points of the compass, as illustrated in the following table.

Nominative	Compound form	Illative	Locative	Essive	Ablative
alli 'high up'	**alá-**	**alás** 'to high up'	—	**allin** 'high up, from high up'	**alil** 'in, from the general area of high up'

8 Adverbs

badji 'up, above'	**bajá-**	**bajás** 'upwards'	—	**badjin** 'in, from above'	**bajil** 'in, from the general area of above'
duohki 'in back'	**duogá-**	**duohkái** 'to the back'	—	**duohkin, duohken** 'in, from the back'	—
maŋŋe- 'behind, after'	**maŋá-**	**maŋás** 'to behind'	**maŋis** 'in, from behind'	**maŋŋin** 'in, from behind'	**maŋil** 'in, from the general area of behind'
olgu- 'out, outside'	**olggo-**	**olggos** 'to outside'	—	**olgun** 'in, from outside'	**olggul** 'in, from the general area of outside'
ovda- 'before'	**ovdda-**	**ovdii** 'to the front'	**ovddas** 'in, from the front'	**ovdan** 'in, from the front'	**ovddal** 'in, from the general area of the front'
siski-, sis- 'in'	**siskká-, siskko-**	**sisa** 'to inside'	**siste** 'inside, from inside'	—	**siskkil** 'in, from the general area of inside'

vuolli 'down, below'	vuolá-	vuolás 'downwards'	—	vuollin 'in, from below'	vuolil 'in, from the general area of below'

Points to note:

- The compound form can be used in conjunction with a noun, typically -**bealli** '-side' or -**geahči** 'end', e.g. **olggobeallái** 'to the outside', **ovddageažis** 'at the front end'.
- The essive functions in a locative sense, equivalent to 'in' or 'from'.
- The ablative likewise functions in a locative sense, but denotes a bigger or more imprecise area than the essive, equivalent to 'in or from the general area of'.

The following examples illustrate the use of these adverbs.

Ii dárbbaš nu **guhkás** vuolgit.	It's not necessary to go so far.
Dál easkka lean beassan oaidnit **siskkil** Sajos-guovddaža.	Just now I have managed to see the Sajos Centre from the inside.
Oaiveskálžžut goivo uvvojedje **bajás** hávddiin jagi 1915 arkeologalaš goaivumiin.	The skulls were dug up from graves in 1915 archaeological digs.

Like the points of the compass, these adverbs have comparative forms, shown here.

Genitive	Ilative singular	Illative plural	Locative
allil 'farther along high up'	**allelii** 'to higher up'	**alleliidda** 'to higher up'	**allelis** 'higher up, from higher up'

8
Adverbs

8 Adverbs

badjel 'farther along the upper side'; 'past'	**badjelii** 'to farther up'	**badjeliidda** 'to farther up'	**badjelis** 'farther up, from farther up'
maŋŋil 'after' (temporal only)	**maŋŋelii** 'to farther behind'	**maŋŋeliidda** 'later' (temporal only)	**maŋŋelis** 'farther behind, from farther behind'
olgul 'farther along the outside'	**olgolii** 'to farther outside'	**olgoliidda** 'to farther outside'	**olgolis** 'farther outside, from farther outside'
ovdal 'before' (temporal only)	**ovdalii** 'to farther in front'	**ovdaliidda** 'to farther in front'	**ovdalis** 'farther in front, from farther in front'
siskil 'farther along the inside'	**siskelii** 'to farther inside'	**siskeliidda** 'to farther inside'	**siskelis** 'farther inside, from farther inside'
vuollil 'farther along the lower side'	**vuollelii** 'to farther down'	**vuolleliidda** 'to farther down'	**vuollelis** 'farther down, from farther down'

Points to note:

- The genitive form is used to indicate a pathway, like the English 'along', 'by', or 'via'.
- The illative form has singular and plural variants. The plural variants are used to indicate a larger or more nonspecific area.
- The nominative forms **ovdal** 'before' and **maŋŋil** 'after', as well as the illative plural form **maŋŋeliidda** 'later', are not used as adverbs of place but rather of time.
- The form **badjelis** can also mean 'on' with reference to clothes.

The use of these comparative forms is illustrated in the following examples.

Dat lei golgan Gáŋgaviikka gáddái, ja lei **vuollil** ulleráji.	It had flowed to the Gamvik shore, and was farther along the lower side of the border of the high tide.
Dan girjjis son guoskkaha diktemuša vejolašvuođa ollet **olgolii**.	With that book she touches on the potential of poetry to reach farther out.
Šaldi huksejuvvui maŋŋil seamma báikái ja loktejuvvui **badjeliidda**.	The bridge was built afterwards in the same place and was raised farther up.
Finnmárkku bálkkát leat gal **vuollelis** go muđui Norggas.	Finnmark's salaries are lower than elsewhere in Norway.
Dan viđanuppelogi jagis go mus leamaš gákti **badjelis** lea goitge ollu buorránan.	In the fifteen years in which I have had a gákti on, a lot has improved.
Ii justa dán fielmmá bokte gal, muhto doppe **badjelis** han gullo guoika.	It's not just through those quiet waters, but farther up rapids can be heard.

Like the adverbs derived from demonstrative pronouns described at the beginning of this section, the adverbs denoting the points of the compass and location also have diminutive variants that are used to indicate the sense of 'a bit'. Thus, just as **dobbil** 'farther along that way' has the diminutive variant **dobbelaččas** 'a bit farther along that way', so **badjil** 'farther along the upper side' has the diminutive variant **badjelaččas** 'a bit farther along the upper side'.

In addition, many North Sámi adverbs of place have comparative forms that are used to denote the sense of 'farther' or 'more'. These comparatives are formed in the same way as comparative adjectives (see section 4.3). The comparatives have a similar function to the genitive forms of the adverbs discussed earlier.

8 Adverbs

Positive	Comparative nominative	Comparative illative	Comparative locative
badjel 'up, above'	**badjeleabbo** 'farther up, farther above'	**badjelebbui** 'to farther up, to farther above'	**badjeleappos** 'in/from farther up, in/from farther above'

Likewise, many adverbs of place have superlative forms that are used to denote the sense of 'farthest' or 'most'. These superlatives are formed in the same way as superlative adjectives (see section 4.4).

Positive	Superlative nominative	Superlative illative	Superlative locative
davvi 'north'	**davimus** 'the most northern'	**davimussii** 'to the most northern'	**davimusas** 'in/from the most northern'

The use of these comparative and superlative forms is illustrated in the following examples.

Geasset mannet **badjelebbui** ja lagabui jiehki gosa sii ceggejit lávu.	In the summer they go farther up and closer to the glacier, where they put up a tent.
Davimusas lea vuos beahce- ja guossavuovdi Alaskas Sibirijá rádjái.	In the most northern [regions] there are still pine and spruce forests from Alaska as far as Siberia.

North Sámi also possesses a number of adverbs of place that have a single shared form in the nominative, illative, essive/locative, and prolative. These are listed here.

birra	around
buohta	above

gasku	in the middle
guovdu	in the middle
lahka	nearby
miehtá	throughout

The following adverb has only an illative form:

ruoktot	homewards, towards home

The following adverb has two forms, an illative and an essive.

guhkás	to far (away) (illative)
guhkkin	far (away), from far (away) (essive)

The use of these adverbs is illustrated in the following examples.

Soai viegaiga **ruoktot**.	The two of them ran home.
Gasku govas lea Sámi joatkkaskuvla ja boazodoalloskuvla.	In the middle in the photo is the Sámi High School and Reindeer Herding School.
Silbajávri lea muhtin sajes **guhkkin** davvin.	Silbajávri is somewhere far in the north.
Soai mihtideigga man **lahka** guovža lei leamaš.	They measured how close the bear had been.
Guovdu lea dollasadji.	In the centre there is a fireplace.

There are also adverbs of place derived from natural phenomena. These have several different case forms.

Base noun	Compound form	Illative	Ablative	Genitive
miehti 'tailwind'	**mieđa-, mieđá-**	**mieđás** 'against the tailwind'	**mieđil** 'from the tailwind'	**miehtil** 'farther along the tailwind side'

8 Adverbs

vuosti	vuosttá-	vuosttás	vuosttil	vuostil 'farther
'headwind'		'against the headwind'	'from the headwind'	along the headwind side'

The use of these forms is illustrated in the following example.

Danin čáziid alde johtaleaddji šaddá dábálaččat johtit juogo **vuosttás** dahje **mieđás**.	Therefore someone travelling on the water usually has to travel either in the headwind or in the tailwind.

Point to note:

- The adverbs **ovddos** 'forwards' and **maŋos** 'backwards' can be used as compounds with **guovlu** 'area, direction' in the sense of 'to/in/from the direction of', as in the second example here.

Son vázzá **ovddos maŋos**.	S/he is walking forwards and backwards.
Ain hui morašlaš miella, ii meidne beassat **ovddosguvlui** jurdagiiguin.	Still in a very melancholy mood, s/he doesn't imagine being able to progress ahead with [his/her] thoughts.

8.4 Degree, measure, and quantity

The North Sámi adverbs of degree, measure, and quantity can be used to modify adjectives or adverbs or can appear in conjunction with a verb. The most commonly used adverbs of this type are listed here.

ain	even more (+ comparative adjective)
arvat	loads, quite a lot
áibbas	really, completely
áinnas	with pleasure, gladly; especially
beare	too

8 Adverbs

buot	the very most (+ superlative adjective)
eanas, eanaš	most
eanet	more
hárve	rare
hui	very
ii eisege	not at all
ii heađisge	not at all
ii ollenge	not at all
ii oppage, ii obage	not at all
ilá	too
liiggás	too much/many, a surplus of
masa	almost
measta	almost
menddo	too
mihá	considerably
nu	so (+ adjective or adverb, e.g. **nu ollu** 'so much')
oalle	quite
oba, oppa	rather
obage, oppage	even (in questions)
ollásii	completely
ollenge	at all (in questions)
ollu	much more (+ comparative adjective)
sakka	very

8 Adverbs

uhcán, unnán	little
vehá	a bit
velá(ba)	even more (+ comparative adjective)
viehka	quite

The use of these adverbs is illustrated in the following examples.

Lea čáppa dálki – **hui** goalki ja beaivváš báitá.	It's beautiful weather – really calm and the sun is shining.
Oba ártet gullat su ruotasteame Sámedikkis.	It's very strange to hear him/her speaking Swedish in the Sámi Parliament.
Odne Čeavetjávrris arvá **vehá**.	Today it's raining a bit in Čeavetjávri.
Iešaldraddes guovllus eai leat dáid áiggiidge **liiggás** olbmot.	In the Iešaldraddes area there aren't too many people these days.
Čázis leat **ilá** olu baktearat.	There is too much bacteria in the water.
Suoidnemánus leat várra **buot** eanemus geassebargit, go fásta bargit leat luomus.	In July there are probably the very most summer workers, as the permanent workers are on holiday.
Ja dat lea **velá** stuorit mearka, ahte sámit leat orron guhká ovttat sajiin.	And that's an even bigger sign that the Sámi have lived in one place for a long time.
Otná skuvlagirjjiin leat **uhcán** dieđut mearrasámiid birra.	In today's schoolbooks there is little information about the Sea Sámi.
Eanas Ruota nuorat eai beroš risttalašvuođas.	Most Swedish young people don't care about Christianity.
Lea go mis **ollenge** vejolašvuohta sámástit?	Will we even have the opportunity to speak Sámi?

Finally, certain nouns and adjectives can be used as intensifying adverbs in conjunction with other adjectives and adverbs. In such cases the intensifying nouns appear in the accusative-genitive, while the intensifying adjectives appear in the attributive case. The most commonly used intensifying nouns and adjectives meaning 'terribly, extremely' are **hirbmat, jalla, issoras, máilmmi**, and **mielahis**. The following examples illustrate the use of this type of adverb.

In mun gal jáhke diet dal lea dakkár **máilmmi** stuorra ášši.	I don't believe that it's such a terribly big issue.
Hoteallas gullo konsearta, oba **jalla** váttis nohkkat dál.	In the hotel there's a concert on; it's really terribly difficult to go to sleep now.
Dat lea 15 000 euro, mii lea **mielahis** stuorra ruhta unna searvái.	It's 15,000 euros, which is terribly big money for a small society.

8.5 Interrogative

The North Sámi interrogative adverbs are listed here.

gos	where, where from
gosa	where to
gallii	how many times
goabbil	along which of the two ways
goabbelii	to which of the two sides
goabbelis	on/from which of two sides
goappil	on/from which side
goas	when
goassážii	until when

goassážis	since when
gokko	what way
man + adjective/adverb	how (e.g. **man stuoris** 'how big')
mo(vt), mot	how
manin, manne	why
maid	why (rhetorical question)
goal	whereabouts
goppos, goappos	in which of the two directions

The following examples illustrate the use of the interrogative adverbs.

Gos don orut?	Where do you live?
Gosa son vulggii?	Where did he/she go?
Goas Elle boahtá ruoktot?	When is Elle coming home?
Manne dihtor galgá máhttit grammatihka?	Why should a computer know grammar?
Mo manná?	How is it going?
Gallii don leat fitnan Suomas?	How many times have you been to Finland?

These interrogative adverbs are also used in the beginning of subordinate clauses, as illustrated in the examples here.

Mun in muitte **gos** son orru.	I don't remember where s/he lives.
Ruotta lea dat davviriika **gosa** ollu báhtareaddjit bohtet.	Sweden is the Nordic country to which many refugees come.

8 Adverbs

Lea eahpečielggas **goas** musea rahppo.	It's unclear when the museum will be opened.
Ráđđehus háliida diehtit **manin** vuođđoskuvlaoahppit eai dáhto oahppat sámegiela.	The government wants to know why primary school pupils don't want to learn Sámi.
Njuorggámis fállet veahki, **movt** gieđahallat losses dáhpáhusaid.	In Nuorgam they are offering help with how to handle the difficult events.
Ohcamis fertet muitalit **man guhká** leat duojárin bargan.	In the application you have to say how long you've worked as a duodji-maker.

The interrogative adverbs are combined with the particle -**ge** to form indefinite adverbs which are used in negative clauses, in questions, and in conditional clauses. This usage corresponds to the use of indefinite pronouns with -ge in the types of clauses (see section 5.6).

(ii) **gosage**	to nowhere, to anywhere
(ii) **gostege**	(from) nowhere, (from) anywhere
(ii) **goassege**	never, ever
(ii) **moge, movtge**	in no way, in any way
(ii) **manin**	for no reason, for any reason

The use of the indefinite adverbs is illustrated in the following examples.

Mus **ii** leat miella mannat **gosage**.	I don't feel like going anywhere.
Mii **eat** leat **goassage** vuovdán min eatnama.	We have never sold our land.
Sus ii lean **gokkoge** šat bávččas!	S/he didn't have pain anywhere anymore!

8 Adverbs

Su mielas dán jagi dilli ii leat **movtge** erenoamáš.	In his/her opinion this year's situation is not special in any way.
Leatgo **goassege** gullan dáid gielaid birra?	Have you ever heard about these languages?
Muhto jus dat **gostege** galgá dáhpáhuvvat, de sáhtášii Guovdageainnus gos leat stuora sogat.	If it is to happen anywhere, it could be in Kautokeino, where there are large extended families.

The interrogative adverbs can be used as distributive adverbs with the addition of -**ge**. In the West -**nai** is also used.

Bohccot manne Norgga beallái ja dohko jámadedje vehá **gosanai**.	The reindeer went to the Norwegian side and died there, a bit here and there.
Sii leat ožžon dan doarjaga, maid sii leat ain **goasge** dárbbašan.	They received the support that they needed on each occasion.

Furthermore, the interrogative adverbs can be augmented by particles to form indefinite adverbs. The particles **vaikko** and **feara** precede the interrogative adverb, whereas the particles **beare**, **fal**, **nu**, and **ihkinassii** follow the adverb.

Vaikko/feare + adverb

vaikko/feara goas	whenever
vaikko/feara gosa	to wherever
vaikko/feara gos	wherever, from wherever
vaikko/feara mo(vt)	in whichever way
vaikko/feara gallii	however many times

Adverb + **beare/fal/nu/ihkinassii**

goas beare/fal/ nu/ihkinassii	whenever
gosa beare/fal/ nu/ihkinassii	to wherever
gos beare/fal/ nu/ihkinassii	wherever, from wherever
mo(vt) beare/ fal/nu/ihkinassii	in whichever way
gallii beare/fal/ nu/ihkinassii	however many times

The use of these indefinite adverbs is illustrated in the following examples.

Váhnemat álge bidjat mánáid skuvllaide **feara gosa**.	The parents started to send [their] children to school wherever.
Mis lea sierra appa, nu ahte sáhtát gullat Sámi Grand Prix **vaikko gos** máilmmis.	We have a special app so that you can hear the Sámi Grand Prix anywhere in the world.
Danin lea nu dehálaš ahte sámegiella oidno ja gullo juohke sajis **gos fal** lea vejolaš.	That's why it's so important that the Sámi language is seen and heard in every place, wherever it's possible.
Oahpaheaddjeoahpuin dus lea sihkkaris boahtteáigi, **gos ihkinassii** orožat.	With a teaching qualification you have a secure future, wherever you might live.

The indefinite particles may sometimes be combined with no change in meaning, e.g. **gos fal ihkinassii** 'wherever'.

8 Adverbs

8.6 Other

North Sámi has several other types of adverbs that can be grouped together by their form but do not readily fit into a single thematic category. The first is formed by the suffix **-lagaid** (or the rarer variants **-laga**, **-la**, and **-l**). This type of adverb often derives from nouns and usually has a reciprocal or distributive sense. The formation of these adverbs is shown here.

Base noun	Adverb
badji 'something which is above'	**badjálagaid** 'on top of each other'
bálda 'side'	**bálddalagaid** 'next to each other'
buohta 'the place opposite'	**buohtalagaid** 'opposite each other'
giehta 'hand'	**giehtalagaid** 'hand in hand'
lahka 'vicinity'	**lahkalagaid** 'near each other'
maŋŋe- 'behind'	**maŋŋálagaid** 'one after the other'
veahkki 'help'	**veahkkálagaid** 'with reciprocal help'

The use of these adverbs is illustrated in the following examples.

Bearrašii riegádedje ovcci máná, main golmmas jápme **maŋŋálagaid**.	Nine children were born to the family, of which three died one after the other.
Man **lahkalagaid** leat sámegielat, ja gulat go don erohusa nuortalaš- ja anárašgielas?	How close to each other are the Sámi languages, and do you hear a difference between Skolt and Inari Sámi?

Máŋgga báikkis orrot sámit ja dážat **bálddalagaid**.	In many places Sámis and Norwegians live next to each other.	**8** **Adverbs**

Another type of adverb is formed by means of the suffix **-naga** (or the variants **-na** or **-n**, the latter being identical to the essive suffix). This type of adverb is typically derived from nouns and adjectives, and usually serves to denote a state or condition. The formation of this type of adverb is shown here.

Base noun	Adverb
muohta 'snow'	**muohtanaga** 'covered in snow'
varra 'blood'	**varranaga** 'covered in blood'
báhkas 'warm'	**báhkasnaga** 'whilst warm'
varas 'fresh'	**varasnaga** 'in a fresh state; raw'
ealli 'living'	**eallinaga** 'alive'

The use of this type of adverb is illustrated in the following examples.

Háliida vihkket bohccuid **eallinaga**.	S/he wants to weigh the reindeer alive.
Go bohten lagabui, de oainnán ahte lea **varranaga** stuora guovlu dákko.	When I came closer, I saw that a big area around here was covered in blood.
Čielgedeahkki lea hirbmat njálggat ja dimis ja ollusat borret dan **varasnaga**.	The loin is very tasty and soft, and many people eat it raw.

Finally, there are some adverbs that modify the whole sentence rather than a particular element within it. Some of the most common of these are listed here.

čielga, čielgasit	clearly
dađi bahábut	unfortunately

8 Adverbs

eahpitkeahttá	doubtlessly
goitge	nevertheless
lihkus	luckily, fortunately
mahká(š)	allegedly, supposedly
sihkkarit	certainly
várra	probably
vejolaččat	possibly
vissát, vissásit	certainly

The following examples illustrate the use of this type of adverb.

Birrasiid 90% bargiin Norggas juhket alkohola, muhto **goitge** eai báljo huma dan birra.

Around 90% of workers in Norway drink alcohol, but nevertheless they hardly ever talk about it.

Njuorggáma čáhcedilli ii **vejolaččat** buorrán ovdalgo muohta suddá.

The water situation in Nuorgam may possibly not improve before the snow melts.

Leat **várra** juo fuomášan ahte gávpoga namma Tromsø lea sámegillii Romsa.

You've probably already noticed that the name of the city Tromsø is Romsa in Sámi.

Lihkus lea dál dilli nu ahte sámit ieža leat dutkagoahtán sámi áššiid.

Fortunately, the situation is now such that the Sámi have started to investigate the issues themselves.

Chapter 9

Adpositions

The term adposition covers both prepositions (which precede their associated noun) and postpositions (which follow their associated noun). North Sámi has both prepositions, e.g. *gaskkal* **Guovdageainnu ja Máze** 'between Kautokeino and Masi' and postpositions, e.g. **vári** *duohken* 'behind the mountain'. In addition, some North Sámi adpositions can function as either prepositions or postpositions (sometimes with a slightly different meaning in each case), e.g. *birra* **máilmmi** 'throughout the world', **máilmmi** *birra* 'around the world'. Etymologically, many adpositions derive from nouns (e.g. the postposition **sajis** 'instead of' derives from the noun **sadji** 'place'). The noun associated with an adposition is typically in the accusative-genitive case. Note that many adpositions can also function as adverbs, e.g. **son manai sisa** 's/he went inside'.

9.1 Adpositions of place

The following table lists the most common North Sámi adpositions (generally postpositions) with spatial meaning. Postpositions with spatial meaning typically occur in two or three forms, depending on whether they refer to movement or not. The movement can be either towards (labelled as 'destination' in the following table), along, or across (labelled as 'pathway'), or away from (labelled as 'origin'). Spatial adpositions that do not refer to movement are labelled as 'location'.

9 Adpositions

Postpostions of place with different forms

Destination	Location/origin	Pathway	English translation
(n)ala	(n)alde	—	on(to)
báldii	bálddas	báldda	next to
badjelii	badjelis	bajil	above, over
beallái	bealde	beale	next to, on the side of
duohkái	duohken/ duohkin	duogi/ duoge	behind
fárrui	fárus	—	along with
gaskii	gaskkas	gaskka, gaskal	among, amidst
geahčái	geahčen	geaže	to/at the end of
gurrii	guoras	guora	next to, to/on the edge of
lusa	luhtte	—	to, at
maŋŋái	maŋis	maŋil	after, behind
ollái	olis	—	to/in the vicinity of
ovdii	ovddas	ovddal	towards, in front of, before
rádjái	rájes, rájis	ráje	up to, until
sisa	siste	—	inside, out of
vuollái	vuolde	vuole/ vuoli, vuolil	under

9 Adpositions

The principle of these parallel forms is illustrated in the following examples:

Beana manai lávu **duohkái**.	The dog went behind the tent.
Beana lea lávu **duohken**.	The dog is behind the tent.
Beana boahtá lávu **duohken**.	The dog is coming from behind the tent.
Beana manai lávu **duogi**.	The dog went along the back of the tent.
Sáhpán ruohtai viesu **vuollái**.	The mouse ran under the house.
Sáhpán lea viesu **vuolde**.	The mouse is under the house.
Sáhpán bođii viesu **vuolde**.	The mouse came out from under the house.
Sáhpán ruohtai viesu **vuoli**.	The mouse ran along under the house.
Son fárre su vánhemiid **lusa**.	S/he is moving to his/her parents'.
Son orru su vánhemiid **luhtte**.	S/he lives at his/her parents'.
Son boahtá su vánhemiid **luhtte**.	S/he is coming from his/her parents'.
Son manai hirbmat guhkás vuovddi **sisa**.	S/he went very far inside the woods.
Son lea vuovddi **siste**.	S/he is inside the woods.
Son viegai eret vuovddi **siste**.	S/he ran away from inside the forest.

Some spatial adpositions only appear in one form, as in the following. Note that all forms listed are solely postpositions unless otherwise indicated.

badjel (pre/postposition)	over (with verbs of motion)
badjin	up, on the upper part of

9 Adpositions

báldal	along and past
bearrái	after (in abstract sense)
birra	around (locative)
bokte	through, past, via
buohta	opposite
čađa	through
gaskkal	(somewhere) between
gasku (preposition)	to/in/from the middle of
gitta (preposition)	right up to; all the way from
guovddáš (pre/postposition)	in the middle of
guovdu (preposition)	to/in/from the middle of
guovdu	across (i.e. to come across something), with respect to
labi	along the surface of
lahka (pre/postposition)	near, to/in/from the vicinity of
meaddel (pre/postposition)	past
meattá (pre/postposition)	past
miehtá (preposition)	through, throughout
mielde	along, alongside
njeaiga	up against
olggul	outside of
ovddal	towards, in front of
rastá	over, across
seahká	into the midst of, in the midst of

siskkil	on the inside of	
vuollái (preposition)	to the bottom of	
vuostá, **vu**ostái (pre/postposition)	against, up against, towards	

The use of spatial adpositions is illustrated in the following examples.

Norggas áigot vuovdigoahtit bohccobierggu **birra** máilmmi.	Norway is going to start selling reindeer meat around the world.
Mun vudjen Álahedjui Máze **bokte**.	I drove to Alta via Masi.
Viessosadji lea ođđa gávpotguovddáža **buohta** Gironis.	The building plot is opposite the new town centre in Kiruna.
Doaivvu mielde bohtet nuorat geasseleirii, **gitta** Helssegis Ohcejohkii.	Hopefully young people will come to the summer camp, all the way from Helsinki to Utsjoki.
Filbma čájehuvvo **miehtá** Sámi.	The film is being shown throughout Sápmi.
Eallu manai ráji **rastá**.	The herd went across the border.
Lávvordateahkeda vujii biillain ealgga **njeaiga**.	On Saturday evening s/he ran into an elk with a car.
Skuvllat galge huksejuvvot girkobáikkiid **lahka**.	Schools had to be built near church sites.

9.2 Adpositions of time

Another group of North Sámi adpositions has temporal meaning. The most common of these are listed here. As in the previous list, the forms appearing here are all solely postpositions unless otherwise indicated.

9 Adpositions

áigi	ago
bale	while, during
čađa	throughout
gaskan (preposition)	in the midst of
gaskka	between
gaskkal	(sometime) between
geažes	after, in (a length of time)
gitta (preposition)	right up to; all the way from
guovdu	right in time for
maŋŋil, maŋŋá (pre/postpostion)	after
miehtá (pre/postposition)	throughout, through the whole
mielde	in the course of
ovdal (pre/postposition)	before
rádjái	until
vuollái	towards

The following examples illustrate the use of the temporal adpositions.

Beassážiid **ovdal** lea jaskes vahkku.	Before Easter it's a quiet week.
Dán **rádjái** čavčča guovžabivddus leat goddon guokte guovžža.	Up until now in the autumn bear hunt two bears have been killed.

Njealji jagi **geažes** suoma-ugralaš álbmogiid kongreassa lágiduvvo fas Suomas.	In four years' time the Finno-Ugric peoples' conference will be held in Finland again.	**9** **Adpositions**
Sámegiella lei beaivválaš giellan osiin suohkanis **gitta** nuppi máilmmisoađi rádjái.	Sámi was a daily language in parts of the county right up until the Second World War.	
Maŋŋil vuođđoskuvlla vázzen ovcci vahku joatkkaskuvlla.	After primary school I attended nine weeks of secondary school.	

9.3 Adpositions with other meanings

Not all North Sámi adpositions have spatial or temporal meaning. Below is a list of common adpositions with other meanings. As earlier, all forms listed are solely postpositions unless otherwise indicated.

aisttan, aistton (preposition)	to quote
bealis	as far as . . . is concerned
birra	about
bokte	by means of
dáfus	regarding, with respect to
dihtii, dihte	because of, for
ear(r)et (preposition)	except, apart from
ektui	with respect to
geažil	because of
gullut, gulu	in the presence of

219

9 Adpositions

haga	without
hárrái	regarding
ládje	in the manner of
láhkái	in the manner of
mielas	in the opinion of
mielde	with, by means of
nammii	for the sake of
oaidnut	in the presence of
oaivái	in the name of
oskálii	with confidence in
ovdasii	as a sign/indication of
ovddas	on behalf of, for
ovdii	for, because of
sadjái	instead of
sajis	in the place of
várás	for, for the sake of, for the benefit of
veagas	with the support of
vehkii	with the support of (following verbs requiring an illative)
vuođul	on the basis of, based on
vuolis	as a sign/indication of
vuostá, vuostái (pre/postposition)	against

The following examples illustrate the use of this type of adposition.

Vuolgge mu **mielde** girkui.	Come with me to the church.
Mun lean dan **vuostá**.	I'm against it.
Sámediggi bivdá árvalusaid Sámi dutkama ja alit oahpu **hárrái**.	The Sámi Parliament is seeking proposals regarding Sámi research and higher education.
Mu **mielas** lea leamaš hui somá blogget.	In my opinion, it has been a lot of fun to blog.
Guovža galgá birget guhká biepmu **haga**.	A bear has to manage a long time without food.
Rabas alit almmi **sádjái** oidnen boares ránesmála internáhta dáhkis.	Instead of the open blue sky I saw the old grey paint on the ceiling of the dormitory.

9.4 Adpositions with possessive suffixes

Like nouns, adpositions can be used with possessive suffixes. In some cases the adposition undergoes consonant and/or vowel changes when the possessive suffix is added. The following table illustrates some of the more common changes that occur. Note that the use of this type of suffixed adposition is relatively restricted in everyday speech. See section 5.2.2 for a complete table of the possessive suffixes.

Adposition	Adposition stem before suffix	Example with first person suffix
alde 'on'	**aldd-**	**alddán** 'on me'
badjelii '(to) over'	**badjelas-**	**badjelasan** '(to) over me'
badjelis 'over'	**badjelistt-**	**badjelisttán** 'over me'

9 Adpositions

báldii '(to) next to'	**báldas-**	**báldasan** '(to) next to me'
bálddas 'next to'	**bálddast-**	**bálddastan** 'next to me'
bealde 'on/from the side of'	**beald-**	**bealdán** 'on/from my side'
beallái 'to the side of'	**beallás-**	**beallásan** 'to my side'
birra 'around, about'	**birra-**	**birrasan** 'around me, about me'
dáfus 'with regard to'	**dáfust-**	**dáfustan** 'with regard to me'
duohkái '(to) behind'	**duohkás-**	**duohkásan** '(to) behind me'
duohkin 'behind'	**duohkin-**	**duohkinan** 'behind me'
gaskan 'in the midst of'	**gaskan-**	**gaskaneamet** 'with each other'
gaskkas 'between, among'	**gaskkast-**	**gaskkasteamet** 'between us'
hárrái 'regarding'	**hárrás-**	**hárrásan** 'as far as I am concerned'
luhtte 'at'	**luht-**	**luhtán** 'at mine'
lusa 'to'	**lusa-**	**lusan** 'to me'
maŋis 'behind, after'	**maŋist-**	**maŋistan** 'behind me, after me'
maŋŋái '(to) behind'	**maŋŋas-**	**maŋŋásan** '(to) behind me'

mielde 'with'	mieldd-	mielddán 'with me'
ovddas 'before, instead of'	ovddast-	ovddastan 'before me, instead of me'
ovdii '(to) in front of'	ovdas-	ovdasan '(to) in front of me'
sisa 'to the inside of'	sisa-	sisan '(to) inside me'
siste 'inside of, out of'	sistt-	sisttán 'out of me'
vuolde 'under'	vuoldd-	vuolddán 'under me'
vuollái '(to) under'	vuollás-	vuollásan '(to) under me'

Points to note:

- Certain adpositions appear in the weak grade before a possessive suffix, e.g. **mielde** 'with' : **mieldd-**.
- Adpositions whose stems end in a consonant in this table have the linking vowel -á- or -a- before the first and second person singular suffixes and the linking vowel -i- before the third person singular suffixes.

The following examples illustrate the formation of this type of suffixed adposition.

Boađe **mielddán** johkagáddái.	Come with me to the riverside.
Jesus gohčui mánáid **lusas**.	Jesus called the children to him. (Luke 18:16)
Dađe mielde go oahpaimet dárogiela, de dárosteimmet **gaskaneamet**.	The more Norwegian we learned, the more we spoke Norwegian amongst ourselves.

Chapter 10
Conjunctions

10.1 Coordinate

The most common North Sámi coordinate conjunctions are as follows

dahje, dáikke, dehe	or
dahje ... dahje	either ... or
dahjege, dehege	that is, in other words
de	so
ja	and
juo ... ja	both ... and
muhto	but
sihke ... ja	both ... and
vai	or (in questions)

The following examples illustrate the use of some of these conjunctions.

Mun liikon **sihke** gáffii **ja** dedjii.	I like both coffee and tea.
Máret orru Guovdageainnus, **muhto** su isit orru Ruoŧa bealde.	Máret lives in Kautokeino, but her husband is living on the Swedish side.
Vuolggát go mearragáddái geassemánus **vai** suoidnemánus?	Are you going to the seaside in June or July?

Don sáhtát vázzit dohko **dahje** vuodjit.　　You can walk there or drive.

10.2 Subordinate

Here are the most common subordinating conjunctions, categorised by function.

10.2.1 Complementisers

North Sámi has the following two complementisers, which have slightly different uses.

ahte　　that

go　　that

Ahte is used in subject, object, and attributive clauses, as in the following examples, respectively.

Leago duohta, **ahte** leat fárreme Ruonáeatnamii?　　Is it true that you're moving to Greenland?

Mun jurddašin, **ahte** leat juo geargan goarrut dan gávtti.　　I thought that you had already finished sewing that gákti.

Lea vejolaš, **ahte** mun deaivvan muhtima feasttas.　　It's possible that I'll meet someone at the party.

By contrast, **go** is typically reserved for subject and object clauses with a temporal dimension, e.g.:

Lea buorre **go** geassi boahtá.　　It's good that summer is coming.

Oidnen, **go** son vuodjá jávrris.　　I saw that s/he was swimming in the lake.

10 Conjunctions

10.2.2 Adverbial

North Sámi has a number of different adverbial conjunctions, discussed here.

Causal

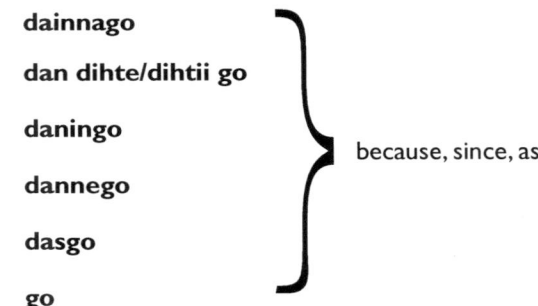

dainnago
dan dihte/dihtii go
daningo   because, since, as
dannego
dasgo
go

The following examples illustrate the use of the causal conjunctions.

Sii mannet dávjá dápmohiid bivdit **dainnago** lea jávri lahkosiin.	They often go trout fishing because there's a lake nearby.
Mun lean válljen čállit sámegillii **dan dihte go** dat lea mu eatnigiella.	I've chosen to write in Sámi because it's my mother tongue.
Biret-Elle vulggii Guovdageidnui **go** su irgi lea doppe.	Biret-Elle went to Kautokeino as her boyfriend is there.

Comparative

go	as, than
nugo	such as, like
dego	like, as if
mađe – dađe, mađi – dađi	the – the

The following examples illustrate the use of the comparative conjunctions.

Guovdageaidnu lea stuorit **go** Ohcejohka.	Kautokeino is bigger than Utsjoki.
Lullisámegiella lea seamma miellagiddevaš **go** davvisámegiella.	South Sámi is as interesting as North Sámi.

Nugo eatnasat dan áigge, son jurddašii ahte ferte oahpahit mánáidasas dárogiela.

Like most people at that time, s/he thought that s/he had to teach his/her children Norwegian.

Dearvvahedje su **dego** son livččii gonagas.

They greeted him as if he were a king.

Ohcalit dán gease ivnniid ja stiillaid – **mađe** hálbbit **dađe** buoret.

This summer we're looking for colours and styles – the cheaper the better.

Concessive

vaikko (-ge)
jos de vel -ge   } even if, although, even though
jus juo, jos juo

The following examples illustrate the use of the concessive conjunctions.

Vaikko lei**ge** dáruiduhttinproseassa jođus, de lei sámegiella beaivválaš giellan.

Even though the process of Norwegianization was underway, Sámi was the language of daily use.

Jos de vel boahtá**ge**, de in huma suinna.

Even if s/he comes, I won't talk to him/her.

Conditional

jos, jus	if
go	if
sahte fal	as long as
beare	if only

The following examples illustrate the use of the conditional conjunctions. Note that **jus/jos** is the most commonly used. **Go** often has a temporal dimension, overlapping with its use in the sense of 'when'.

10 Conjunctions

Jos in livčče váiban, de vuolggášin du mielde.	If I weren't tired, I'd go with you.
Riŋge munnje **go** sáhtát.	Phone me if you can.
Mun vuolggášin olgoriikii, **beare** mus livčče ruđat.	I'd go abroad, if only I had money.

Purpose

vai	so that
amas	so that not

The following examples illustrate the use of the purpose conjunctions.

Mii merket misiid **vai** diehtit geasa dat gullet.	We mark reindeer calves so that we know whom they belong to.
Bija bierggu jiekŋaskáhpii **amas** billašuvvat.	Put the meat into the fridge so that it doesn't go off.

Result

nu(vt) ahte	so that

The following example illustrates the use of **nu(vt) ahte**.

Mun gudđen uvssa rabas **nu(vt) ahte** beana manai olggos.	I left the door open so that the dog went out.

Temporal

go	when
goas	when (a specific time)
ovdal go, ovdalgo, ovdal	before
maŋŋil go, maŋŋilgo	after
dassá(žii) go, dassá(žii)go	until
dan rájes go	since, starting from

dan botta go	while	
dalle go	at the time when	

The following examples illustrate the use of the temporal conjunctions.

Mun adden biepmu beatnagiidda **go** bohten ruoktot.	I gave the dogs food when I came home.
Sii háliidit maid diehtit **goas** don leat riegádan.	They also want to know when you were born.
Mii vuoššaimet gáfe **ovdal go** bođiidet.	We made coffee before you came.
Ráđđehus mearrida áššis **maŋŋil go** suohkan lea ohcan.	The government decides on the matter after the county has made an application.
Mu boahtteáigásaš isit orru Durkkas **dassážii go** moai náitaletne.	My future husband is living in Turkey until we get married.
Dán jagi lea 70 jagi áigi **dan rájes go** dáiddár Nils-Aslak Valkeapää (Áillohaš-rohkki) riegádii.	This year is seventy years since the artist Nils-Aslak Valkeapää (the late Áillohaš) was born.
Dan botta go bargen doppe bessen čuovvut duodjegurssa.	While I was working there I could attend a duodji course.
Dalle go mun ledjen mánná mis ii lean viessu oppanassiige.	At the time when I was a child, we didn't have a house at all.

10
Conjunctions

Chapter 11

Particles

Particles are small indeclinable words. In North Sámi particles can be divided into discourse (modal) particles and interjections. There are two types of discourse particles based on their form: enclitic particles and independent particles.

11.1 Discourse particles

11.1.1 Enclitic particles

North Sámi has a relatively large number of enclitic particles. Enclitic particles are suffixed to a preceding word, and they lack stress. Note that sometimes, especially in the West, enclitic particles may be written as independent words. Some enclitic particles are used only in statements, some only in questions, and some are used in both. The most common enclitic particles are discussed here.

-ba

The enclitic particle -ba is usually attached to the first constituent in a clause. It highlights and draws attention to the word it is attached to. It can have a slightly confrontational nuance. The particle -ba appears both in statements and questions. The use of this particle is illustrated in these examples.

| Mas **ba** munges dihten mii dat lei lávlagiid go in lean gullan dan goassege? | How was I supposed to know what that song was when I had never heard it? |
| Ii **ba** olu turista bissánge dáidda sámi báikkiide. | Not many tourists stop here in the Sámi places. |

-bat

The enclitic -**bat** is attached to the first constituent in the sentence. It is used only in questions. It serves to express surprise, scepticism, and reproach. The use of -**bat** is illustrated in these examples.

| Gos **bat** sámediggi gávnnalii dasa ruđaid? | Where in the world did the Sámi Parliament find the money for this? |
| Gii **bat** don leat? | Who might you be?/Who are you then? |

-ge

The enclitic particle -**ge** can be attached to any constituent in the clause. It has two functions: in affirmative clauses its meaning corresponds to the English 'indeed' or 'also, too', and in negative clauses and in questions its meaning correponds to the English 'even, at all'. In the West the particle -**nai** can be used instead of -**ge** in the sense of 'also, too'. It emphasises the constituent to which it is attached. In conjunction with the negative verb, -**ge** functions as a conjunction combining clauses in the sense of 'and so'. In conjunction with **vaikko/vaikke** 'even though', -**ge** expresses concession in the sense of 'admittedly'.

Son lei buori vuoimmis ja bođii **ge** nuppi sadjái.	S/he was in good form and indeed came second.
Mu eallin livččii lean earálágan ja sámi musihkkakultuvra**ge**.	My life would've been different and Sámi music culture also.
– Máhtát go ruonáeatnangiela? – In máhte, in sáni **ge**.	– Do you know Greenlandic? – I don't, not even a word.
Mii dovddaimet dušše muhtuma sis, eat **ge** mannan nu lahka.	We only knew some of them, and so we didn't go so close.
Vaikke vel ovdáneapmi lea **ge** leamaš positiiva, de váillui ollu.	Even though the development was admittedly positive, a lot was still missing.
Dát lea buorre oahppu munnje **nai**.	This is a good lesson for me too.

11 Particles

11 Particles

-gis

The enclitic particle -**gis** can be any constituent in the clause, and it can be used in statements and questions. It is used to contrast and highlight the noun to which it is attached with something else that has been previously mentioned.

Liikon buoremusat leat luonddus, nugo viehkat meahcis ja dálvet **gis** čuoigat.	I like being in nature the best, such as running in the woods and then skiing in the winter.
Maid dál **gis** leat hutkan?	What have you come up with this time?

-go

The enclitic particle -**go** is used in closed (polar) questions (both direct and indirect). It is attached to the first constituent in the clause and marks this element out as the topic of the question. Usually -**go** is attached to the main verb, in which case the question is about the entire clause. The use of this interrogative particle is illustrated in these examples.

Lea **go** dus miella bargat journalistan sámi stuorámus mediaásahusas?	Would you like work as a journalist for the biggest Sámi media establishment?
Mun in dieđe lean **go** vel dan ipmirdan.	I don't know if I've understood it yet.

The particle can also be used as a substitute for **man** 'how' in certain question, e.g. **ollugo** = **man ollu** 'how much', **guhkágo** = **man guhká** 'how long'.

-han

The enclitic particle -**han** is attached to the first constituent in the clause. It is used in statements and indicates that the information to which it refers is or should be obvious or known to the interlocutor. The following examples illustrate its use.

Ja dát **han** lea hirbmat ilolaš ášši.	And that, as we know, is a very happy matter.
Don **han** barggat bohccuiguin birra jagi, lávet go muhtumin dolkat?	And after all, you work with reindeer all year round; do you sometimes get tired?

Sámegiella **han** lea mu eatnigiella ja dat giella maid mun geavahan beaiválaččat.	And Sámi is after all my mother tongue, and the language which I use daily.

-son

The enclitic particle -**son** is used in questions and is typically suffixed to the first constituent. It indicates uncertainty on the part of the speaker, and is often used in rhetorical questions. The following examples illustrate its use.

Lea go **son** dat rivttes olmmoš?	Is that the right person, I wonder?
Ii go **son** dábálaš eisseváldi sáhte bargat sámeáššiiguin?	Can't a normal authority work with Sámi issues?

In addition, North Sámi has a number of other less frequently used enclitic particles, listed here.

-**ban**	gives emphasis
-**hal**	a) makes questions more polite/friendlier b) indicates that the speaker believes the statement to be true
-**gos**	contraction of -**go** (interrogative particle) + **dus** 'at/with you'
-**mat**	a) 'in any case; irrespectively' b) makes imperatives more polite
-**mis**	a) indicates a realisation on the part of the speaker; gives a conciliatory nuance b) makes imperatives more polite
-**s**	gives a friendlier tone to a question

Some enclitics form a lexicalised unit together with the word to which they are attached, e.g. **dego** 'like, as', **diedusge** 'of course', **ii headisge** 'not at all', **naba** 'what about, how about'. All indefinite pronouns and adverbs ending in -**ge** and -**nai** (e.g. **giige** 'whoever', **gosnai** 'wherever' – see sections 5.6 and 8.5, respectively) could be regarded as lexicalised units encorporating these enclitic particles.

11 Particles

11.1.2 Independent particles

In addition to enclitic particles, North Sámi has a number of independent discourse particles. These can appear anywhere in the clause unless otherwise indicated. Some of the most common of the independent discourse particles are listed here.

almma, am(m)a	introduces a question to which one expects a positive answer
baicca, baicce	rather, instead, actually (i.e. contrary to expectations)
beare	makes a request friendlier
dal	a) is used to seek clarification about an uncertain point b) is used to highlight a particular element of the clause c) makes a request more polite
dat	highlights the preceding element of the clause (often used with a topicalised constituent)
de	is used to strengthen an utterance
fal	a) is used to confirm the preceding element in the clause, often in a response to a polar question b) makes a request friendlier/more polite
gal	extremely commonly used particle with a variety of functions, including confirming or reinforcing the truth or obviousness of a statement and indicating an assumption (equivalent to the English construction 'it must be' or 'isn't it')
hás	appears at the beginning of a statement to lend a challenging or suggesting tone, equivalent to English 'I bet …' or 'how about …'

j(u)o	is used in chains of particles to add weight to the utterance
na	used in a similar manner to English 'well' but with higher frequency; can have a variety of nuances of uncertainty, scepticism, hesitation, doubt, etc.; can also be used to confirm a previous statement and initiate or close a sequence of utterances
naba	introduces a question, equivalent to English 'what about'
oainnat	equivalent to English 'you see'
vai	appears at the beginning of a statement to indicate slightly surprised confirmation, equivalent to English 'so' or 'so that's how it is'

The use of these particles is illustrated in the following examples.

Sámi goahkka **oainnat** ii fuola guobbariid.	A Sámi cook doesn't care for mushrooms, you see.
Naba don?	What about you?
Ledje **baicca** ollu oaivilat plánaid birra.	There were actually a lot of opinions about the plans.
Máhtát go čuoigat? **Na**, dieđusge.	Do you know how to ski? Well, of course.
Mun in **gal** háliit doppe fitnat.	I really don't want to go there.
– Leago duohta? – **De** lea.	– Is it true? – It is.
Máret **dat** gal fuomášii dan feailla.	Máret was the one who noticed the mistake.

11 Particles

11.2 Interjections

The following is a list of common North Sámi interjections.

fiš	yuck
fuoi	yuck
gea	look
gul	listen
hei, he-hei	my, my
(h)o-hoi	expresses tiredness
huh	phew
iš	yuck
j(u)o	yes, yeah
uš	yuck
vuoi	oh my goodness, oh no

Chapter 12
Clauses

This section is dedicated to the features of basic clauses. Information on complex clauses can be found in the sections on relative pronouns (5.5), conditional verb forms (7.2.3), non-finite verb forms (7.4), and subordinate conjunctions (10.2).

12.1 Word order

The basic word order in North Sámi clauses is SVO (subject + verb + object), e.g.:

Risten-Iŋgá vuoššai gáfe.	Risten-Iŋgá made coffee.
Son dovdá mu oambeali.	S/he knows my cousin.

If an adverbial is placed at the beginning of the clause, the word order is not affected, e.g.:

Iđđes Risten-Iŋgá vuoššai gáfe.	In the morning Risten-Iŋgá made coffee.

Note, however, that due to interference from Norwegian and Swedish, there is a tendency among some North Sámi speakers to place the verb in the second position when the clause starts with an adverbial or a question word, e.g.:

Iđđes **vuoššai** Risten-Iŋgá gáfe.	In the morning Risten-Iŋgá made coffee.
Maid **muitala** Johan Turi sámi identitehta birra?	What does Johan Turi say about Sámi identity?

12 Clause types

There are several exceptions to the basic SVO word order. First, imperative clauses lack an explicit subject and thus start with the verb, e.g.:

Vuošša gáfe!   Make coffee!

Second, negative clauses often start with the negative verb (though they may alternatively start with the subject), e.g.:

In mun dieđe.   I don't know.

Third, in clauses with compound verbal structures (i.e. those containing both a finite and non-finite component), there is a strong tendency to place the object before the non-finite verbal component, e.g.:

Sii leat **skuvlla vázzime**.   They are attending school.

Mun lean **gáfe vuoššan**.   I've made coffee.

Son háliida **suomagiela oahppat**.   S/he wants to learn Finnish.

Finally, note that any element of a clause can be fronted for purposes of topicalisation, e.g.:

Dihtora mun osten.   It was a computer that I bought.

Na, čáppat dat gal lea.   It sure is *beautiful*.

12.2 Intransitive

A North Sámi intransitive clause consists of a subject plus a verb. The verb may be accompanied by an adverbial phrase (e.g. an adverb of place or time or an inflected noun) but never by a direct object. The following examples illustrate intransitive clauses.

Beana ciellá.   A/the dog is barking.

Moai dánsejetne.   The two of us are dancing.

Son orru Guovda-geainnus.	S/he lives in Kautokeino.	**12** Clause types
Mánát leat olgun.	The children are outside.	

12.3 Transitive

A transitive clause consists of a subject, a verb, and a direct object. It may additionally be accompanied by an optional adverbial phrase. The following examples illustrate transitive clauses.

Áhkku vuoššá aďďamiid.	Grandma is cooking marrowbones.
Elle-Márjá Vars lea máŋga nuoraidgirjji čállán.	Elle-Márjá Vars has written many novels for young people.
Mu oabbá lei huksen oďďa viesu.	My sister had built a new house.

12.4 Other two-place verbal clauses

Some North Sámi verbs take a subject and another obligatory argument in the illative or locative case. Each of these verbs determines the case in which the argument appears. Some of these verbs have been mentioned in the sections on the illative and locative cases (3.2.4 and 3.2.5, respectively). The following examples illustrate this type of clause.

Mun liikon goikebirgui.	I like dried meat.
Son lea dolkan skuvlii.	S/he is sick of school.

12.5 Habitive

The habitive construction is used to indicate that someone (or something) has something (or someone). The person (or thing) who has something is in the locative case and appears at the beginning of the clause. The thing (or person) that they have is the subject of the clause, and as such is in the nominative case. It appears at the end of the clause. The two parts of the

12 Clause types

construction are linked by the verb **leat** 'to be'. If the subject is plural, the verb **leat** 'to be' appears in the plural as well. The following examples illustrate habitive clauses.

Ristenis lea biila.	Risten has a car.
Jovnnas leat ollu ustibat.	Jovnna has a lot of friends.
Mus ii leat oabbá.	I don't have a sister.

12.6 Existential

Existential clauses are used to indicate that something or someone exists. They are equivalent to the English construction 'there is/there are'. They are typically composed of an adverbial of place (e.g. an adverb or a noun in the locative) followed by the verb **leat** 'to be' in the appropriate form and finally a subject. If the subject is plural, the verb **leat** 'to be' will also be plural. In some cases other verbs with a similar meaning to **leat** 'to be' may be used, e.g. **gávdnot** 'to be located', **orrut** 'to live', etc. The following examples illustrate the use of existential clauses.

Guovdageainnus lea čáppa girku.	There's a pretty church in Kautokeino.
Doppe eai leat muorat.	There are no trees there.
Beavddi alde leat golbma gohpu.	There are three cups on the table.

12.7 Predicative

Predicative clauses typically consist of a subject (in the nominative case), the verb **leat** 'to be', and a noun (also in the nominative case) or adjective. The following examples illustrate this type of predicative clause.

Son lea oahpaheaddji.	S/he is a teacher.
Beana lea čáhppat.	The dog is black.
Skohterat leat ođđasat.	The snowmobiles are new.

In some cases predicative clauses may use the verb **šaddat** 'to become' instead of **leat** 'to be'. There are two types of predicative constructions with this verb. In the first, the subject is in the nominative and the noun following the verb is in the essive, e.g.:

Boares skuvla šattai sámi hoteallan.	The old school became a Sámi hotel.

In the second (which has the same meaning as the first), the noun before the verb is in the locative and the noun following it is in the nominative, e.g.:

Boares skuvllas šattai sámi hotealla.	The old school became a Sámi hotel.
Sus šattai sámemusihka ođasteaddji.	He became a revitaliser of Sámi music.

12.8 Subjectless

North Sámi clauses may lack an explicit subject. Such subjectless constructions correspond to English clauses starting with 'it', as in 'it's raining'. They may begin with an adverb. The following examples illustrate this type of clause:

Arvá.	It's raining.
Odne lea buolaš.	It's very cold today.
Lea juo bearjadat.	It's already Friday.

There are also subjectless clauses involving a physical or emotional experience, in which the experiencer is in the accusative and the verb is in the third person singular. The following example illustrates this type of clause.

Mu vuovssihii.	I felt sick (lit: it made me feel sick).

12.9 Interrogative

North Sámi has two types of interrogative clause, closed (also known as polar or yes/no) and open (formed with a question word). Closed interrogative clauses are composed of a positive or negative verb followed by

12
Clause types

the interrogative particle **go** (which may be independent or suffixed to the verb). The following examples illustrate closed interrogative clauses.

Lea go dus beana?	Do you have a dog?
Boahtá go son juovlastállu dán jagi?	Is the Christmas troll coming this year?
It go bora bierggu?	Don't you eat meat?
Orru go Biret Mázes?	Does Biret live in Masi?

The particle **bat** (discussed in section 11.1.1) can be used instead of **go** to express surprise, scepticism, or reproach in a question, e.g.:

Nie divrras biillabat don ostet?!	Did you buy such an expensive car?!

Closed interrogative clauses are answered by repeating the main verb of the question in the appropriate person, often preceded by a discourse particle such as **de** or **na**, e.g.:

– **Orru go Biret Mázes?**	– Does Biret live in Masi?
– **(De) orru. / – Ii (oro).**	– Yes, she does. / – No, she doesn't.

Note that closed interrogative clauses may alternatively be answered by **j(u)o** 'yes', e.g.:

– **Orru go Biret Mázes?**	– Does Biret live in Masi?
– **Juo.**	– Yes.

Note that a closed interrogative clause may begin with a constituent other than the verb (e.g. the subject or an adverbial) in order to indicate that the question is focused on it. The following examples illustrate this:

Don go boađát?	Are you the one coming?
Mázii go manat?	Is it Masi that you're going to?

The answer to this type of interrogative clause will typically begin with the word to which the interrogative particle is attached, often followed by the discourse particle **fal** (discussed in section 11.1.2), e.g.:

– **Don go boađát?**	– Are you the one coming?
– **Mun fal.**	– Yes, I am.

Open questions are formed with question words, i.e. interrogative pronouns (see section 5.4) or interrogative adverbs (see section 8.5). The question word is placed at the beginning of the sentence, followed by the subject and verb (as in statements).

Gos don orut?   Where do you live?

12
Clause types

Chapter 13
Word formation

13.1 Derivative suffixes

North Sámi possesses a wide variety of suffixes that can be used to create new verbs, nouns, and adjectives from other verbs, nouns, and adjectives. Some of these derivative suffixes are extremely widely used and very productive, while others are more limited in scope. In the following section the main North Sámi derivative suffixes will be examined, with the most attention given to the more frequently occurring ones.

13.1.1 Verb suffixes

North Sámi verbs can be derived from other verbs, nouns, or adjectives. The key types of derived verbs will be discussed in turn here. Note that many of the suffixes presented here are multifunctional and are often lexicalised to a certain degree rather than being completely productive. These points will be explained in more detail.

13.1.1.1 Verbs derived from verbs

North Sámi contains a large number of suffixes that serve to derive verbs from other verbs. These suffixes can be divided into two categories, a) valency-changing suffixes, which create e.g. passive, reflexive, causative, and reciprocal verbs, and b) aspectual suffixes, which change the way in which the action of a given verb is presented, e.g. progressive, habitual, etc.

13.1.1.1.1 Valency-changing suffixes

North Sámi possesses a number of valency-changing derivative verbal suffixes, meaning suffixes that change type and number of arguments (i.e. participants) in the sentence. These suffixes are examined in turn here.

13.1.1.1.1.1 Passive

In North Sámi, as in English, the direct object of a transitive clause becomes the subject of a passive clause, as in the following example.

Transitive	**Olmmái bassá biilla.**	The man washes the car.
Passive	**Biila bassojuvvo.**	The car is washed [by the man].

There are two main differences between North Sámi and English regarding the passive. First, in North Sámi the agent of a passive clause cannot be expressed, in contrast to English (as in 'by the man' in the example).

Second, in North Sámi the passive is formed by adding a derivative suffix to the stem of a verb. The passive suffix has slightly different forms depending on whether it is added to an even-syllable, odd-syllable, or contracted verb, as illustrated here.

Even-syllable

The passive suffix for even-syllable verbs is **-ojuvvot**.

Active verb	Passive verb
dahkat 'to do, to make'	**dahkkojuvvot** 'to be done, to be made'
buktit 'to bring'	**buktojuvvot** 'to be brought'
goarrut 'to sew'	**gorrojuvvot** 'to be sewn'

Points to note:

- When the passive suffix is added, the **-at**, **-it**, and **-ut** endings disappear.
- The verbal stem is in the extra strong grade where applicable. Note that in some cases the extra strong grade is not indicated in the orthography and looks identical to the strong grade (e.g. **gorrojuvvot** 'to be sewn').
- Diphthongs simplify before -o-, e.g. **gorrojuvvot**.

Even-syllable verbs ending in -**at** and -**it** also commonly have a variant short passive form ending in -**ot**, as follows.

Active verb	Passive verb
dahkat 'to do, to make'	**dahkkot** 'to be done, to be made'
buktit 'to bring'	**buktot** 'to be brought'

In some cases these short passive forms in -**ot** have a specialised meaning indicating a passive action that happens automatically or spontaneously with no involvement from outside forces. Examples of the automative passive in contrast to its active and standard passive equivalents can be found in the following table. Note that sometimes the automative passive has a lexicalised meaning which differs somewhat from that of the active or standard passive.

Active	Passive	Automative passive
oaidnit 'to see'	**oidnojuvvot** 'to be seen'	**oidnot** 'to be visible'
gávdnat 'to find'	**gávdnojuvvot** 'to be found'	**gávdnot** 'to be located'
gullat 'to hear'	**gullojuvvot** 'to be heard'	**gullot** 'to be audible'

The difference in meaning between the standard and automative passive is further illustrated in the following examples.

Guovža **oidnojuvvui** márkanis.	The bear was seen in town.
Guovža **oidnui** muora duoge.	The bear was visible from behind the tree.

Note that an active third person plural verb form without a subject is commonly used instead of the standard passive, e.g. **guovžža oidne márkanis** 'the bear was seen in town', literally 'they saw the bear in town'.

Odd-syllable

The passive suffix for odd-syllable verbs is **-uvvot**, as illustrated in the following table.

Verb	Passive
muitalit 'to tell'	**muitaluvvot** 'to be told'
geavahit 'to use'	**geavahuvvot** 'to be used'
billistit 'to destroy'	**billistuvvot** 'to be destroyed'

Contracted

The passive suffix for contracted verbs is **-juvvot**, as illustrated in the following table.

Active verb	Passive verb
čilget 'to explain'	**čilgejuvvot** 'to be explained'
diŋgot 'to order'	**diŋgojuvvot** 'to be ordered'

Point to note:

- Verbs ending in -át are often intransitive and therefore unlikely to appear in the passive.

The passive suffix ends in -ot, and as such all passive verbs conjugate like contracted verbs. The following table illustrates the conjugation of a passive verb in the present tense.

oidnojuvvot 'to be seen'

	Singular	Dual	Plural
First	**oidnojuvvon** 'I am seen'	**oidnojuvvojetne** 'we are seen'	**oidnojuvvot** 'we are seen'
Second	**oidnojuvvot** 'you are seen'	**oidnojuvvobeahtti** 'you are seen'	**oidnojuvvobehtet** 'you are seen'
Third	**oidnojuvvo** 's/he is seen'	**oidnojuvvoba** 'they are seen'	**oidnojuvvojit** 'they are seen'

**13
Word
formation**

The following table illustrates the passive in various tenses and moods (affirmative and negative).

Negative present	**mun in oidnojuvvo** 'I am not seen'
Past	**mun oidnojuvvojin** 'I was seen'
Negative past	**mun in oidnojuvvon** 'I was not seen'
Perfect	**mun lean oidnojuvvon** 'I have been seen'
Negative perfect	**mun in leat oidnojuvvon** 'I have not been seen'
Pluperfect	**mun ledjen oidnojuvvon** 'I had been seen'
Negative pluperfect	**mun in lean oidnojuvvon** 'I had not been seen'
Conditional	**mun oidnojuvvošin** 'I would be seen'
Negative conditional	**mun in oidnojuvvoše** 'I would not be seen'

Point to note:

- The past participle of the passive has a short variant form ending in -**jun**, e.g. **oidnojun** 'seen', which is particularly common in the spoken language.

The following examples illustrate the use of the passive.

Sámi kultuvrra ávnnaslaš vuođđu ii galgga **billistuvvot**.	The material basis of Sámi culture must not be destroyed.
Luonddubuktagat leat dávjá **ráhkaduvvon** oljjus, ovdamearkka dihtii kokosoljjus.	Natural products are often made from oil, for example coconut oil.

Sámi gávpi **rahppojuvvo** Jielleváris.	A Sámi shop is opening in Gällivare.	**13** **Word formation**
Čájálmas **čájehuvvui** vuosttaš geardde 1994:s.	The performance was shown for the first time in 1994.	
Jagi 1939 rájes gárjilgiella **čállojuvvui** kyrillalaš alfabehtain.	From 1939 Karelian was written in the Cyrillic alphabet.	
Njuovvanbohccot **buktojuvvojedje** Bálojávrri gili gárdái.	The reindeer destined for slaughter were brought to the Palojärvi village enclosure.	

Note that, in contrast to English, North Sámi passive sentences do not always have an expressed subject. Such a case is shown in the following example.

Davvi-Sámis **muitaluvvo** čuđiid birra, Mátta-Sámis fas ruottelaččaid birra.

In northern Sápmi [stories are] told about the Chudes; in southern Sápmi about the Swedes.

Certain intransitive verbs may also appear in the passive. In such cases, the passive form has an impersonal meaning, equivalent to the German impersonal pronoun *man* or the French *on*. In impersonal sentences the focus is on the action, and the subject is not specified. Such sentences are difficult to translate literally into English, which lacks an equivalent impersonal construction. The following examples illustrate this usage.

Feasttas **dánsejuvvui**.

There was dancing going on at the party.

Guopparmátkái **vulgojuvvo** skuvlla ovddas dbm. 12.

We'll/they'll be setting out on the mushroom-picking trip from in front of the school at 12 p.m.

Dohko ii **mannojuvvo**.

No one goes there.

13 Word formation

13.1.1.1.1.2 Adversative passive

North Sámi has an additional passive construction which is used to convey adversative actions (i.e. actions that are harmful or unfavourable to the subject). Adversative passives are formed with the suffix -**hallat** or -**haddat**. The subject of an adversative passive verb is always animate (i.e. a living being). The formation of the adversative passive is illustrated here.

Active verb	Passive verb
borrat 'to eat'	**borahallat** 'to be eaten'
goddit 'to kill'	**gottáhallat** 'to be killed'
vuodjit 'to drive'	**vuojáhallat** 'to be run over'

Points to note:

- The stem of the verb in the adversative passive is in the weak grade.
- Stem-final -**i**- becomes -**a**- or -**á**- when the adversative passive suffix is added.
- Adversative passives conjugate like even-syllable verbs.
- In contrast to the standard passive, the adversative passive suffix can be attached to intransitive verbs (such as **vuodjit** 'to drive'). In such cases, the meaning of the resulting adversative passive verb is not always completely predictable.

In contrast to the standard passive verbs discussed earlier, adversative passives can appear in conjunction with an agent, which is in the illative case. The following examples illustrate this:

Maid galgá dahkat ovdalaš juovllaid amas **borahallat** stállui?	What must one do before Christmas in order not to be eaten by a troll?
9-jahkásaš **vuojáhalai** biilii.	A nine-year-old was run over by a car.
Guossámis **gottáhalai** guovža disdaga ja Anáris gaskavahku.	A bear was killed in Kuusamo on Tuesday, and one in Inari on Wednesday.

13.1.1.1.1.3 Reflexive

In North Sámi, like in English, reflexive constructions are typically conveyed by means of a subject and verb in conjunction with the object **ieš** 'self', e.g. **várašit** 'to protect' vs. **várašit iežas** 'to protect oneself'.

In addition, North Sámi possesses a number of intrinsically reflexive verbs, i.e. verbs whose subject is the same as their object. North Sámi reflexive verbs typically correspond to English reflexive constructions with '-self', e.g. 'to wash oneself'. North Sámi reflexive verbs can be formed with various suffixes, discussed in turn here.

The suffixes **-dit** and **-addat** are found with reflexive meaning in conjunction with certain verbs. (Note that **-dit** can also have causative meaning, discussed later.) The suffix **-dit** is attached to verbs whose stem ends in a vowel, while **-addat** is attached to verbs whose stem ends in a consonant. The following table illustrates this type of verb.

Transitive verb	Reflexive verb
bassat 'to wash'	**basadit** 'to wash oneself'
čuohppat 'to cut'	**čuohpadit** 'to cut oneself'
luoitit 'to let go, to drop'	**luoitádit** 'to go down, to let oneself down'
vealuhit 'to lay (something) down'	**vealuhaddat** 'to lie down, to stretch oneself out'

Point to note:

- When **-dit** is attached to an even-syllable verb ending in **-it**, the stem remains in the strong grade and the final **-i-** becomes **-á-**.

There are also several other suffixes that can have a reflexive sense in conjunction with certain verbs. Like **-dit/-addat**, these suffixes are somewhat

13 Word formation

lexicalised and relatively limited in their use. These suffixes include -**alit**/-**allat**, -**šit**, and -**sit**, as in the following examples:

Transitive verb	Reflexive verb
báitit 'to shine, to warm'	**báitalit** 'to warm oneself'
boaldit 'to burn'	**boalddašit** 'to burn oneself'
rahpat 'to open'	**rahpasit** 'to open (itself)'

13.1.1.1.1.4 Reciprocal

Reciprocal meaning (i.e. 'each other') in North Sámi is often conveyed by means of the reciprocal pronouns **nubbi nuppi, goabbat guoibmi**, and **guhtet + guoibmi +** 'each other' (discussed in section 5.9). However, there are also several suffixes that can be used to transform (typically transitive) verbs into reciprocal ones. The main reciprocal suffixes are -**(a)dit**/-**addat**, -**alit**/-**allat**, -**ašit**, -**hallat**, -**haddat**. Note that, as in the case of the reflexive suffixes, many of these can also have other meanings, and their use is limited to certain verbs. Moreover, sometimes the meaning of a derived reciprocal verb is not entirely predictable.

Transitive verb	Reciprocal verb
gávdnat 'to find'	**gávnnadit** 'to meet each other'
liikot 'to like'	**liikodit** 'to like each other'
náitit 'to marry off'	**náitalit** 'to get married (to each other)'
oaidnit 'to see'	**oaidnalit** 'to see each other'
addit 'to give'	**attašit** 'to give each other'
gullat 'to hear'	**gulahallat** 'to understand each other'

13.1.1.1.1.5 Causative

North Sámi possesses a causative suffix, which serves to indicate that the subject of the verb is causing someone or something else to perform the action. This is often equivalent to the English construction 'to make X do Y'. The function of the North Sámi causative is illustrated in the following example.

| Base verb | Mánná **čaimmai**. | The child laughed. |
| Causative | Mun **čaimmahin** máná. | I made the child laugh. |

The main North Sámi causative suffix has slightly different forms depending on the type of verb to which it is attached, as illustrated here.

Even-syllable

The causative suffix for even-syllable verbs is **-hit**.

Base verb	Causative verb
oahppat 'to learn'	**oahpahit** 'to teach' (i.e. 'to make someone learn')
diehtit 'to know'	**dieđihit** 'to inform' (i.e. 'to make someone know')
goarrut 'to sew'	**goaruhit** 'to have someone sew'

Point to note:

- The causative suffix is attached to the weak grade of the verbal stem.

Odd-syllable

The causative suffix for odd-syllable verbs is **-ahttit**.

Base verb	Causative verb
ráhkadit 'to make'	**ráhkadahttit** 'to have someone make'
guldalit 'to listen'	**guldalahttit** 'to make someone listen'

suoládit 'to steal'	**suoládahttit** 'to make someone steal'

Contracted

The causative suffix for contracted verbs is **-hit**.

Base verb	Causative verb
čohkkát 'to sit'	**čohkkáhit** 'to make someone sit'
čilget 'to explain'	**čilgehit** 'to make someone explain'

The following examples illustrate the use of causative verbs.

Politiijat **dieđihedje** ahte nuppi biilla vuoddji lea duššan.	The police informed [the public] that the other car's driver had died.
Mun **oahpahan** sámegiela vuosttaš giellan.	I teach Sámi as a first language.

Note that while in many cases the direct object of a North Sámi causative verb is a person who is made to do the action of the verb, in some cases the direct object is someone or something that the subject causes someone to make or do. In such cases the person who is made to carry out the action appears in the illative. The following example illustrates this type of causative clause.

Oahpaheaddji **logahii** girjji studeanttaide.	The teacher made the students read a book.

Causative verbs referring to mental or physical experiences often appear in impersonal clauses lacking an expressed subject. In such cases the person experiencing the action of the verb is in the accusative-genitive. The following example illustrates this type of clause.

Mu **vuovssiha**.	I feel sick. (Lit: [Something] is making me vomit.)
Mu **čaimmaha**.	I feel like laughing. (Lit: [Something] is making me laugh.)

Finally, some causative verbs can be used to indicate that something is possible or permissible, corresponding to the English suffixes -able and -ible. This usage is relatively restricted, and causative verbs with this type of permissive meaning (in addition to their usual causative meaning) must be learned individually. The following examples illustrate this type of verb.

Base verb	Permissive verb
borrat 'to eat'	**borahit** 'to be edible' (can also mean 'to feed')
vuodjit 'to drive'	**vuojihit** 'to be possible to drive' (can also mean 'to make someone drive')

13.1.1.1.1.6 Applicative

In North Sámi, an applicative is a transitive verb that is derived from an intransitive verb of motion. In some cases North Sámi applicative verbs correspond to English transitive verbs of motion such as 'to walk someone/something', 'to drive someone/something'. In other cases, North Sámi applicative verbs have the meaning of 'to go somewhere with someone/something' or 'to follow someone/something', but nevertheless take a direct object instead of an indirect one. The North Sámi applicative suffixes are the same as the causative ones, namely -**hit** (for even-syllable and contracted verbs) and -**ahttit** (for odd-syllable verbs). This is illustrated here.

Base verb	Applicative verb
vuodjit 'to drive'	**vuojihit** 'to transport, to give a ride'
vázzit 'to walk'	**váccihit** 'to walk someone somewhere, to take something somewhere on foot, to follow someone on foot'

13 Word formation

> **viehkat** 'to run'
>
> **viegahit** 'to run somewhere with something, to run after someone'

Like many other North Sámi derived verbs, applicatives are quite restricted in scope. The following examples illustrate their use.

Mun **váccihin** mána skuvlii.	I walked the child to school.
Máret **viegahii** oasti gávppi uksii.	Máret ran after the customer to the door of the shop.

13.1.1.1.1.7 Anti-applicative

The North Sámi anti-applicative is typically derived from intransitive verbs that denote weather conditions or natural processes. The anti-applicative serves to indicate that the subject is the victim of unpleasant circumstances. Anti-applicatives are formed with the suffix **-ot** (attached to even-syllable verbs in the extra strong grade) or **-uvvat** (attached to odd-syllable verbs), as illustrated here.

Base verb	Anti-applicative verb
dálvat 'to become winter'	**dálvot** 'to be caught unprepared for winter'
arvit 'to rain'	**arvot** 'to get soaked by rain'
dulvat 'to flood'	**dulvot** 'to be flooded'
sevnnjodit 'to get dark'	**sevnnjoduvvat** 'to be caught out by the darkness'

Points to note:

- Anti-applicatives ending in **-ot** conjugate like contracted verbs.
- Anti-applicatives ending in **-uvvat** conjugate like even-syllable verbs.

The following examples illustrate the use of the anti-applicative.

Hánsa vikkai ceahkkut dan stobu, muhto **dálvu** .	Hánsa tried to build the cabin, but he was caught unprepared by the winter.
Šilju **dulvui**.	The field got flooded.

13.1.1.1.1.8 Desiderative

The desiderative suffix serves to indicate that the subject has a desire to perform the action of the base verb. The desiderative suffix is -**stuvvat**, added to the weak grade of the verbal stem. The following table illustrates this.

Base verb	Desiderative verb
borrat 'to eat'	**borastuvvat** 'to feel like eating'
juhkat 'to drink'	**jugastuvvat** 'to feel like drinking, to get thirsty'

The object of the desiderative verb appears in the illative. The following example illustrates the use of this construction. Note that the desiderative is extremely limited in scope; the construction **mus lea miella** 'I feel like' followed by an infinitive is much more commonly used.

Mun **jugastuvven** vuollagii.	I felt like drinking beer.

13.1.1.1.2 Aspectual suffixes

In addition to the suffixes discussed previously, North Sámi has a substantial number of suffixes that lend a specific aspectual nuance to the verb in question. These aspectual suffixes are examined in turn here.

13.1.1.1.2.1 Subitive and diminutive

Subitive verbs express immediate, sudden, or hurried actions. Diminutive verbs express actions that take place for only a short period of time or in a small degree. Subitive verbs can be formed by adding the suffix -**lit** to the strong grade of even-syllable verbs, as shown below.

Base verb	Subitive verb
borrat 'to eat'	**borralit** 'to eat quickly'
jápmit 'to die'	**jápmilit** 'to die suddenly'

In addition, subitive and diminutive verbs can be formed with the suffix -**stit**, which is attached to the weak grade of even-syllable verbs and to contracted verbs, or -**astit**, which is attached to odd-syllable verbs. Some common subitive and diminutive verbs are shown here.

Base verb	Subitive/diminutive verb
bargat 'to work'	**barggastit** 'to work a little bit'
lávlut 'to sing'	**lávllostit** 'to sing a little bit'
muitalit 'to tell'	**muitalastit** 'to tell quickly'
čilget 'to explain'	**čilgestit** 'to explain quickly'
čohkkát 'to sit'	**čohkkástit** 'to sit for a little while'
dánset 'to dance'	**dánsestit** 'to dance a little bit'

Point to note:

- When the diminutive suffix is added to even-syllable verbs, stem-final -**i**- becomes -**e**-, and stem-final -**u**- becomes -**o**-.

Finally, diminutive verbs may sometimes be formed with the suffix -**ašit**, which is attached to the weak grade of even-syllable words ending in -**it**.

Base verb	Diminutive verb
addit 'to give'	**attašit** 'to give little by little, to hand out'
vázzit 'to walk'	**váccašit** 'to walk a bit'

13.1.1.1.2.2 Momentaneous

North Sámi has various momentaneous suffixes that are used to indicate actions that happen once, are of extremely short duration, and possibly happen suddenly. The momentaneous suffixes are -**et**, -**dit**, -**alit**, -**ádit**, and -**ihit**. Momentaneous verbs are formed from base verbs that have an inherently continuative or aspectually neutral sense. The following table illustrates some momentaneous verbs.

Base verb	Momentaneous verb
čuorvut 'to shout'	**čurvet** 'to shout out, to shout once'
doallat 'to hold'	**dollet** 'to take hold of'
čorbmat 'to punch'	**čorbmadit** 'to punch once'
šloaŋkit 'to slam'	**šloaŋkalit** 'to slam shut'
civkit 'to chirp'	**civkkádit** 'to chirp suddenly once'
jávkat 'to disappear'	**jávkkihit** 'to disappear suddenly'

13. .1.1.2.3 Frequentative

Frequentative suffixes are used to indicate actions that happen many times, continue for an extended period, and/or are performed by multiple subjects (either simultaneously or sequentially). The frequentative suffixes are -**alit**, which is attached to the strong grade of even-syllable verbs, -(**a**)**dit**, which is attached to the weak grade of even-syllable verbs and to contracted verbs, and **-addat** or **-allat**, which are attached to odd-syllable verbs. There is also a diminutive frequentative suffix, **-(i)ldit**, and a frequentative and applicative suffix in **-(u)hit** that is used exclusively with verbs denoting sounds.

Base verb	Frequentative verb
giitit 'to thank'	**giitalit** 'to thank repeatedly, to thank many people'
addit 'to give'	**addalit** 'to keep giving, to hand out, to give away'
jápmit 'to die'	**jámadit** 'to die (of multiple people), to be dying'
čuožžut 'to stand'	**čuččodit** 'to keep standing'
čohkánit 'to sit down'	**čohkánaddat** 'to keep sitting down, to sit down one after the other'
muitalit 'to tell'	**muitaladdat** 'to keep telling'
addit 'to give'	**attildit** 'to keep on giving a little bit away, to give away little by little'
bávkit 'to bang'	**bávkkuhit** 'to bang many times with something'

In some cases a frequentative verb may have a conative nuance, meaning 'to try to do something', e.g.:

Base verb	Frequentative (conative) verb
boktit 'to wake up'	**boktalit** 'to try and wake someone up'
nohkadit 'to put someone to bed'	**nohkadaddat** 'to try and put someone to bed'

13.1.1.1.2.4 Inchoative

The inchoative suffix is used to indicate an action that begins, equivalent to the English construction 'to start to'. The inchoative suffix takes the form -**goahtit**, which is attached to the strong grade of even-syllable verbs and to contracted verbs, and -**išgoahtit**, which is attached to odd-syllable verbs. In the East the form -**šgoahtit** is used instead of -**goahtit**. Note that, in contrast to many of the derived aspectual verbs, the inchoative suffix is productive and very widely used.

Base verb	Inchoative verb
lohkat 'to read'	**lohkagoahtit** 'to start to read'
vuolgit 'to leave'	**vuolgigoahtit** 'to start to leave, to set out'
čierrut 'to cry'	**čierrugoahtit** 'to start to cry'
muitalit 'to tell'	**muitališgoahtit** 'to start to tell'
dánset 'to dance'	**dánsegoahtit** 'to start to dance'

In addition, in the West inchoative verbs can be formed by changing an even-syllable verb into a contracted one. The ending of the resulting contracted verb is not predictable. The following examples illustrate this type of inchoative verb.

Base verb	Inchoative verb
buollat 'to burn'	**buollát** 'to start to burn'
arvit 'to rain'	**arvát** 'to start to rain'
čierrut 'to cry'	**čirrot** 'to start to cry'

Similarly, -**lit** can be used as an inchoative suffix in conjunction with verbs of motion. It is attached to the strong grade of even-syllable verbs. This is illustrated here.

13 Word formation

Base verb	Inchoative verb
vázzit 'to walk'	**vázzilit** 'to start walking'
viehkat 'to run'	**viehkalit** 'to start running'

In addition, certain other suffixes may appear with inchoative meaning. These include -**iidit** and -**stit**.

Base verb	Inchoative verb
golgat 'to flow' (of water)	**golggiidit** 'to start to flow' (of water)
bieggat 'to blow' (of wind)	**biekkastit** 'to start to blow' (of wind)

13.1.1.2 Verbs derived from nominals

North Sámi has a large number of verbs derived from nouns and adjectives. The most common suffixes used to derive such verbs are listed here.

-ut

    jalla 'stupid, crazy'   **jallut** 'to become stupid, to become crazy'

    buoidi 'fat'   **buoidut** 'to get fat, to put on weight'

    ruoinnas 'thin'   **ruoidnut** 'to get thin, to lose weight'

    márfi 'sausage'   **márfut** 'to make sausages'

-et

    muorra 'wood'   **murret** 'to chop wood'

    nanus 'sturdy, solid'   **nannet** 'to affirm, confirm'

    čielggas 'clear'   **čilget** 'to explain, to clarify'

    goikkis 'dry'   **goiket** 'to dry something'

-dit/-tit

    jeagil 'lichen'   **jeagildit** 'to pick lichen'

    vuođđu 'base'   **vuođđudit** 'to found, to establish'

    jietna 'sound'   **jietnadit** 'to make a sound'

    buorre 'good'   **buoridit** 'to improve'

    máinnas 'story'   **máinnastit** 'to tell a story'

13 Word formation

-(a)stit

    leaika 'joke'   **leaikkastit** 'to joke'

    márkan 'town centre'   **márkanastit** 'to visit the town centre'

    meahcci 'forest'   **meahcástit** 'to hunt in the forest'

-nit

    headju 'bad'   **hedjonit** 'to become bad, worse'

    luovus 'loose'   **luovvanit** 'to become loose'

    davvi 'north'   **davvánit** 'to move northwards'

-uvvat

    vealgi 'debt'   **vealgáduvvat** 'to get into debt'

    nubbi 'other'   **nuppástuvvat** 'to change'

    boaris 'old'   **boarásmuvvat, boarásmit** 'to grow old(er)'

Point to note:

- This suffix can be preceded by another consonant or consonant cluster such as -st-, -d-, -l-, -š-, -m-, -n-, etc. Note that verbs ending in **-muvvat** have an alternative variant **-mit**.

-stallat

gáffe 'coffee'	**gáfestallat** 'to have coffee'
lávvu 'tent'	**lávostallat** 'to stay in a tent'

Other suffixes used to derive verbs from nominals include -(l)uddat, -át, -istit, -iidit, -agit, -odit, -stahttit, -(a/o)šit, -ihit, -uhit, -ildit.

13.1.2 Noun suffixes

13.1.2.1 Nouns derived from verbs

North Sámi possesses a variety of suffixes that are used to derive nouns from verbs. These suffixes are listed and illustrated here.

-n, -eapmi

This suffix is used to form verbal nouns (see section 7.4.2 for details). The **-n** suffix is attached to the stem of even-syllable verbs in the strong grade and to the stem of contracted verbs, while the **-eapmi** suffix is attached to the stem of odd-syllable verbs.

Verb	Derived noun
borrat 'to eat'	**borran** 'eating'
čállit 'to write'	**čállin** 'writing'
goarrut 'to sew'	**goarrun** 'sewing'
oahpahit 'to teach'	**oahpaheapmi** 'teaching'
čohkkát 'to sit'	**čohkkán** 'sitting'

-upmi

This suffix is attached to the stem of odd-syllable verbs with a reflexive or reciprocal meaning, and to passive verbs in **-uvvot** and **-uvvat**. Note that **-uvvot** and **-uvvat** are replaced by the **-upmi** suffix.

Verb	Derived noun
beroštit 'to care, to be interested'	**beroštupmi** 'caring, interest'
bovdejuvvot 'to be invited'	**bovdejupmi** 'invitation'
molsašuvvat 'to be changed'	**molsašupmi** 'change'

-muš, -eamoš

This suffix is used to form nouns referring to a verbal action. The **-muš** suffix is attached to the stem of even-syllable verbs in the strong grade and to the stem of contracted verbs, while the **-eamoš** suffix is attached to the stem of odd-syllable verbs.

Verb	Derived noun
borrat 'to eat'	**borramuš** 'food'
soahpat 'to agree'	**soahpamuš** 'agreement, contract'
viggat 'to try'	**viggamuš** 'goal, attempt'
cealkit 'to utter'	**cealkámuš** 'statement'
muitalit 'to tell'	**muitaleamoš** 'story'
birget 'to get by'	**birgemuš** 'livelihood'

Point to note:

- Occasionally there is a vowel change when the derivative suffix is added, as in the case of **cealkit** 'to utter' : **cealkamuš** 'statement'.

13 Word formation

13 Word formation

-a

This suffix is attached to the stem of even-syllable verbs in the weak grade.

Verb	Derived noun
oahppat 'to learn'	**oahpa** 'studies'
sirdit 'to move (transitive)'	**sirdda** 'a short move'
cealkit 'to utter'	**cealkka** 'sentence'

-as

This suffix can be attached to even-syllable, odd-syllable, and contracted verbs. The resulting noun is odd-syllable. In some cases it is preceded by a verbal derivative suffix such as -n- or -lm- (which may not be visible in the base verb shown here).

Verb	Derived noun
biktit 'to warm'	**bivttas** 'garment'
gossat 'to cough'	**gosanas** 'a cough'
dutkat 'to investigate'	**dutkkalmasat** 'interrogation' (always plural)

-at

This suffix can be attached to even-syllable, odd-syllable, and contracted verbs. In some cases it is preceded by a verbal derivative suffix such as -ld-, -st-, or -h- (which may not be visible in the base verb shown here).

Verb	Derived noun
čuggestit 'to sting, to stab'	**čuggestat** 'sting'; 'impulse'
gahčat 'to ask'	**gažaldat** 'a question'
orrut 'to live'	**orohat** 'dwelling-place'

-u

This suffix is attached to the stem of even-syllable verbs in the strong grade.

Verb	Derived noun
bargat 'to work'	**bargu** 'work'
lohkat 'to read, to count'	**lohku** 'number'
atnit 'to use'	**atnu** 'use'
doaivut 'to hope'	**doaivu** 'hope'

-a

This suffix is attached to the stem of even-syllable verbs ending in -**it** and -**ut**. The resulting nouns are odd-syllable.

Verb	Derived noun
čállit 'to write'	**čála** 'written communication'
muohttit 'to snow'	**muohta** 'snow'

-us, -hus

The -**us** suffix is attached to the stem of even- and odd-syllable verbs, and the -**hus** suffix is attached to the stem of contracted verbs.

Verb	Derived noun
čoaggit 'to gather'	**čoakkus** 'gathering'
rihkkut 'to break (the law)'	**rihkus** 'crime'
bálvalit 'to serve'	**bálvalus** 'service'
čilget 'to explain'	**čilgehus** 'explanation'

13.1.2.2 Nouns derived from nouns

North Sámi has a number of suffixes used to derive nouns from other nouns. The most common of these are discussed here.

-laš

This suffix is very commonly used and relatively productive. It is typically attached to placenames and serves to denote an inhabitant of that place. It can also be attached to other nouns, in which case it usually indicates a person who has the property denoted by the base noun. The derived noun is often in the strong grade but in some cases is in the weak grade; note that there may be vowel changes before the suffix.

Base noun	Derived noun
Sápmi 'Sápmi'	**sápmelaš** 'Sámi person'
Ruotta 'Sweden'	**ruottelaš** 'Swede'
dállu 'house, farm'	**dálolaš** 'farmer'
sohka 'extended family'	**sogalaš** 'distant relative'

-š

This is the diminutive suffix. It is extremely productive. It is attached to the accusative-genitive form of the noun. Note that final -i and -u change to -á- and -o- respectively when the diminutive suffix is attached.

Base noun	Derived noun
nieida 'girl'	**nieiddaš** 'little girl'
bárdni 'boy'	**bártnáš** 'little boy'
beana 'dog'	**beatnagaš** 'little dog'
suolu 'island'	**sulloš** 'little island'

Sometimes plural nouns with the diminutive suffix have a reciprocal sense, e.g. **vieljažat** 'brothers with each other'.

-has

This suffix indicates belonging. It is added to the weak grade of nouns. Note that final -i and -u change to -e- and -o-, respectively, when the suffix is attached.

Base noun	Derived noun
gáddi 'shore'	**gáttehas** 'landlubber'
suolu 'island'	**suolohas** 'island dweller'

-odat

This suffix often has a collective sense. It is attached to the strong grade of even-syllable nouns ending in -i. The final -i is replaced with the -o- of the suffix, which causes diphthong simplification.

Base noun	Derived noun
áigi 'time'	**áigodat** 'epoch, period'
searvi 'association'	**servodat** 'society'

-ádat

This suffix is attached to the weak grade of even-syllable nouns referring to weather. The final vowel of the noun is replaced by the -á of the suffix.

Base noun	Derived noun
dálki 'weather'	**dálkkádat** 'climate'
dálvi 'winter'	**dálvvádat** 'wintery weather'

In addition, there are a number of other suffixes that can be used to derive nouns from other nouns. These are much less productive and less frequently used than those discussed earlier. Such suffixes include -**stat**, -**uš**, -**dat**, -**l**, -**lat**, -**at**, -**s**, and -**t**.

13 Word formation

13.1.2.3 Nouns derived from adjectives

North Sámi has a number of derivative suffixes used to create abstract nouns from adjectives. The most common of these are discussed here.

-vuohta

This is the most productive and commonly used abstract noun suffix. It is attached to even-syllable and odd-syllable adjectives without any changes to the adjective, e.g.:

Base adjective	Derived noun
liekkas 'warm'	**liekkasvuohta** 'warmth'
boaris 'old'	**boarisvuohta** 'old age'
friddja 'free'	**friddjavuohta** 'freedom'

Note that when -**vuohta** is attached to adjectives ending in -**heapmi**/-**heapme** and -**haš**, -**heapmi**/-**heapme** and -**haš** change to -**his**, e.g.:

mielaheapme 'insane'	**mielahisvuohta** 'insanity'
oanehaš 'short'	**oanehisvuohta** 'shortness'

-odat

This suffix is likewise used to form abstract nouns from adjectives. It is less productive than -**vuohta**. The resulting abstract noun is in the strong grade (or extra strong, where applicable).

Base adjective	Derived noun
jalla 'stupid, crazy'	**jallodat** 'madness'
guhkki 'long'	**guhkkodat** 'length'

-ádat

This is another suffix used to form abstract nouns. The resulting noun is in the weak grade.

Base adjective	Derived noun
goikkis 'dry'	**goikkádat** 'dry spell, drought'

In addition, there are a number of less frequently used suffixes including -**at**, -**ut**, and -**as** that can be used to derive nouns from adjectives. These suffixes often indicate a person or thing that possesses the quality denoted by the adjective, e.g.:

Base adjective	Derived noun
sáhppat 'bluish'	**sáhpadas** 'bruise'

13.1.3 Adjective suffixes

13.1.3.1 Adjectives derived from verbs

North Sámi has a number of suffixes that are used to derive adjectives from verbs. The most common of these are listed here.

-meahttun

This is a negative suffix corresponding to the English prefixes 'un-' and 'in-'. It can be attached to all types of verbs. Even-syllable verbs are in the strong grade, and there may be vowel changes when the suffix is attached.

Base verb	Derived adjective
dovdat 'to know'	**dovdameahttun** 'unknown'
jáhkkit 'to believe'	**jáhkkemeahttun** 'unbelievable'
ipmirdit 'to understand'	**ipmirmeahttun** 'incomprehensible'

13 Word formation

-(e)vaš

This suffix is added to the strong grade of even-syllable verbs. Note that the final vowel of the verb may change when the suffix is attached.

Base verb	Derived adjective
duhtat 'to be satisfied'	**duhtavaš** 'satisfied'
čuovvut 'to follow'	**čuovvovaš** 'following'
bissut 'to stay'	**bissovaš** 'permanent, stable'

-as

This suffix is used to derive adjectives from verbs. The adjective is in the weak grade.

Base verb	Derived adjective
váibat 'to get tired'	**váibbas** 'tired'

-eš, -oš

These suffixes are used to indicate someone or something possessing a quality denoted by the action of the verb. It is attached to even-syllable verbs. In some cases the verb is in the weak grade and in others it is in the strong grade. There may be vowel changes and diphthong simplification when the suffix is added.

Base verb	Derived adjective
buollit 'to burn'	**buleš** 'inflammable'
diehtit 'to know'	**dihtteš** 'knowing, informed'

In addition, there are a number of rarer suffixes that can be used to form adjectives from verbs. These include -**l**, -**las**, -**ahkes**, -**heapmi**, and -**as**.

13.1.3.2 Adjectives derived from nouns

The most common North Sámi suffixes used to derive adjectives from nouns are listed here.

-heapmi

This is a negative suffix that corresponds to the English prefixes 'un-' and 'in-', and the suffix '-less'. It is relatively productive and is attached to even-syllable nouns in the weak grade (unless the noun does not gradate, as in the final example here) and to contracted nouns. Note that final -i and -u become -e- and -o- respectively when the suffix is added.

Base noun	Derived adjective
fápmu 'power'	**fámoheapme** 'powerless'
bargu 'work'	**bargguheapme** 'jobless, unemployed; lazy'
veahkki 'help'	**veahkeheapmi** 'helpless'
gudni 'honour'	**gudneheapmi** 'without honour'

The **-heapmi** suffix changes to **-his** in the attributive, e.g. **fámohis olmmoš** 'a powerless person'. If an adjective ending in **-heapmi** appears in a compound or takes an additional derivative suffix, **-heapmi** likewise changes to **-his**, e.g. **bargguhisvuohta** 'unemployment'. Note that the variant **-heapme** is also used with certain words, e.g. **lihkuheapme** 'unhappy'.

-meahttun

This is likewise a negative suffix that corresponds to the English prefixes 'un-' and 'in-', and the suffix '-less'. It is attached to odd-syllable nouns.

Base noun	Derived adjective
Ipmil 'God'	**ipmilmeahttun** 'godless'
heahpat 'shame, disgrace'	**heahpatmeahttun** 'shameless'

13 Word formation

-laš

This suffix is attached to even-syllable nouns in the weak grade and to odd-syllable nouns. It is used to indicate that the adjective has the quality of the noun from which it is derived.

Base noun	Derived adjective
mirku 'poison'	**mirkkolaš** 'poisonous'
mánná 'child'	**mánálaš** 'childish'
stáhta 'state'	**stáhtalaš** 'of the state'
dovdu 'feeling'	**dovddolaš** 'conscientious'

-saš

This suffix is used to create adjectives that denote time. It is attached to even-syllable nouns in the strong grade. Final -i and -u become -á- and -o-, respectively, when the suffix is attached.

Base noun	Derived adjective
jahki 'year'	**jahkásaš** 'year-old; annual'
vahkku 'week'	**vahkkosaš** 'week-old; weekly'

-at, -ot

These suffixes are used to indicate someone or something that possesses the quality of the noun from which it is derived. They commonly refer to physical qualities and are often used in compounds. They are suffixed to even-syllable nouns in the weak grade. There may be vowel changes when the suffix is attached. The suffix -ot is a variant of -at, which is used with nouns ending in -u.

Base noun	Derived adjective
čalbmi 'eye'	**čáhppesčalmmat** 'black-eyed'
juolgi 'leg, foot'	**guhkesjuolggat** 'long-legged'
šaddu 'growth'	**beallešattot** 'half-grown'

-i, -eaddjái

These suffixes are used to create adjectives whose meaning corresponds to the English expression 'rich in . . .'. The suffix **-i** is attached to even-syllable nouns (usually in the extra strong grade); in some cases final **-i** changes to **-á-** before it. The suffix **-eaddjái** is attached to odd-syllable nouns.

Base noun	Derived adjective
vuodja 'butter, fat'	**vuoddjái** 'fatty, rich in fat'
guolli 'fish'	**guollái** 'rich in fish'
jeagil 'lichen'	**jeahkáleaddjái**, **jeageleddjái** 'rich in lichen'

Note that when used attributively, the **-i** suffix becomes **-s**, e.g. **guollás jávri** 'a lake rich in fish'.

In addition, there are a number of other suffixes that can be used to form adjectives from nouns. These include **-es**, **-as**, **-geahtes**, **-keahtes**, and **-olaš**.

13.1.3.3 Adjectives derived from adjectives

North Sámi has several suffixes that can be used to derive adjectives from other adjectives. These are listed here.

-meahttun

This is a negative suffix that corresponds to the English prefixes 'un-' and 'in-', and the suffix '-less'. The suffix is added to the predicative singular form of the adjective.

Base adjectives	Derived adjective
dearvvaš 'healthy'	**dearvvašmeahttun** 'unhealthy'
čorgat 'tidy'	**čorgatmeahttun** 'untidy'
stáđis 'stable'	**stáđismeahttun** 'unstable'

13 Word formation

-lágán, -lágan, -lágáš, -lágaš

This suffix corresponds to the English adverbs 'quite' or 'pretty'. The suffix is usually added to the attributive singular form of the adjective.

Base adjective	Derived adjective
boaris 'old'	**boareslágán** 'quite old'
stuoris 'big'	**stuorralágán** 'quite big'
headju 'bad'	**heajoslágán** 'quite bad'

-osaš

This suffix is used to indicate a specific measure of a physical quality, e.g. **23-km guhkosaš mátki** 'a 23-km-long trip'. It is attached to even-syllable and odd-syllable adjectives in the strong grade and may be accompanied by a vowel change.

Base adjective	Derived adjective
guhkki 'long'	**guhkkosaš** 'of X length'
čieŋal 'deep'	**čikŋosaš** 'of X depth'

13.1.3.4 Adjectives derived from adverbs

North Sámi has a few suffixes that can be used to derive adjectives from adverbs, listed here.

-laš

As in the case of adjectives derived from nouns, this suffix can be attached to an adverb to indicate belonging. The derived adjective is in the strong grade.

Base adverb	Derived adjective
dáppe 'here'	**dábbelaš** 'belonging to here'
doppe 'there'	**dobbelaš** 'belonging to there'

-áš

This suffix is attached to adverbs of time. The derived adjective is in the weak grade and may be accompanied by a vowel change.

Base adverb	Derived adjective
odne 'today'	**otnáš** 'today's'
ikte 'yesterday'	**ivttáš** 'yesterday's'
dál 'now'	**dáláš** 'current'
diibmá 'last year'	**diimmáš** 'last year's'

13.2 Compounding

North Sámi is rich in compounds. The most common types of compounds are discussed here.

13.2.1 Compound nouns

Compound nouns are an extremely common feature of North Sámi. Compound nouns can be formed from two nouns or from an adjective plus a noun. The most common types of compound noun are discussed here.

Nominative noun + noun

Compound nouns are often formed by combining two or more nouns in the nominative case. Final -i and -u in the first noun change to -e and -o, respectively. The first noun may be a common or proper noun. Note that when a person's name is used in a compound, the two nouns are hyphenated.

Base nouns	Compound noun
girji 'book' + **gávpi** 'shop'	**girjegávpi** 'bookshop'
geađgi 'stone' + **áigi** 'time'	**geađgeáigi** 'Stone Age'
dolla 'fire' + **sadji** 'place'	**dollasadji** 'fireplace'

13 Word formation

13 Word formation

lávlun 'singing' + **gilvu** 'competition'	**lávlungilvu** 'singing competition'
Biret 'Biret' + **muottá** 'aunt'	**Biret-muottá** 'Aunt Biret'
Deatnu 'Tana river' + **gáddi** 'shore'	**Deatnogáddi** 'the shore of the Tana river'

Accusative-genitive noun + noun

The first noun in a compound may appear in the accusative-genitive. In such cases there is usually no vowel change.

Base nouns	Compound noun
eadni 'mother' + **giella** 'language'	**eatnigiella** 'mother tongue'
mánát 'children' + **gárdi** 'garden'	**mánáidgárdi** 'kindergarten'
boarrásat 'old people' + **siida** 'collective home, village'	**boarrásiidsiida** 'old people's home'
boazu 'reindeer' + **biergu** 'meat'	**bohccobiergu** 'reindeer meat'
riika 'nation' + **rádji** 'border'	**riikkarádji** 'national border'
johka 'river' + **njálbmi** 'mouth'	**joganjálbmi** 'river mouth'
Suopma 'Finland' + **giella** 'language'	**suomagiella** 'Finnish (language)'

Noun in other case + noun

Occasionally a noun in another case may be compounded, e.g.:

Base nouns	Compound noun
okta 'one' + **bargu** 'work'	**ovttasbargu** 'cooperation'
okta 'one' + **geassu** 'pulling, drawing'	**oktiigeassu** 'summary'
albmi 'sky, heaven' + **mannan** 'going' + **beaivi** 'day'	**albmáimannanbeaivi** 'Ascension Day'

Adjective, adverb, or pronoun + noun

An adjective, adverb, or pronoun may serve as the first element of the compound. In such cases the adjective is usually in the attributive form. Examples include the following.

Base forms	Compound noun
rávis 'grown-up' + **olmmoš** 'person'	**rávesolmmoš** 'grown-up'
boaris 'old' + **bárdni** 'boy'	**boaresbárdni** 'bachelor'
ođas 'new' + **jahki** 'year'	**ođđajahki** 'New Year'
olggos 'towards out' + **addi** 'giver'	**olggosaddi** 'publisher'
sis- 'inside' + **eanan** 'land'	**siseanan** 'inland'
ieš 'self' + **dovdu** 'feeling'	**iešdovdu** 'self-confidence'

13
Word formation

Note that compounds can be composed of a large number of elements, e.g.:

Base forms	Compound noun
boazu 'reindeer' + **doallu** 'holding, keeping, herding' + **láhka** 'law, legislation'	**boazodoalloláhka** 'reindeer herding legislation'
mánát 'children' + **gárdi** 'garden' + **oahpaheaddji** 'teacher' + **oahppu** 'studies'	**mánáidgárdeoahpaheaddjioahppu** 'kindergarten teacher training'

13.2.2 Compound adjectives

Compound adjectives are typically formed from a derived adjective preceded by a noun, adjective, adverb, pronoun, or numeral. When a noun appears as the first element of the compound it is usually in the accusative-genitive but is in the nominative preceding adjectives ending in -**at** or -**ot**. When an adjective appears as the first element of the compound it is usually in the attributive form. The following are some common compound adjectives.

Base forms	Compound adjective
bealli 'half' + **šaddu** 'growth'	**beallešattot** 'half-grown'
golbma 'three' + **jahkásaš** 'year-old'	**golmmajahkásaš** 'three-year-old'
ruoksat 'red' + **vuovttat** 'haired'	**ruksesvuovttat** 'red-haired'
olgo- 'out' + **riikalaš** 'national'	**olgoriikalaš** 'foreign'
ieš 'self' + **sihkkar** 'sure'	**iešsihkkar** 'self-confident'

13.2.3 Compound verbs

Some North Sámi verbs can be combined with a preceding adverb to form a compound with a more specific meaning. In some of these compounds the adverb can be separated from the verb, but in others the two components are inseparable.

Some of the more common compound verbs are shown here.

Base forms	Compound verb
bajás 'towards up' + **šaddat** 'to grow, to become'	**bajásšaddat** 'to grow up'
vuollái 'towards down' + **čállit** 'to write'	**vuolláičállit** 'to sign'
vuostái 'towards against' + **váldit** 'to take'	**vuostáiváldit** 'to receive'
badjel 'over' + **geahččat** 'to look'	**badjelgeahččat** 'to look down on, to scorn'

Suggested resources

There are at present no published English-language grammars or textbooks of North Sámi. However, the following resources (some of which are written in Norwegian, Swedish, or Finnish) may be of use to readers.

General introduction

Fernandez-Vest, M. M. Jocelyne. 2012. *Sami: An Introduction to the Language and Culture.* Helsinki: Finn Lectura.

Grammars

Aikio, Ante. 2009. *The Structure of North Sámi.* Also available at http://cc.oulu.fi/~anaikio/materials/structure_NS.pdf

Nickel, Klaus Peter and Pekka Sammallahti. 2011. *Nordsamisk grammatik.* Karasjok: Dávvi Girji.

Phrasebooks

Dauch, Bettina. 2005. *Samisch für Lappland – Wort für Wort.* Bielefeld: Peter Rump.

Textbooks and online courses

Bartens, Hans-Hermann. 1989. *Lehrbuch der saamischen (lappischen) Sprache.* Hamburg: Helmut Buske.

Berg, Tor Magne, Mariana Blind, and Per Stefan Labba. 2006. *Gulahalan 1.* Inari: Sámediggi. Also available at http://www.ur.se/webbplatser/gulahalan/

Suggested resources

Berg, Tor Magne, Mariana Blind, and Per Stefan Labba. 2010. *Gulahalan 2*. Inari: Sámediggi. Also available at http://www.ur.se/webbplatser/gulahalan/

Guttorm, Inga, Johan Jernsletten, and Klaus Peter Nickel. 1992. *Davvin* 4 volumes. Oslo: Folkets Brevskole.

Hedlund, Cecilia and Lars-Gunnar Larsson. 2011. *I dušše duoddaris! Lärobok i nordsamiska*. Uppsala: Uppsala universitet.

http://oahpa.no: Online Sámi grammar with some exercises and a paradigm generator created and managed by the University of Tromsø.

Dictionaries

Sammallahti, Pekka. 1993. *Sámi-suoma-sámi sátnegirji/Saamelais-suomalainen-saamelainen sanakirja*. Utsjoki: Girjegiisá.

Linguistic overviews

Sammallahti, Pekka. 1998a. *The Saami Languages: An Introduction*. Karasjok: Dávvi Girji.

Sammallahti, Pekka. 1998b. Saamic. In *The Uralic Languages*, ed. Daniel Abondolo, 43–95. London: Routledge.

Online press, radio, and TV

The following websites contain North Sámi-language written news as well as radio and TV programming.

http://yle.fi/uutiset/sapmi/

http://www.nrk.no/sapmi/

http://sverigesradio.se/sameradion

http://avvir.no/

Online bookshops

http://www.idut.no/

http://www.davvi.no/

http://www.calliidlagadus.org/

Index

ablative 174, 188–9, 193, 195–7, 201–2
accusative 51–2
actio comitative 160–1
actio essive 126–8
actio locative 158–60
adjectives 60–8; attributive 61–4; comparative 64–5; compound 280; demonstrative 67–8; derived 271–7; predicative 60–1; superlative 66–7
adpositions 213–23; place 213–17; postpositions 213–23; prepositions 213–23; spatial 213–17; suffixed 221–3; temporal 217–19; time 217–19
adverbial conjunctions 226
adverbs 174–212; comparative 174–5, 197–200; degree 202–5; frequency 185; indefinite 207–9; interrogative 205–7; manner 175–9; measure 202–5; place 188–202; quantity 202–5; superlative 200; temporal 180–7; time 180–7
adversative passive 250
affricates 16
alphabet 13
anti-applicative 256–7
applicative 255–6
aspect 257–62
attributive adjectives 61–4

cardinal numerals 110–13
cases 27–8, 51–9; accusative 51–2; comitative 57–8; essive 58–9; genitive 52–3; illative 53–5; locative 55–7; nominative 51
causative 252–5
clause types 237–43; existential 240; habitive 239–40; interrogative 241–3; intransitive 238–9; predicative 240–1; subjectless 241; transitive 239
comitative 57–8

comparative: adjectives 64–5; adverbs 174–5, 197–200; conjunctions 226–7
complementisers 225
compound: adjectives 280; nouns 277–80; verbs 281
compounding 277–81
concessive conjunctions 227
conditional: conjunctions 227–8; verbs 133–7, 146–7
conjunctions 224–9; adverbial 226; comparative 226–7; complementisers 225; concessive 227; conditional 227–8; coordinate 224–5; purpose 228; result 228; subordinate 225–9; temporal 228–9
consonant gradation 20–6
consonant length 16
consonants 14–18
consonant-stem 27
coordinate conjunctions 224–5

demonstrative: adjectives 67–8; pronouns 95–6
derivation: adjective 271–7; noun 264–71; numeral 115–16; verb 244–64
derivative suffixes 244–77
derived: adjectives 271–7; nouns 264–71; numerals 115–16; verbs 244–64
desiderative 257
diminutive: nouns 268; verbs 257–9
diphthong 14
distributive: adverbs 208; pronouns 103–4

enclitics 230–3
existential clauses 240

frequentative 259–60

genitive 52–3
gerund 161–3

Index

habitive clauses 239–40

illative 53–5
imperative 137–41, 147–8
inchoative 261–2
indefinite: adverbs 207–9; pronouns 99–103
indicative 117–28, 129, 144–5
infinitive 148–54
interjections 236
interrogative: adverbs 205–7; clauses 241–3; pronouns 96–8
intonation 19
intransitive clauses 238–9

locative 55–7

momentaneous 259
mood 129–42; alternative ways of expressing 142; conditional 133–7, 146–7; imperative 137–41, 147–8; indicative 117–28, 129, 144–5; potential 129–33, 145–6

negation 143–8; of the conditional 146–7; of the imperative 147–8; of the indicative 144–5; of the potential 145–6; of the progressive 147; of the purposive 168–9
nominative 51
nouns 27–59; contracted 27, 47–50; even-syllable 27, 28–37; odd-syllable 27–8, 37–47
numerals 110–16; cardinal 110–13; derived 115–16; ordinal 114–15

oblique stem 27
ordinal numerals 114–15
orthography 6–8, 13

participles 169–73; past 171–3; present 169–71
particles 230–6; discourse 230–5; enclitic 230–3; independent 234–5; interjections 236
passive 245–50; adversative 250
past tense 120–4
perfect tense 124–5
phonology 13–26
pluperfect tense 125–6
possessives 71–94
postpositions 213–23
potential 129–33, 145–6
predicative: adjectives 60–1; clauses 240–1

prepositions 213–23
present tense 117–20
prolative 174, 188–9, 200
pronouns 69–109; demonstrative 95–5; distributive 103–4; indefinite 99–103; interrogative 96–8; personal 69–70; possessive 71–94; reciprocal 105–9; reflexive 104–5; relative 98–9
purpose conjunctions 228
purposive 168–9

reciprocal: pronouns 105–9; verbs 252
reflexive: pronouns 104–5; verbs 251–2
relative pronouns 98–9
reported speech 128–9
result conjunctions 228

stops 16
stress 18, 230
subitive 257–9
subjectless clauses 241
subordinate conjunctions 225–9
suffixes: aspectual 257–62; case 27–8 derivative 244–77; possessive 71–94; valency-changing 244–57
superlative: adjectives 66–7; adverbs 200
supine 168–9
syllables 18–19, 37, 47

temporal: adverbs 180–7; conjunctions 228–9
tense 117–28; alternative ways of expressing 128; past 120–3; perfect 124–5; pluperfect 125–6; present 117–20; progressive 126–8; in reported speech 128–9
transitive clauses 239
translative 174

valency-changing suffixes 244–57
verbal abessive 165–7
verbal genitive 163–4
verbal nouns 45, 126–8, 154–5, 158, 160, 264
verbs 52, 54, 56, 58, 59, 117–72, 244–64, 281
vowel changes 39, 118, 121, 161, 221, 265, 268, 271, 272, 274, 276, 277, 278
vowels 13–14
vowel-stem 27

word order 237–8

286

Printed in Great Britain
by Amazon

29917176R00167